The Second Gulf War

The Second Gulf War

About the
Liberation
of Kuwait

(August 1990 – March 1991)

by

Edgar O'Ballance

GALAGO

Published by Galago Books
42 Palace Grove, Bromley, Kent, BR1 3HB

Photosetting in 10½/12pt Melior
WHM Photosetting
David Mews, 11a Greenwich South Street, London, SE10 8NW

Printed in England by Antony Rowe Limited

Edgar O'Ballance

Served in the British and Indian Armies as a regular officer; reaching the rank of Colonel.

During World War II served in France — East African Campaign — in the Western Desert — in West Africa — in the Middle East — in India — in Burma — and Sumatra; alternating combat postings with staff appointments, the latter mainly in field intelligence.

Since 1948 has worked as a Journalist, first for a US Wire Service; and since 1962 as a Freelance; specialising in reporting current wars and low insurgency conflicts; international relations; strategic studies; geo-strategic analysis; general defence problems and international terrorism.

Has taken part in a number of International seminars, study groups and discussions, and lectured at a number of staff colleges and similar institutions.

Since 1948 has covered and reported on 19 different wars, campaigns and low intensity operations, and has "looked-in" on another seven or more.

A Member of the London-based International Institute for Strategic Studies — the Royal United Services Institute for Defence Studies — and is Chairman of the London-based Military Commentators' Circle.

Books by Edgar O'Ballance

The Gulf War — Brassey's Defence Publishers (1988)
The Cyanide War — Brassey's Defence Publishers (1989)

Terrorism in the 1980s — Arms & Armour Press (1989)

Wars in Vietnam (1954-60) — Ian Allan (1975)

No Victor, No Vanquished: The Middle East War 1973 — Presidio Press USA (1978)
The Language of Violence — Presidio Press USA (1979)
Terror in Ireland: The Story of the IRA — Presidio Press USA (1981)
Tracks of the Bear: US-USSR Relations in the 1970s — Presidio Press USA (1982)

The Arab-Israeli War: 1948-9	— Faber & Faber (1956)
The Sinai Campaign: 1956	— Faber & Faber (1959)
The French Foreign Legion	— Faber & Faber (1961)
The Red Army of China	— Faber & Faber (1962)
The Red Army of Russia	— Faber & Faber (1964)
The Indo-China War: 1946-54	— Faber & Faber (1964)
The Malayan Insurrection: 1948-60	— Faber & Faber (1966)
The Greek Civil War: 1944-49	— Faber & Faber (1966)
The Algerian Insurrection: 1954-62	— Faber & Faber (1967)
War in the Yemen: 1962-69	— Faber & Faber (1971)
The Third Arab-Israeli War: 1967	— Faber & Faber (1972)
The Kurdish Revolt: 1961-70	— Faber & Faber (1973)
Arab Guerrilla Power	— Faber & Faber (1974)
The Electronic War in the Middle East: 1968-70	— Faber & Faber (1974)
The Secret War in Sudan: 1955-72	— Faber & Faber (1977)

To be published – Autumn 1992

Wars in Afghanistan: 1839-1992

by Brassey's Defence Publishers (London)

Abbreviations

ACC — Arab Co-operation Council
ADJ — Asian Defence Journal
AFJI — Armed Forces Journal International
ALARM — Air Launched anti-radiation missile
ALF — Arab Liberation Front
AMU — Arab Magreb Union
AP — Associated Press
AFP — Agence France-Presse
ARCENT — Commander of the Army component
ASARS — Advanced Synthetic Aperture System

BBC — British Broadcasting Corporation

CENTAF — Commander of the Air Force component
CENTCOM — Central Command
CIA — Central Intelligence Agency
C-in-C — Commander-in-Chief
CW — Chemical Warfare

DFLP — Democratic Front for the Liberation of Pallestine
DIA — Defense Intelligence Agency
DMZ — De-Militarised Zone
DoD — Department of Defense
DPK — Democratic Party of Kurdistan
DSP — Defense Support Program

EC — European Community
ERINT — Extended Range Interceptors

Fatah-RC — Fatah Revolutionary Council
FLIR — Forward Looking Infra-Red

GCC	—	Gulf Co-operation Council
GCI	—	Ground Control Interceptor
GPALS	—	Global Protection Against Limited Strikes
GPS	—	Global Positioning Systems
HAS	—	Hardened Air Shelters
HE	—	High Explosive
HUM/INT	—	Human Intelligence
IAEA	—	International Atomic Energy Agency
IAF	—	Iraqi Air Force
ICO	—	Islamic Conference Organisation
ICRC	—	International Committee of the Red Cross
IDF	—	Israeli Defence Force
IFF	—	Identification — Friend or Foe
IING	—	Iraqi Independent National Group
IISS	—	International Institute for Strategic Studies
IMF	—	International Monetary Fund
INA	—	Iraqi News Agency
IRNA	—	Islamic Republican News Agency
JACIO	—	Joint Action Committee of the Iraqi Opposition
JCS	—	Joint Chiefs of Staff
JDW	—	Jane's Defence Weekly
KIO	—	Kuwait Investment Office
KTO	—	Kuwait Theatre of Operations
LANTIRN	—	Low Altitude Navigation and Targeting Infra-Red at Night
MARCENT	—	Commander of Marine component
MNF	—	Multi-National Force
MRLS	—	Multiple Rocket Launcher System
MSP	—	Meteorological Satellite Programme
NATO	—	North Atlantic Treaty Organisation
NAVCENT	—	Commander of the Naval contribution
NBC	—	Nuclear, Biological and Chemical
NDP	—	National Democratic Party
NPF	—	National Progressive Front
OPEC	—	Organisation of Petroleum Exporting Countries
PFKG	—	Provisional Free Kuwait Government
PLF	—	Palestine Liberation Front
PFLP	—	Popular Front for the Liberation of Palestine

PFLP-GC	—	PFLP-General Command
PLO	—	Palestine Liberation Organisation
POW(s)	—	Prisoner(s)-of-War
Psy-Ops	—	Psychological Warfare Operations
PUK	—	Patriotic Union of Kurdistan
RAF	—	Royal Air Force (British)
R & R	—	Rest-and-Recreation
RCC	—	Revolutionary Command Council
RDF	—	Rapid Deployment Force
RDJTF	—	Rapid Deployment Joint Task Force
RUSI	—	Royal United Services Institute for Defence Studies
SAIRI	—	Supreme Association for the Islamic Revolution for Iraq
SAS	—	Special Air Service (British)
SBS	—	Special Boat Service (British)
SOCOM	—	Commander of the Special Forces component
THAAD	—	Tactical High Altitude Air Defence
TIALD	—	Thermal Imagery and Laser Designation
TV	—	Television
UAE	—	United Arab Emirates
UAV	—	Unmanned Aerial Vehicle
UN	—	United Nations
UNIKOM	—	UN Iraq-Kuwait Observation Mission
UNSC	—	Security Council
USA	—	United States of America
USAF	—	United States Air Force
USN	—	United States Navy
USS	—	United States Ship
VIP	—	Very Important Person
WEU	—	Western European Union

Bibliography

I would like to thank the Authors, Editors and Compilers of the following works, which I have read with profit and interest.

Where quotations or matter have been used appropriate credits are given within the script:

Allen, Charles   *Thunder and Lightning — The RAF in the Gulf*
                     — HMSO (UK) 1991

Bullock, John and   *Saddam's War*
    Morris, Harvey   — Faber & Faber (UK) 1991

Cohen, Roger and   *In the Eye of the Storm: The Life of General Schwartzkopf*
    Gatti, Claudio   — Bantam (UK) 1991

Karsh, Efraim and   *Saddam Hussein: A Political Biography*
    Rautsi, Inari   — Brassey's (UK) 1991

Miller, J. and   *Saddam Hussein and the Crisis*
    Mylroie, L.   — Arrow Books (UK) 1990

Parrish, Robert and   *Schwartzkopf*
    Andreachio, N.A. — Bantam (UK) 1991

Simpson, John   *From the House of War*
                     — Hutchinson (UK) 1991

Woodward, Bob   *The Commanders*
                     — Simon & Schuster (USA) 1991

Also: UK House of Commons, Defence Committee (Tenth Report) — *Preliminary Lessons of Operation Granby*

Periodicals and news agencies include:

UK	Daily Telegraph
	Guardian
	Middle East
	Reuters
	Sunday Times
	The Times
USA	Newsday
	New York Time
	Washington Post
	USA Today
Iran	Islamic Republican News Agency
	Kayan
	Tehran TImes
Iraq	Baghdad Times
	Iraqi News Agency
Israel	Jerusalem Post
France	Agence France Presse

Military publications consulted include:

Armed Forces Journal International (USA)

Asian Defence Journal (Malaysia)

Defence Journal (Pakistan)

Flight International (UK)

Jane's Air-Launched Weapons (UK)

Jane's All the World's Aircraft (UK)

Jane's Avionics (UK)

Jane's Defence Weekly (UK)

Jane's Fighting Ships (UK)

Military Balance (IISS) (UK)

RUSI Journal (UK)

Strategic Survey (IISS) (UK)

Survival (IISS) (UK)

Chronology

1752   An As-Sabah appointed 'Sheikh of Kuwait'

1899   British Trucial Treaty with Kuwait

1922   Convention of Uqair

1932   Iraq became Independent
The Kingdom of Saudi Arabia proclaimed

1936   Oil discovered in Kuwait
(did not come into production until 1946)

1961   Kuwait became Independent

1962   Kuwait produced a Constitution

1979   Saddam Hussein becomes President of Iraq

September 1980 – August 1988 — Iran–Iraq War

1981   Gulf Co-operation Council formed

April 1988 — Halabja Incident
(CW used against Iraqi Kurds)

1989   Arab Co-operation Council and Arab Magreb Union formed

1990   London Declaration (end of the Cold War)

1990 – 25th July — American Ambassador meets Saddam Hussein

– 31st July — Taif (Saudi Arabia) meeting

August 1990

– 2nd   — Iraqi armed forces occupy Kuwait

— UN Resolution 660 — condemning Iraqi action

– 6th   — Saudi Arabia asks for military assistance

August 1990 *continued*

- 7th — American troops land in Saudi Arabia
- — Saudi Arabia and Turkey close oil pipelines to Kuwait and Saudi Arabia
- 8th — President Bush makes his 'line in the sand' speech
- — Kuwait declared to be the 19th Governate of Iraq (Formalised on 25th)
- 9th — Kuwait's borders closed
- 10th — Arab League Summit (Changing alliances)
- 12th — Saddam Hussein's 'peace initiative' (includes 'linkage')

September 1990

- 11th — President Bush outlines objectives
- 16th — Saddam Hussein implements his Human Shield policy (ends on 12th December)
- 17th — US General Dugan re-assigned
- 23rd — Saddam Hussein threatens Saudi Arabia and Israel
- 27th — Emir of Kuwait addresses the UN General Assembly

October 1990

- 13th–15th — Kuwaiti Popular Congress held at Jedda (Saudi Arabia)

November 1990

- 5th — Allied troops in Saudi Arabia placed under nominal command of Saudi General
- 28th — President Bush visits US troops in Saudi Arabia (Thanksgiving Day)
- 29th — UN Resolution 667 approved (an 'appointment for war')

January 1991

- 6th — Saddam Hussein promises the 'Mother of all Battles'
- 12th — US Congress authorises use of military force
- 14th — Iraqi National Assembly votes for war
- 15th — UN Deadline for Iraqi troops to quit Kuwait
- — President Bush decides on the military option
- 16th — Allies re-capture Qarah Island

January 1991 *continued*

- 16th – 17th — Allied air offensive begins
- 18th — SCUDs began to fall on Saudi Arabia and Israel
  - Most Western media personnel expelled from Iraq
  - Soviet Peace Plan
- 24th — Saudi pilot achieves only 'double-kill' of the war
- 25th — Allied aircraft begin a 'shelter-busting' campaign
  - Flight of Iraqi aircraft to Iran begins
- 29th — General Schwartzkopf stated that Allied air supremacy had been achieved
- 29th – 2nd February — Battle for Khafji

February 1991

- 24th — Allied ground offensive began
- 27th — Allied troops enter Kuwait City
  - General Schwartzkopf gives his Media presentation
- 28th — Hostilities suspended
  - The 'Turkey Shoot'

March 1991

- 3rd — Formal Cease-Fire
- 11th — UN authorised UNIKOM

September 1991

- 19th — US-Kuwait Defence Agreement signed

Contents

Chapter		Page
1	The Rape of Kuwait	1
2	A Line in the Sand	16
3	Operation Desert Shield	35
4	Strategic Defiance	51
5	The Air War	64
6	The Obstacle Belt	83
7	Operation Desert Sabre	98
8	Praise and Appraisal	110
9	The On-Going Sequel	131
Appendices		157
A	The Arab League	158
B	The Gulf Co-operation Council	159
C	United Nations Security Council Resolutions	160
D	Nations Contributing to the Allied Coalition	161
E	Naval Contributions and Deployment	162
F	Allied Ground Forces	165
G	Operation Desert Storm: Command Structure	166
H	Allied Combat Aircraft Operating in the Gulf	167
I	Order of Battle: Ground Forces	169
J	Further UN Security Council Resolutions	170

Preface

At first sight the Liberation of Kuwait seemed to be a just war, fought for a just cause, as tiny Kuwait had suddenly been occupied by a larger, aggressive neighbour, portrayed as having expansionist ambitions that embraced the Arabian Peninsular. On closer examination the purity of purpose of rushing to the aid of this little-known (to the West), far-away, non-democratic, oil-rich country induced doubts. The covert reason was that the USA was primarily concerned with ensuring that the huge underground reservoirs of cheap, easily obtained oil in the Arabian Peninsular should continue to flow westwards under American influence. If Saddam Hussein, President of Iraq, gained control of these vast oil resources, he would be able to manipulate both the price, and the flow, of oil on to the world market to American detriment. It was an American war, for American empirical economic purposes, and Allies involved were in a subservient, or supporting, role.

Neither President Bush nor President Saddam Hussein though the confrontation would come to war, as each initially was convinced the other would ultimately back away, and it came as a surprise to both when neither did so. Each misjudged the other. This is often how wars start. During the Kuwait Crisis, prior to actual hostilities, Bush continually increased the size of his 'big stick', thinking this would over-awe Saddam Hussein, and do the trick; while Saddam Hussein thought the USA had no stomach for the military option, being psychologically conditioned against war by its own Vietnam experience.

By threats, promises and bribes, a fragile Allied military coalition was cobbled together, consisting of some uneasy bed-fellows, such as Syria, long regarded as a pariah in Western eyes, due to its support for international terrorism. By a miracle of modern transportation the USA air-lifted nearly half-a-million troops and thousands of tons of military material some 8,000 miles to 'defend a line in the sand' in Saudi Arabia.

In confrontation to this build-up, Iraqi troops settled in entrenched defences, at first confident they would win the Mother of all Battles, but eventually fatally resigned to their fate.

The value of Western hostages was vividly demonstrated when Saddam Hussein detained foreign nationals in Kuwait and Iraq to form his defensive Human Shield against any Western attack, holding some of them at, or near, potential military targets. Saddam Hussein was eventually persuaded to release them, and his supporters consider this to be his second big mistake. It was reckoned that President Bush would never have sanctioned bombing Iraqi targets if it would endanger American lives. Had Saddam Hussein retained his Human Shield, it is probable the Kuwait Crisis would have dragged on painfully and indefinitely, as did that when American hostages were seized in Tehran by Islamic Fundamentalist Revolutionary Students, and held for '444 days' (1979-81). This would have been a severe strain on Allied resolve and on the cohesion of the fragile Allied coalition.

The war was fought under the banner of the United Nations, as the ending of the Cold War enabled Bush to harness the UN Security Council to his cause (Pax Americana), persuading it to approve a series of Resolutions isolating Iraq, initiating embargoes against it, and then authorising the use of force to evict Iraqi troops from Kuwait. Bush liked to 'have people running with him'. Previously, the Security Council had been a Cold War pawn between the two main Super Powers, which neutralised its effectiveness. Now the USA 'called the shots'. Desperately needing American economic assistance, the USSR became a compliant supporter of the USA, its former enemy; while enigmatic China, wanting Western technology, trying to remain as neutral as possible, was also compliant to a degree, but abstained from voting on Resolution 678 (for the 'use of force').

The war was resoundingly won by a massive air campaign in which the very latest state-of-electronic art was used to deadly effect, and almost with impunity, as little Iraqi resistance was offered, for the cost of only a tiny handful of Allied casualties.

The effectiveness of American high-flying Stealth-type aircraft, using laser-guided, precision munitions, was the major factor that almost won the war for them, although they only carried out 8% of the bombing sorties, the other 92% being mainly World War II-type bombing, exampled by 'carpet-bombing', elderly B-52 aircraft. The theory that modern wars could be won by air power alone was nearly proved — but not quite. Western 'high-tech' electronics and weaponry were superior to those of the Soviets (Iraqis having mainly Soviet equipment), which was confirmed by Marshal Dimitri Yazov, the (then) Soviet Defence Minister, who openly admitted shortcomings and failures of Soviet air defence weapons in this war.

The anticipated grand air battle, predicted by advocates of the NATO 'Air-Land Battle Strategy' did not happen, as Saddam Hussein kept his air force out of the battle, and still retains over half his combat aircraft, and nearly all his helicopters.

Iraqis, military and civilian alike, suffered heavy casualties, as many as 400,000, or perhaps more, in '40 days' of continual Allied aerial onslaught. The precise toll is still hidden from the Western world by American authorities, as they wanted to persuade everyone they were fighting a clinical war, with precision weapons of fine accuracy, that only struck military buildings. Civilian casualties were disregarded, and if mentioned at all were known as 'collateral damage'. It had been expected that the Head of a totalitarian state at war would manipulate the Media, but it came as rather a surprise-shock to find the Allies using the same means. The fortitude of the Iraqi people under this intense bombardment, confounded the air power theory, as it had done in previous wars.

Stunned by the weight of Allied munitions falling on them, the Mother of all Battles, when it came, was a walk-over for the Allies, as dazed, shell-shocked, bewildered Iraqi troops surrendered in their thousands, although far more managed to hastily scurry back to their own country. The anticipated major tank battle, which it was hoped would prove the superiority of Western tanks, was never fought, and Saddam Hussein still has his 1,000 modern T-72 Soviet tanks intact.

This 'hyper war' or 'North-South war' in the jargon, had absorbed practically all available American (and British) military expeditionary resources, supplemented by drawing on their NATO inventories, and detaching troops from NATO commitments. It had been a one-sided conflict, in which a very heavy 'high-tech' sledge-hammer had been used to crack a conventional nut. Military strategists have searched for 'new lessons' of war, to find none of any significance, just age-old ones that were either applied efficiently, or ignored. The simple answer is that Western weaponry was better than that possessed by the Iraqis; although the cream, of the Iraqi air force and battle-tank fleet were never tested in battle.

Allied military leadership was mainly of a technical nature, epitomised by US General Horner, who directed and co-ordinated over 2,100 Allied aircraft in some 110,000 sorties, which was a masterpiece of organisation and staff work. Opportunity was too brief on the ground, and enemy resistance too slight, for a Patton, Rommel or Montgomery to emerge as a new master of warfare. Extrovert General Schwartzkopf's claim to military fame is that he unified the US separatist armed services into the Total Force concept, and imposed central command in the field — previously two US military weaknesses. Schwartzkopf's 'Media-hyped' grand Deception Plan, of giving the impression he was about to launch a frontal attack, and then made a wide western flanking movement, is not unique in military history. It was the only sensible course to take (as I explained when interviewed by CNN, on the 31st January 1991). Allied Generals were never tested in hard battle, or adversity.

The Iraqis were driven from Kuwait, but Allied success ended there, as a Pandora's Box of problems sprang open. The so-called Hidden Agenda had not been accomplished: and Saddam Hussein, who remained in power, turned to crush his southern Shia and northern Kurdish insurgencies with customary brutality. Saddam Hussein continued to operate his Strategic Defiance as UN monitoring teams sought to prise open his secret Aladin's Cave of non-conventional weaponry. Experts agree that he was 'only months away' from perfecting a nuclear warhead. The Middle East arms race simply gathered more momentum.

It is often said that Generals sit and plan to fight the 'last war' again one day, who ever-fascinated by 'combat-proven' new weaponry, is what they seem to be doing now, by putting all their 'high-tech' eggs in one basket, at the expense of other military requirements. The circumstances of the Liberation of Kuwait were unusual, and may never be repeated. Next time, the Generals may meet serious opposition, both 'high-tech' and 'low-tech' combined.

As time goes by, elation, chagrin, disillusionment or disappointment may subside, or alternately harden into bitterness. History will be the arbiter of the future reputation of the Liberation of Kuwait war. Like the truth it purports to be, history is many faceted, often politically biased, and usually written, and at times re-written, to make it palatable for comfortable, morale-boosting national purposes.

In the USA, the Liberation of Kuwait will long be regarded as a glorious military victory, full of righteous motivation. The British and French may regard it just as just another footnote to their military history, a repeat of many long-past, largely forgotten colonial campaigns and battles. They both were certainly in a hurry to get their 'Victory Marches' over and done with, so their governments could get on with reducing their armed forces. Other European participants may find it embarrassing in future, and want to quietly forget all about it.

In the ever-changing swirl of Arab rivalries, both Egypt and Syria may be uneasy at having fought a brother Arab State at the bidding of a Western nation, and will play down its significance. Others in the military coalition, who restricted themselves to the 'defence of Saudi Arabia only', may regard it as a bright moment in their dull military histories when "they marched to right a wrong". Non-committed countries, Islamic and non-Islamic, some inherently anti-Western and anti-Imperialist may see it as just one more Pax Americana step to gain control over the whole of the Arabian Peninsular.

Kuwait may regard the war as a near fatal watershed in its short history, which must not re-occur, but lacking faith in brother Arab States, and wishing to remain independent and secure, it concluded a 10-year US-Kuwait Defence Agreement in September, even though this meant accepting an American arms stock-pile, joint American-Kuwaiti military exercises on its sand, and having to open its port to USN battle ships. In Iraq, Saddam Hussein is already persuading his people they have won a great victory by standing up alone, like a David facing Goliath, against American Imperialism. Stories of wars and campaigns invariably contain elements of truth, laced with varying amounts of fiction. This account outlines facts and facets of this war, several uncomfortable and embarrassing, as clearly, factually and analytically as possible, before they become too deformed, or obscured by partial governments or historians.

August 1992   Edgar O'Ballance
                                               Wakebridge, Derbyshire

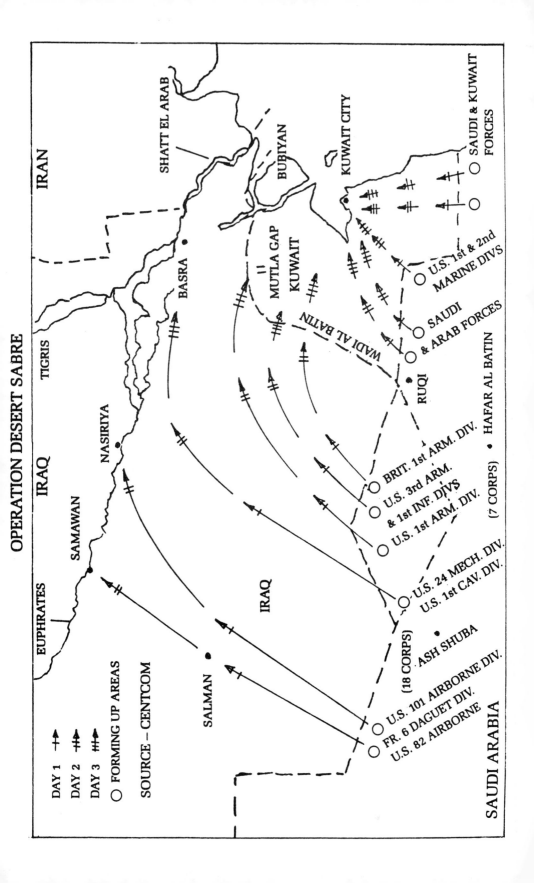

OPERATION DESERT SABRE

KUWAIT — DEFENSIVE POSTURE

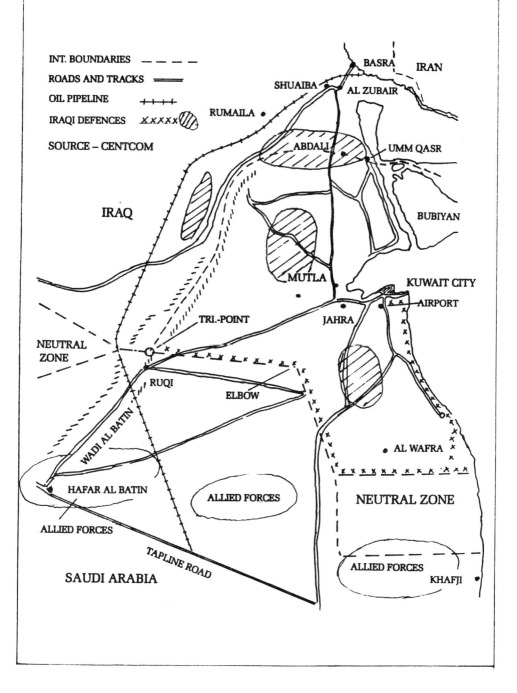

INT. BOUNDARIES — — —
ROADS AND TRACKS ═══
OIL PIPELINE ┼┼┼┼
IRAQI DEFENCES ✗✗✗✗✗
SOURCE – CENTCOM

IRAQ

BASRA

IRAN

SHUAIBA

AL ZUBAIR

RUMAILA

ABDALI

UMM QASR

BUBIYAN

MUTLA

KUWAIT CITY

AIRPORT

TRI.-POINT

JAHRA

NEUTRAL ZONE

RUQI

ELBOW

WADI AL BATIN

AL WAFRA

HAFAR AL BATIN

ALLIED FORCES

NEUTRAL ZONE

ALLIED FORCES

ALLIED FORCES

KHAFJI

TAPLINE ROAD

SAUDI ARABIA

1

The Rape of Kuwait

While the complacent, unsuspecting population of Kuwait City slept peacefully in their beds, at 0200-hours (local time), on Thursday, 2nd August 1990, two Iraqi Republican Guard armoured divisions, and other formations (140,000 troops in all: *General Powell*), in five mobile columns, swept into Kuwait across its land frontier. The main column moved southwards down the highway that led from Basra to Kuwait City, while the other four spread out invading from the north-west to move along roads across desert terrain to overwhelm towns, oil installations and key communications.

Despite being on a State of Alert since the 16th July, detachments of the army, frontier guards and police posts were quickly brushed aside. The main column reached the outskirts of Kuwait City at 0440-hours, when Iraqi combat aircraft began to bomb key targets. Kuwait Radio did not announce the invasion until 0630-hours, and Iraqi bombing seems to have little disturbed the people, many of whom first heard of their disaster when on their way to work, or when they reached their work place. By nightfall Iraqi troops were in possession of the city, its suburbs and adjacent oil installations. Telecommunications with the outside world were severed. Despite ominous warning signs the ostrich-like Kuwait authorities had been taken completely by surprise.

Awakened as soon as it was known that hostile Iraqi troops had crossed the frontier into Kuwait, the Emir, Sheikh Jaber al-Ahmad al-Jaber as-Sabah, his family, Ministers and other VIPs, hastily bundled themselves into an instant black limousine motorcade, which suggested that this was an ever-ready precaution always available to the Emir in case of an emergency, which this certainly was. Fleets of black, bullet-proof limousines, with darkened windows, swiftly and silently sped away southwards, to be well clear of Kuwait territory when dawn broke. An exodus by helicopter might have awakened, and alerted, the sleeping city.

1

The Emir, and the Crown Prince, Sheikh Saad al-Abdullah as-Selim as-Sabah reached the safety, and luxury, of a first class modern hotel in Taif, a Saudi mountain resort, over 300 miles from home, where they stayed for the duration of the Crisis and War.

Back in Kuwait City, Kuwait armed forces put up only brief resistance to the invaders, mainly it was said at the Shuwaikh main army barracks on the northern outskirts of the city, the Jahra barracks; and by the Palace Guard, at the Dasman Palace, the Emir's official residence, but little seems to be known about this in detail, although local legends are being manufactured. Iraqi aerial and ground attacks quickly smothered Kuwaiti opposition, causing some casualties. The semi-official Iraqi estimate of 400 dead was considered to be much too low, and locals insist that the figure of 4,000 was a more realistic one. Certainly, Iraqi troops operated with a heavy hand.

Much later, according to one source (*Guardian*: 7th June 1991), after the Emir and his entourage eventually returned to Kuwait City, with his government unchanged in composition, angry Kuwaiti military officers circulated two Petitions, which stated they would quit if the post-war government administration did not include military leadership changes. They wanted an immediate investigation, and removal if necessary, of the Chief-of-Staff, his senior staff officers, and others responsible, for abandoning their country when it was attacked — this embraced some 20 Generals and 75 Colonels. The Kuwaiti Defence Minister, Sheikh Nawaf as-Sabah, declined to discuss the 'army revolt'.

The Iraqis enforced an immediate curfew in Kuwait City, and in compliance the majority of inhabitants remained in their houses and apartments. Those who ventured out on to the streets were shot at, or rounded up and put into impromptu detention buildings. The population of Kuwait was about 1.9-million (1989 figures), but only about 650,000 of them were "first class citizens" with full civil rights and privileges, being Kuwaitis proper. It was the hot season and many Kuwaitis proper were absent on business, leisure or pleasure, and in the following days many began slipping away from Kuwait into Saudi Arabia.

Kuwait was both oil-rich and investment-rich, and so Kuwaitis proper were a cosseted and pampered community, which generally led an indolent life. As they could well afford to hire 'foreign' expertise, management and labour for all inconvenient or distasteful jobs, Kuwaitis did little for themselves. About 400,000 Palestinians lived in Kuwait, unable to obtain Kuwait citizenship, largely forming a middle management strata of government, commerce, trade, transportation and other enterprises, while over half-a-million Asian workers were employed on service and menial jobs.

With prepared lists ready, personnel of the Iraqi Military Intelligence Service (Mukhabarat) accompanying the invasion force, immediately began to round up anti-Iraqi exiles, and other subversives, who were detained, interrogated, and then sent off to Baghdad. Many 'wanted persons' were found in the Bnaid al-Gar district, inhabited mainly by Shia Muslims. The ruling as-Sabah family and the majority of inhabitants were of the Sunni persuasion. Additionally, about 8,000 Kuwaiti civilians were also taken off to the Iraqi Capital as hostages as well as all captured Kuwait military personnel.

The Central Prison was opened, all prisoners were screened, and common criminals and anti-Sabah offenders, released. Anti-Iraqi terrorists were sent to Baghdad, probably never to be seen again. These included members of the notorious 'Kuwaiti-17 martyrs', being originally 17 members of the anti-Saddam Hussein 'Dawa' (Hizb al-Daawa al-Islamiya — Islamic Call) terrorist organisation that had developed in the 1960s, convicted of attempting to assassinate the Emir in 1987. The Dawa committed several spectacular terrorist exploits, taking hostages, and each time demanding the release of the Kuwaiti-17 in exchange for their safety. Each time the Emir refused, and was commended for his resolute stand by Western nations.

The exception was in April 1988, when a Kuwaiti airliner, flying from Bangkok, was hijacked and diverted to Mashad (Iran), and then to Algiers, where a 16-day siege ensued. The hijackers again demanded the release of the Kuwaiti-17, and on this occasion, as members of the as-Sabah family were among the hostages, two of the Kuwaiti-17 were quietly released in exchange for them. The remaining '15' were seized by the Iraqis. There was silence for a while about their fate, until January 1992 (Washington Post), when it was revealed they had been handed over by the Iraqis to the Iranian government, probably their paymaster, as part of the price for concluding the formal Cease-Fire in the Iran-Iraq War (1980-88), to be freed into anonymity.

Next, the Iraqis set about officially, systematically and thoroughly, looting Kuwait City, stripping it of everything of any value that was movable, especially if it belonged to the as-Sabah family, or to the 'government', which was pretty much the same thing. Buses, commercial vehicles, private cars, tractors, machinery and apparatus from the oil, water and sewerage installations were removed. Within hours convoys of trucks, heavily laden with looted goods were on their way to Baghdad, a process that continued for many days.

Also looted were supermarkets, shops and stores, packed full of goods attractive to rich Kuwaitis, that included televisions, radios, stereo-systems, video cameras, mobile telephones, jewellery and watches, as well as packaged foods, household furniture and fittings, many of which later ended up in the 'Thieves' Market' in Baghdad. Street salesmen of this stolen property, quoted the previous owner as being 'Ali Baba', but few questions were asked by the Iraqi authorities, as long as the items were not required for 'official purposes'. It was said that two Iraqi Generals personally oversaw the removal of over 70 Rolls-Royce cars and quantities of spares, as well as a number of Bentleys and Jaguars. Later, some of the Jaguars were traced to a motor sale-room in Beirut, but the Rolls-Royces and Bentleys have been much harder to trace.

Gold and foreign currency deposits were seized from the Kuwaiti Treasury. Later (in July and August 1991), Iraq returned to Kuwait '1,216 gold bars, each weighing 28.6-lbs, worth more than $500-million (AP). The Kuwait National Museum was stripped bare of its priceless exhibits, objects d'art, antiques, tapestries, jewels and Islamic artifacts, which were all trucked off to Baghdad. It was later stated by the Kuwaitis that the nominal value of the goods taken by the Iraqis in this gigantic looting spree exceeded $3-billion. Vindictiveness and heavy-handedness accompanied the looting as some buildings were deliberately damaged, set on fire, or demolished. Items not wanted or immovable, were often smashed or made inoperative and valueless.

Later, the Kuwaiti Ambassador to the UN (Mohammed Abdul Hassan) declared "Iraqi occupation forces have mounted a looting and plundering operation designed to achieve nothing less than the complete removal of all Kuwaiti assets".

On the 4th August, units of the People's Army, a mustered militia, were drafted in to garrison Kuwait City, and some of their less well disciplined personnel, seeing what their government was doing, joined in and began looting for private gain. The People's Army seemed to concentrate on breaking into shuttered and locked, empty houses and apartments, to steal household items such as televisions, radios, tape-recorders, refrigerators, furniture and ornaments. Rooms were often wrecked, floor-boards torn up, and walls smashed in search of suspected hiddeen jewellery, money or valuables.

The Iraqi military commander ordered that looting by the People's Army must stop, but found this difficult to enforce. Eventually, on the 14th August, an Iraqi officer was publicly hanged near his pile of looted items, as a warning to others, and the photograph of this salutary execution widely distributed. As well as incidents of wanton damage there were also many of rape, assault and ill-treatment of inhabitants, for which generally the People's Army was blamed, but perhaps army formations that replaced Republican Guard ones, which had headed the invasion force, and which had moved out southwards towards the Saudi border, were just as guilty.

An aftermath problem of female victims of rape, was explained by a Kuwaiti Doctor (Mansour Sarkhou), who remained in Kuwait throughout the seven-month Iraqi Occupation, who said (*Daily Telegraph*: 6th November 1991), that "some 5,000 Kuwaiti women were made pregnant, most in repeated mass rapes of extreme violence"; and he added that

4

"When liberating forces of the coalition came through they reported finding naked girls held prisoner in the dug-outs of the Iraqi troops". These human outrages were compounded as abortion is illegal in Kuwait, and of course, contrary to Islamic law.

The enormity of the Rape of Kuwait does not always seem to be fully appreciated universally. It was as if a group of professional thieves descended like a group of vultures on a dead carcase, to strip the whole city of everything of value, damage what they could not take with them, and abuse the population, without regard to Human Rights. It was said that if the American CNN *(Cable Network News)* television organisation (which actually had a team in Baghdad at that moment which later covered Allied munitions hitting targets in that city), had also had one in Kuwait able to transmit, it would have made a much deeper impression on international opinion. It would have marked the actual start of the Kuwait War more indelibly. Mistakenly, many now tend to think the Kuwait War did not begin until the 17th January 1991: for the Kuwaitis it began on the 2nd August 1990, with the Rape of Kuwait.

Occupation of Kuwait City

Many 'wanted persons' and 'foreigners' fearing arrest sought shelter in the apartments of friends, Kuwaitis and expatriate alike, and many remained safely hidden for some time. Apart from periodic house searches by the Iraqi Mukhabarat and the People's Army, and occasional looting forays, the major part of the population was generally left alone to survive as best it could.

Arms in plenty were to be had in Kuwait City, at least initially, and a few bolder Kuwaiti spirits tried to form resistance groups in their own localities, but scope was limited, the Iraqi military presence heavy, curfews were in force, and retribution was deadly. A resistance radio station, "This is Kuwait — Huna Kuwait", did surface to broadcast intermittently for a while.

Soon some inhabitants began to collaborate with the occupying Iraqi authorities, the finger being pointed mainly at the Palestinians, as Yasir Arafat, leader of the Palestinian Liberation Organisation *(PLO)*, had virtually thrown in his lot with Saddam Hussein, but some Kuwaitis also collaborated, not all being firmly enamoured with the autocratic rule of the as-Sabah family. Apart from such individuals the large majority of the inhabitants, Kuwaitis and non-Kuwaitis, for their own safety and in their own self interest, remained passive. On the 5th August, the curfew was relaxed slightly, and key workers were urged to return to their jobs.

The previous day, the so-far unknown 'Provisional Free Kuwait Government' *(PFKG)* appeared, which was alleged to be composed of

'Iraqis pretending to be Kuwaitis', headed by Colonel Ali Hussein, son-in-law of Saddam Hussein. It was said that several prominent Kuwaitis who refused an invitation to join the PFKG were detained, together with other Kuwaitis regarded as being 'uncooperative'. In fact, in the early hours of the Iraqi invasion, *Radio Baghdad* had insisted that Iraq was simply responding to a request from the PFKG for military asistance — which puzzled many.

On the 7th August, the PFKG announced the advent of the independent 'Republic of Kuwait', but it had to turn about face quickly as the following day Saddam Hussein annexed Kuwait, and it had to state that Kuwait had become the '19th Governate of Iraq'. General Ali Hassan al-Majid, regarded as a hard man, who had been an Army Corps commander in northern Iraq in 1987-8, when chemical warfare means were used against the Kurds, was appointed Governor of the Kuwait Governate.

Members of the short-lived PFKG were rewarded. Colonel Ali Hussein became a Deputy Prime Minister, and the eight others were appointed Advisers to the Presidential Office in Baghdad, with full Ministerial rank. None appeared to be Kuwaiti. All foreign embassies and legations in Kuwait were ordered to move to Baghdad, but most hesitated.

On the 9th August, the borders of Kuwait were closed to foreigners trying to leave the country. It was estimated there were about 4,000 British and 2,500 American nationals in Kuwait, and also about 600 British and 600 American citizens in Iraq. On the 12th, a Briton (Donald Croaskery) was shot dead near the frontier while escaping. On the 16th, all British and American nationals in Kuwait were ordered to surrender to the authorities.

Kuwaiti Armed Forces

The Kuwait armed forces were small, numbering in all about 20,300 all ranks (IISS), sustained by, and reliant upon, several hundred foreign advisers and technicians. They lack combat experience. Top heavy with Kuwaiti 'Top Brass', despite a facade of a two-year period of conscription, the Kuwaiti element within them was remarkably small, but undefined. Few Kuwaiti citizens were attracted to a military career in a desert setting. Many of the middle and junior grade officers were expatriate Muslims, such as Pakistanis on 'contract' engagements, while the ranks contained a very high proportion of 'Bidoun', that is 'stateless' Arabs who resided in Kuwait. The Bidoun (lit:, 'without') numbered over 200,000, and also largely filled the lower ranks of the police, other para-military services, and many were employed as private security guards.

Billions of dollars had been expended by the Kuwaitis in purchasing prestige armaments, such as modern aircraft, tanks and missiles, and millions of dollars worth were still in the pipeline. For their size, the Kuwaiti armed forces were over-armed, and indeed could not absorb all the weaponry that had been acquired, much of which still lay in crates in store.

The Kuwaiti Army, about 16,000 strong (IISS), consisted basically of two armoured and three mechanised units, formed into two brigades, one of which was detached to the Gulf Co-operation Council (GCC) Rapid Deployment Force (RDF), at Hafar al-Batin, in northern Saudi Arabia. It was equipped with about 625 armoured vehicles of different types, which included 165 Chieftain, 40 Centurion and 170 Mark-1 Vickers main battle tanks; 36 self-propelled guns; HOT, TOW and Vigilant anti-tank missiles; and also 12 Soviet FROG-7 launchers, and some missiles.

The Kuwaiti Air Force, with about 2,000 personnel, had about 40 combat aircraft, that included Mirage F-1s and Hawk trainers, some of which were due to be replaced by US F-18s, and 24 helicopters. Kuwait had an integrated Air Defence Control System, with US HAWKs, and other anti-aircraft weaponry. Other missiles included the French Super R-530 and R-550 Magic. The Kuwaiti Navy, about 2,000 strong, had eight missile-craft, some with Exocet missiles, and 14 smaller craft, which operated from the two small naval bases at Shuwaikh and al-Adami. The Kuwait National Guard, which included the Palace Guard and the Border Guard, was about 1,500 strong, armed with light weapons, having about 80 light armoured vehicles.

According to one source (Strategic Survey: IISS), the Kuwaiti armed forces received 'a few hours warning of the invasion, thanks to a newly arrived surveillance radar on a tethered balloon', but did not state exactly how much warning had been given. Whatever it was, no doubt it was swiftly passed on to the sleeping Emir. It certainly seems to have circulated within the armed forces like wild-fire. This was an airborne Early Warning balloon, equipped with radar for low-level air defence, provided by the US Navy. It was captured by invading Iraqis.

It is now known that a number of high ranking Kuwaiti officers, with some servicemen, about 3,000 perhaps, in over 50 tanks and other vehicles, were able to hastily decamp into Saudi Arabia. Kuwait Air Force pilots managed to fly out 15 combat aircraft, and most of the helicopters, and all eight of the Navy's missile-craft made it to the security of Saudi harbours. The first impression was that many senior Kuwaiti officers gave more attention to flight than to fight. In November, the Kuwaiti government-in-exile, in its Taif hotel, stated that '4,200 Kuwaitis had been killed, and 12,000 soldiers captures by the Iraqis'.

Gleefully, the Iraqis scooped up this haul of abandoned aircraft, weaponry, missiles, vehicles, ammunition and military equipment, which together with hundreds of unopened crates, was quickly dispatched to Baghdad. It was a valuable addition to the Iraqi arsenal, and included the HAWK launchers and over 150 missiles, as well as the FROG launchers and their missiles. There appears to be little, if any, evidence of any Kuwaiti attempts to destroy any of the modern weaponry or munitions to prevent them falling into the hands of the invaders.

The Iraqis did obtain one more valuable windfall, finding 15 Kuwait civilian airliners on the ground at the Kuwait International Airport (out of a fleet of 23). Additionally, a British airliner, on a scheduled flight, had just landed, to find the airport in Iraqi hands, when all on board became Iraqi hostages. Controversy arose afterwards, it being alleged that the airport authorities had sufficient warning of the situation on the ground to have diverted it elsewhere while still in the air.

The Iraqi Armed Forces

It is sufficient to say for the moment that in comparison to the tiny, not all that effective, Kuwaiti armed forces, those of Iraq were very, very large, well armed and combat experienced.

Reason for the Iraqi Invasion

In short, the real reasons for the Iraqi military invasion of Kuwait were Saddam Hussein's naked expansionist ambitions and Iraqi economic need. In September 1980, he had led his country into a war with neighbouring Iran, which lasted for eight years, and had a very debilitating effect on both countries. In this war Saddam Hussein posed as the 'Defender of the Arab Nation' against Iranian Islamic Fundamentalist expansion. Certain Arab Gulf States, being under this impression, gave him interest free loans.

The Iranian government eventually sued for a cease-fire, which came into effect on the 20th August 1988. Kuwait then demanded repayment of its loans. Pre-war Iraq had been the second largest oil exporter in the Organisation of Petroleum Exporting Countries (OPEC), a cartel to maintain price stability, but its oil installations had been largely devastated in the conflict. Saddam Hussein refused to pay, demanding instead that the debts be cancelled as he had been "defending the Arab Nation". Kuwait re-issued its demand.

Additionally, Saddam Hussein alleged that Kuwait had moved into Iraqi territory during the war to establish military posts and oil installations, and had 'stolen' oil from the Iraqi Rumaila oil-field. He costed this loss at $2-billion, and demanded payment. He also blamed Kuwait for 'over-production' of oil above its OPEC quota, which caused world oil prices to slump, consequently reducing Iraq's income. He valued this lost revenue at $25-billion, and demanded payment. Once again Kuwait refused, and continued to disregard its OPEC quota. Saddam Hussein added another $5-billion for the loss of oil revenue from the Neutral Zone, of which he had been entitled a half share.

By early 1990, Iraq's foreign debts amounted to approximately $80-billion, over half of which was owed to Arab States, while its income from oil revenues was only $15-billion, of which some 30% was needed to service debts (IISS). There were also long-standing border disputes between Kuwait and Iraq, which after a period of quiescent during the war, reared up again.

Caught by Surprise

Saddam Hussein had made his accusation of 'stealing oil' speech in May 1990, and during the following weeks he reiterated several times his demands for money from Kuwait, making wild threats of what he would do if he did not obtain satisfaction. July was a tense month in which Saddam Hussein moved troops towards the Kuwaiti border. Affluent and imbued with the belief that money could buy anything, Kuwaitis tended to be arrogant and condescending, and were unmoved by his threats. The general Arab impression was that Saddam Hussein was simply sabre-rattling, hoping to frighten tiny Kuwait into compliance by scare tactics.

On the 24th July, President Mubarak, of Egypt, visited Saddam Hussein in Baghdad, and was assured by the Iraqi President that he would not launch a military invasion of Kuwait. Mubarak told King Fahd, of Saudi Arabia, and through his contacts passed this information on to King Hussein, of Jordan. Mubarak believed what Saddam Hussein had said. At an OPEC meeting (26th/27th), while the price of oil was raised from $18 to $21 pb (per barrel), output quotas remained the same, with the slight exception of an upward adjustment in the case of the United Arab Emirates (UAE). Iraq's oil output quota remained at 2.5-million bpd (barrels per day), and that of Kuwait at 1.5-million bpd.

King Fahd tried to become a peace-maker in this issue, and on the 31st July invited representatives of both Iraq and Kuwait to Taif. The Kuwaiti Crown Prince, who was also Prime Minister, and the Iraqi Deputy Chairmen of the Iraqi Revolutionary Command Council (RCC), attended this meeting. Talks stumbled along, and then broke down. The participants embraced each other in the Arab fashion, and returned to their respective countries. A few brief hours later the Iraqi military invasion of Kuwait was under way.

Many national leaders were completely taken by surprise, their respective intelligence services having let them down. The US Central Intelligence Agency (CIA) was afterwards taken to task, and censured for its failure, admitting that it "Did not have the complete picture of Iraqi movements" *(Washington Post)*. Some hours before the invasion a well-known American analyst *(Pat Lang)* warned that Saddam Hussein was about to march into Kuwait, but this was disregarded by the US Defense Secretary, Richard Cheney, who thought the Iraqi President was bluffing.

Arab leaders tended to blame the USA for encouraging Saddam Hussein to attack Kuwait, being of the opinion that President Bush had deliberately given him the green light. With his large, combat-experienced armed forces, Saddam Hussein was not afraid of any Arab military opposition, but was apprehensive in case the United States would intervene, as it had done in Lebanon previously, especially as cheap oil was at stake.

On the 25th July, the American Ambassador to Iraq, Ms. April Glaspie, saw Saddam Hussein, and in the course of their meeting allegedly told him (according to Saddam Hussein, who claimed he had a recording of the conversation) that "The United States has no opinion on Arab-Arab conflicts, like your border disagreement with Kuwait". Glaspie, who spoke fluent Arabic, did not make notes at the time, and this comment became controversial, as later, US Secretary of State, James Baker, tried rather unfairly to blame her for virtually giving the Iraqi President the go-ahead. Had this comment not been made, it is possible that Saddam Hussein might have hesitated.

Kuwait

On the 1st August 1990, Kuwait was a tiny independent sovereign Arab State, comprising some 11,200 square miles, wedged between Iraq and Saudi Arabia. It was a member of the United Nations, the Arab League, the Gulf Co-operation Council, and OPEC. Virtually a city state, it was known derisively to its many enemies and detractors as an 'oil well with a national flag'. It was a 'traditional' Arab Gulf State, governed autocratically by the Emir (Amir), Sheikh Jaber al-Ahmad al-Jaber as-Sabah, who acceded in 1978, and who appointed, and dismissed, Ministers at will.

For centuries during which the vast deserts of the Arabian Peninsular were inhabited by small tribes, forever on the move in search of grazing for their herds of animals. Kuwait was one of the very few settled habitations, which necessarily rested on an adequate supply of drinking water. Its position was favourable in that it was on traditional camel-train routes, carrying spices, incense and other eastern commodities, from south-eastern Arabia to Syria, Mesopotamia and East Mediterranean ports and cities. Although Basra was an ancient, well established Arab port in the region, Kuwait attracted a good deal of small-boat traffic across the Gulf from the east. Kuwait developed both a thriving market place, and a small pearl-diving industry.

At the turn of the 18th Century the as-Sabah tribe began to settle on Kuwait. It is recorded that in 1752, the Ottoman authorities appointed Sheikh as-Sabah to be 'Sheikh of Kuwait'; successive Sheikhs, or 'Governors', became autonomous. The as-Sabah family has held the 'Emirate', as it became, ever since. In 1899, the British made a Trucial (Truce) Treaty with the Emir of Kuwait, virtually turning it into a 'British Protectorate', and making it completely independent of the Basra Wilayat, the Ottoman Empire being too weak to object to such British incursions into the Gulf area. In 1913, the British drew wide boundaries in the sand around Kuwait City, to enhance the importance of their Protectorate, this being one of the first introductions of the Western concept of 'fixed national boundaries' in this part of the Arabian Peninsular.

On the dissolution of the Ottoman Empire after World War I, the British formed the new state of Iraq, mainly from the territory of Mesopotamia, but ensured that their Kuwait Protectorate remained independent of it. At the Convention of Uqair (1922), the British re-defined boundaries between Iraq, Kuwait and the 'Emirate of Nejd' (now part of Saudi Arabia). To avoid conflicting tribal claims on certain disputed terrain, the British formed two 'Neutral Zones'. One was directly south of Kuwait (between Kuwait and Nejd), and the other was to its west (between Iraq and Nejd), which would belong to neither country, but which nomadic tribes could continue to use as their traditional seasonal grazing grounds. The oil factor was not then a consideration for Imperial map-makers, but later when oil production developed in the area, that pumped from the two Neutral Zones, was to be shared equally between adjacent countries.

Mandated to Britain, Iraq protested that as Kuwait had originally been in the Ottoman Wilayat of Basra (perhaps itself in dispute), it should have been incorporated into the new Kingdom of Iraq, but this was over-ruled by the British. This Iraqi claim was raised periodically, but owing to British objections, came to nothing. Having only the narrow Shatt al-Arab channel as the marine outlet from Basra, on the east side of which sat their traditional enemies, the Persians, Iraqis cast covetous eyes on Kuwait's large open harbour. Iraq's small naval base at Umm Qasr, on the narrow Khor Abdullah channel, was masked off from the Gulf proper by the two Kuwaiti Islands of Bubiyan and Warba.

In June 1961, Britain granted full independence to Kuwait, and the Trucial Treaty was replaced by one of Friendship and Assistance, which included defence support. Instantly, President Kassem of Iraq, pressed his claim on Kuwait, and made threatening military moves, causing the Emir to call for British military assistance. Some 6,000 British troops arrived, and took up positions facing the Iraqi frontier, which deterred Kassem's expansionist ambitions. British troops were relieved by military contingents from Arab League States, all of which had departed by January 1963.

In June that year, Iraq was persuaded to recognise the independent sovereignty of Kuwait, and in return Kuwait reputedly paid a bribe of £30-million to Iraq; and shortly afterwards paid another bribe of £25-million to Egypt (when that country briefly formed a Federation with Iraq and Syria); large sums of money in those days for a small developing country to pay out. The British 'defence agreement' expired in 1971. The following year, Iraq demanded permission to install an oil pipeline through Kuwaiti territory, and to construct an oil terminal on Bubiyan Island, but this was rejected. In 1973, Iraqi armed forces occupied a small portion of Kuwaiti territory near this Island, but withdrew again in the face of general Arab disapproval. It is believed the Saudis suggested, at the Taif meeting (31st July), that Iraq should recognise the existing land border with Kuwait in return for Warba Island and a lease of part of Bubiyan Island. Kuwait refused.

Kuwait produced a written Constitution in 1962, which catered for an elected National Assembly, but this early trial of democracy did not survive long. It was not until February 1985, that another National Assembly appeared, in which 50 members were elected and 50 were nominated. The electorate was tiny, only some 90,000 'first class' Kuwaiti citizens being entitled to vote, of whom a number had not even bothered to register. This National Assembly was dissolved in July 1986, owing to the Members' criticism of the as-Sabah family in government.

Public meetings and demonstrations were forbidden, but a number of discontented ex-National Assembly Members began meeting at each others' homes in the traditional 'Diwabiya' manner, to discuss political matters, and from December 1989, onwards these seemed to develop into a movement of protest. In June 1990, the Emir allowed another election for a National Assembly, but no results were ever published, nor did one materialise. The Emir shuffled a few Ministers, and then reverted to his usual attitude of indifference to democracy. However, he could not completely ignore the growing unease that was becoming openly manifest, and so appointed a 75-member Interim National Assembly, which was only a consultative body, a rubber-stamp, which did not satisfy those seeking a greater democratic leap forward.

Oil in commercial quantities was first discovered in Kuwait in 1938, but production was delayed owing to World War II, and oil production did not come on stream until July 1946. Kuwait is reported to have the fifth largest oil reservoir in the world, and within a few short years became fabulously rich. It became a founder member of OPEC in 1960. Awash with petro-dollars, Kuwaiti oil wealth produced a most luxurious welfare state, which included free medical care, education and other benefits, all tax free, but only for 'first class' Kuwaiti citizens.

Commerce was encouraged and many Kuwaitis individually became very wealthy. The Emir established a government agency, the Kuwait

Investment Office (KIO), based in London, to invest surplus oil profits in world stock markets. It was said that Kuwaiti income from these investments exceeded the sale of oil, and oil-refined products. In 1989, for example, the Kuwaiti annual surplus of income over expenditure was about $855-million *(Financial Times)*. On the 2nd August 1990, the Emir gave the KIO full authority over all Kuwait's financial assets and investments, to prevent them from being taken over by Iraq, or frozen by foreign governments.

Saddam Hussein Takriti

Now we come to the villain of the piece — Saddam Hussein Takriti — a street-wise terrorist fighter in his youth as some would have us believe, who developed into a hard self-seeking Dictator, who rules by a judicious mixture of fear and reward. Having very few confidants, he relies upon his extended family, which has far more than its fair share of public offices and appointments, for loyal support. If he sinks, they all sink with him. Without formal military training (it is reputed he failed to gain entrance to the National Military College), he has shown a flair for strategy, for selecting competent military commanders, for abruptly changing them, and an aptitude for brinkmanship.

His reputation was blood-stained with acts of sadistic cruelty and inhumanity, probably his most notorious being the use of chemical weapons against his own people. *Amnesty International* asserted that his prisons were full of untried dissidents; that secret executions were the order of the day, that torture in them was rife, and that many people simply 'disappeared'. His record of infamy is dark and long, but more than a little blurred, having been doctored by both his supporters and detractors.

Saddam Hussein was born in 1937, in a village near the city of Takrit, on the River Tigris, about 50 miles north of Baghdad. Takrit is also the birthplace of Saladin (a Kurd), the 12th Century Muslim commander who defeated the Crusaders in the Holy Land. Saladin is one of Saddam Hussein's heroes. Conflicting legends about his early life obscure fact, as does the 'official' documentary on his youth, shown on Baghdad TV, in October 1991. Born into a legal family, and educated in Baghdad (and perhaps also in Cairo), as a youth he became involved in the (then) illegal Arab Baath (Renaissance) Socialist Party. His earliest revolutionary violence was in 1959, when he claims to have shot at the motorcade of Prime Minister Abdul Karim Kassem, and was himself wounded by security guards. He had to flee to Egypt, but his reputation as a 'hit-man' had been achieved. After the assassination of Kassem, in 1963, Saddam Hussein returned to Iraq, but his involvement in another plot, meant that he had to stay underground until a General Amnesty was proclaimed. By this time he had become Deputy Secretary General of the Baath Party.

When the Baathists returned to power in Iraq in 1968, by a coup led by General Ahmad Hassan al-Bakh, Saddam Hussein became Director of Security Services, and quickly gained promotion in both political and governmental circles. In 1970, he received an honorary degree from the Iraq National Military College (the one he had failed to gain entrance to as a young man), and assumed the rank of General. Saddam Hussein stayed in the shadow of President al-Bakh, becoming Foreign Minister.

As Foreign Minister he signed the Algiers Treaty, of 1975, under which the Shah of Iran agreed to stop sending arms to Kurdish rebels in northern Iraq. In return, Iraq agreed to forfeit certain rights it had assumed over the Shatt al-Arab, which formed the southern part of the frontier between Iraq and Iran. It was also agreed that the joint boundary should be along the 'thalweg', that is the centre, or deepest part, instead of along the Iranian shore.

On the 17th July 1979, Saddam Hussein pushed President al-Bakh aside, and took his place, becoming President of Iraq, Chairman of the RCC, and Secretary General of the Baath (Regional) Party. In September 1980, he abrogated the Algiers Treaty, and sent Iraqi troops in to Iran, thus starting the nine-year long conflict.

Iraq had been mainly armed by the Soviets, and was considered by some to be a Soviet client state, but during the Iraq-Iran War the West tended to support Saddam Hussein, regarding him as a shield against hostile expansionist ambitions of the Iranian Islamic Fundamentalist Revolution, as preached by Ayatollah Khomeni, fearing it might spill over into the Gulf area, where oil-rich Arab States with small populations, and sketchy defence forces, were extremely vulnerable. Some nations applied economic sanctions against Iraq, but others, such as the USA, Britain, France and other arms-exporting nations, tended to ignore embargoes. In mid-1982, the Iraq-Iran War stalemated roughly along the joint international boundary, and devolved into trench warfare on the World War I model, becoming extremely costly in human life.

After the cease-fire between Iraq and Iran, the arms race began to gain momentum in the Middle East region, involving Iraq, Iran, Israel and Egypt, each of which sought to obtain non-conventional weapons, and improve their military capabilities. Saudi Arabia had unilaterally already obtained medium-range ballistic missiles from China, that could target both Israel and Iran. Certain Arab States purchased more prestige items of sophisticated weaponry. Documents available to the US House of Representatives, indicated that in the 15 days prior to the 2nd August, the Bush Administration approved the sale of advanced technology products, worth $4.8-million, to Iraq, including on one day (17th July 1990) computers to the value of $3.4-million. The US Commerce Department stated it had tried to tighten up policy after Saddam Hussein had threatened to use chemical warfare against Israel (in Spring 1990), but that State Department officials 'didn't want to know' *(Washington Post)*.

In February 1989, Iraq, Egypt, Jordan and North Yemen, formed the Arab Co-operation Council (ACC), which had all the hallmarks of a military coalition framework. (North and South Yemen were unified in May 1990.) Surveying the Gulf scene, and its international background, Saddam Hussein judged the time was ripe to march against Kuwait — and then the Arabian Peninsular would lay open before him.

2

A Line in the Sand

A universal crescendo of condemnation arose over the Iraqi invasion of Kuwait causing mixed responses. Some governments were genuinely concerned by the injustice of a larger neighbour gobbling up a smaller one and the effect this would have on international behaviour, while others apprehensively wondered which country might be the next victim, and yet other governments were more concerned in case oil from Kuwait and other Arab Gulf States might fall into hostile, and exploitive hands. About 60% of known oil reserves in the world are reckoned to be in the Middle East Region, together with huge quantities of natural gas. The main attraction of Middle East oil is that it is easy and economical to extract, unlike for example, that from the North Sea, or from under the Soviet permafrost, and consequently by comparison is extremely cheap.

Few, if any, governments thought Saddam Hussein would resort to the military option, but not only had he shown his teeth, he had shown he could, and would, bite as well. Oil-rich Arab Gulf States, practically defenceless against Iraqi military capability, became extremely apprehensive, dreading the probability that Kuwait was but the first step to their own oil wells.

At particular risk was Saudi Arabia, the largest oil producer in the Middle East, upon which the USA relied for cheap energy. A tacit, unspoken and unwritten, cosy arrangement had developed between the United States and Saudi Arabia, under which if the Americans would not openly criticise, or interfere in its internal affairs, the Americans could have quantities of cheap oil. The Saudis seemed to shelter under the invisible American defence umbrella in the hope it would deter predators, while pretending to be completely neutral.

President Bush and his shrewd and capable Secretary of State, James Baker, both taken by surprise, were quick off the mark to seize this unique opportunity to dominate this Kuwait Crisis. Bush issued an Executive

Order, banning all American trade with Iraq and Kuwait, froze such assets as those two countries had in the USA, and called upon other nations to take similar action.

Baker, who happened to be in Moscow at that moment, persuaded the Soviet Foreign Minister, Edvard Shevardnadze, to join in a USA-USSR call for a universal ban on arms to Iraq and Kuwait. Bush's next step was to try to halt the flow of export oil from Iraq and Kuwait by putting pressure on Saudi Arabia and Turkey to stop this passing through their oil pipeline facilities, but both Saudi Arabia and Turkey hesitated. By fortuitous chance the British Prime Minister, Mrs. Thatcher, was in America at that moment, who conferred with Bush, giving him full support on this issue.

UN Resolutions 660 & 661

Almost without pausing, President Bush mustered an emergency meeting (still on the 2nd August) of the UN Security Council, and succeeded in pushing through Resolution 660, by 14 votes to nil (Yemen abstaining), which condemned the Iraqi invasion of Kuwait, urged a cease-fire, and demanded that Iraqi troops withdraw from Kuwait. The UN Security Council consists of 15 members, including five 'permanent' ones (USA, USSR, UK, France and China), the latter having the power of veto over decisions, while the remaining ten seats rotate amongst all members, as does the Chairmanship. UN Security Council Resolutions are mandatory on all members.

President Reagan had not set much store by the UN forum, or its effectiveness in emergencies, as during the Cold War, both the USA and the USSR had used it in an adversarial manner for their own partisan purposes, or to discredit the other, their power of veto usually nullifying proposed Resolutions. The Cold War had officially been ended by the London Declaration, of the 6th July 1990, a month before the Iraqi invasion, so President Bush was able to view the UN forum in a new light, feeling it could be useful to him. Both the US Senate and the US House of Representatives moved quickly to endorse Bush's action, which pleased the President, who 'liked to have people running with him', spurring him on to take additional measures.

On the 3rd August, there was a meeting of the Arab League in Cairo where Arab representatives had gathered to attend an Islamic Conference Organisation (ICO) meeting, which condemned Saddam Hussein's invasion of Kuwait by a majority vote, calling for an Iraqi withdrawal. The following day (4th) the European Community (EC) broadly approved of what Bush was doing, which pleased him.

President Bush worked hard with his Secretary of State to persuade the UN Security Council to produce a Resolution authorising trade, arms and other embargoes against Iraq and Kuwait, and succeeded on the 6th August, when Security Council Resolution 661 was approved by 13 votes to nil, with Yemen and Cuba abstaining. This authorised a range of economic sanctions against Iraq and Kuwait that included many items, exceptions being medicines and some food commodities. Both Iraq and Kuwait were major oil producers, but had little else of any significance to export, and both countries had to import large quantities of food. Even Switzerland, a traditional neutral (not a member of the UN) joined in the embargo. On the 7th, the Saudis closed their Yanbu oil pipeline, and the Turks closed down the twin oil pipelines from Iraq, at the Yumurtalik terminal, near the Turkish port of Dortyol.

The Saudi Decision

Although at this stage President Bush most probably did not think the Kuwait Crisis would end in war, he intended to wave a big military cudgel at Saddam Hussein. He also saw it as a wonderful opportunity for spreading Pax Americana. He sent his Secretary of Defense, Richard Cheney, on the 6th, to Riyadh (Saudi Arabia), who took with him satellite reconnaissance print-outs, to confer with King Fahd, pointing out that Saddam Hussein's next target might be the eastern Dhahran oil complex.

Saudi armed forces were small, and widely spread across that huge country, and would be incapable of stemming an Iraqi invasion. Cheney offered US troops to defend Saudi terrain. Although some of his advisors were doubtful about the implications of such an offer, King Fahd recognised his danger, and chose what he thought was the lesser of two evils, of opting to have American infidels on his sacred soil in a defensive posture, rather than face hostile, aggressive Iraqi Muslims. This Saudi decision was the 'unthinkable' one, that Muslims everywhere, and non-Muslims too, thought could never happen. It is probably correct to say that not a single 'Arabist', or 'Middle East expert', forecast such an eventuality.

Overjoyed, President Bush moved swiftly, and ordered a squadron of US F-15 combat aircraft and the 82nd Airborne Division, to move to Saudi Arabia, and their advance elements landed on Saudi terrain on the 7th August. On the 8th, President Bush made a nation-wide TV broadcast to the American people to explain what he had accomplished so far, and his reasons. He said, "The sovereign independence of Saudi Arabia is of vital interest to the USA"; adding that "a line has been drawn in the sand". Bush openly entered the lists against Saddam Hussein.

However, Bush was not exactly happy with his unilateral agreement with Saudi Arabia as it seemed to pitch him personally against Saddam Hussein. He wanted other countries 'to run with him' against Iraq, so Baker was instructed to drum up international support, and to form an 'allied coalition' of national military contingents, to give the appearance of unity and broad opposition to Saddam Hussein, and especially to enlist regional Arab States. Thus *Operation Desert Shield* emerged.

The Cairo Summit

On the 10th August, an Arab League Summit was held in Cairo, which produced a Seven-Point Resolution, by a majority vote, 12 members (out of 21) being in favour. Three opposed it (Iraq, Libya and the Palestine Liberation Organisation [PLO]), two abstained (Algeria and Yemen), three expressed reservations (Jordan, Mauritania and Syria), and one (Tunisia) did not attend. The Summit approved sending a pan-Arab armed force to Saudi Arabia and Egypt, Morocco and Syria agreed to contribute to it. The inclusion of Syria in this proposed pan-Arab force was a surprise, and marked a change of alliances within the Arab League.

In response, Saddam Hussein unsuccessfully called for a Jihad (Holy War) against the USA. On the 12th, he unveiled his 'Peace Initiative', saying he would withdraw from Kuwait if the Israelis would withdraw from the Occupied Territories and the Golan area. This was the first mention of the 'Palestine Problem', and this suggestion became known as 'linkage'.

Saudi Arabia

Saudi Arabia is a huge oil-rich country, of some 1.4-million square miles, consisting mostly of expanses of mountainous terrain of arid desert. Scattered parts of the Arabian Peninsular had been brought together after the dissolution of the Ottoman Empire after World War I, by the puritanical Wahabi sect, headed by Abdul Aziz Ibn Saud, who proclaimed the Kingdom of Saudi Arabia in 1932. It remains an autocracy, retaining much of its medieval character. It is a member of the UN, the Arab League, the GCC, and OPEC, but the Saudi regime tended to keep a low profile in international affairs. An abundance of petro-dollars enable this socially and technically undeveloped country to obtain selective Western benefits, that included electricity, modern hospitals, TV and radio services, motor vehicles and domestic luxuries. The Saudis relied heavily on expatriate expertise and labour.

The present Ruler is King Fahd Ibn Aziz, whose official title is 'Custodian of the Two Holy Mosques', meaning those at Mecca and Medina, cities regarded as sacred by all Islam. King Fahd governs through a Council of Ministers, whom he appoints and dismisses at will. Non-Muslims are barred from entering Mecca, and are generally unwelcome elsewhere in Saudi Arabia, unless they have required skills or uses.

Saudi Arabia is strictly governed by the precepts of the Koran. For example, offenders can be decapitated by a sword in public, or even stoned to death, while women remain relegated to a cloistered, subservient existence, much as they have been for centuries. The population is estimated to be about 14-million (*IISS*), which includes about four-million expatriates.

As befitted its excessive wealth, Saudi Arabia in common with certain other oil-rich Arab Gulf States, bought expensive prestige weaponry as symbols of statehood, much of which has to be maintained by expatriates, and some of which, especially spares, remain in mint condition in packing cases. America, Britain and France have sold large quantities of weaponry to Saudi Arabia, but the Soviets, because of their Godless regime, have generally been debarred from this lucrative market.

The pro-Israeli lobby in America has been periodically successful in preventing American arms sales to Saudi Arabia, but less successful in the case of Britain and France. In September (1990) it was reported that the strength of the Saudi army (then about 40,000 *IISS*) was to be doubled, this being linked with a proposed massive arms deal with the USA, reputed to be valued at $20-billion. The pro-Israeli lobby in Washington got to work, and James Baker was forced to admit, on the 23rd September, that this transaction had been scaled down to about $7.5-billion — still a sizable one for a country whose active armed forces numbered only about 67,500 personnel (*IISS*).

Saudi armed forces recruit on a voluntary basis, and although conscription is decreed, this does not seem to have been enforced. The army was formed into nine brigades of various types, with supporting specialist units and sub-units. The army is over-equipped for its size, possessing some 550 main battle tanks, and almost 2,000 other armoured vehicles.

The Saudi air force (some 18,000 personnel) had almost 200 combat aircraft, which included US F-5s, F-15s and Tornados, while more F-15s were in the process of delivery. It also had five AWACS (Airborne Warning and Control System) radar planes, with 16 refuelling aircraft, but no armed helicopters. Saudi Air Defence missiles included the US HAWK and the French Shahine. Its main air bases are at the King Fahd Air Base at Taif; the King Khalid Air Base at Khamis Mushayt; and the King Abdul Aziz Air Base at Dhahran, with smaller ones at Hail and Tabuk.

The Saudi navy (about 9,500 personnel, including 1,500 marines) had eight frigates, nine missile craft, and other smaller and support ships, in two fleets. The Western Fleet was based on Jedda (Jiddah), and the Eastern Fleet at Jabayl. Naval aviation had 24 helicopters. Saudi Arabia was reported to be negotiating to buy submarines (JDW).

The Saudi National Guard (about 55,000 strong), gives personal loyalty to the House of Saud, having an internal security role. It has about 35,000 active members, equipped with light armoured vehicles and light arms; and some 20,000 tribal levies.

Often thwarted by the pro-Israeli lobby in Washington, in 1985, the Saudis turned the tables, and successfully completed a secret deal with the Chinese to buy a job lot (reputed to be about 60) Dong Feng-3 (Western code — CSS-2) intermediate ballistic missiles. These were the first all-Chinese missiles, tested in 1969, and deployed in Tibet facing India, but were regarded as surplus as they were a discontinued line, the Chinese now working on a different technological progression. The Chinese modified the DF-3 rocket to carry a 3,000-kg conventional warhead, instead of a two-megaton nuclear one, for a distance of some 7,000-kms. These DF-3 intermediate range ballistic missiles, using 'storable liquid fuel', were deployed at the Sulayil Oasis, about 285 miles south of Riyadh in silos (ADJ). Regarded as less accurate than the latest state of the rocket art, they were an 'area' weapon that could reach both Iran and Israel.

A tight system of censorship operated in Saudi Arabia to present a picture of a placid, well ordered, contented Islamic country to the outside world, but this masked internal problems. The Sunnis of the western Hajaz, who considered themselves the original Guardians of Mecca and Medina, were uncomfortable under the religious domination of the Wahabis, while the Shias (estimated to be a 15% minority) in the eastern parts of the country were not very happy either, for somewhat similar reasons.

The Saudi regime was badly shaken in November 1979, when a self-proclaimed Mahdi (Prophet), with armed followers, seized the Grand Mosque at Mecca. This was a religious-political rising against the House of Saud, and the seige continued for some days, until it was resolved by a French Special Forces team. There had also been dissident Shia incidents in the eastern provinces, but these were little reported.

During the Iran-Iraq War the Saudi Shias had been subjected to propaganda from Ayatollah Khomeini, of Iran, urging his fellow sectarians to rise up against the Saudi regime, which was supporting Iraq. Next, Khomeini sent his political agitators on the annual Haj, the Pilgrimage to Mecca that all good Muslims should complete at least once during their lifetime, to cause instability. Not only did Khomeini have his eye on Karbala, Nejaf and Jerusalem, but he also had it on Mecca and Medina. A major incident occurred at Mecca in July 1987, on the Haj, when a group of Iranian political pilgrims clashed with Saudi security forces, and over 400 people were killed, mainly Iranians. A two-week siege of the Saudi Embassy in Tehran followed. The Saudis clapped a low pilgrim quota on Iran for its Haj, which caused it to break off diplomatic relations with Saudi Arabia.

Another incident occurred on the Haj at Mecca in July 1989, when two explosions near the Grand Mosque killed one pilgrim and injured many more. In September, 16 Kuwaiti Shia pilgrims were executed for this crime, and four others imprisoned and flogged. It was alleged that from 'confessions' obtained, the guiding hand behind this terrorist exploit was Iranian. Prior to August 1990, it could be said the main external military threat to Saudi Arabia seemed to be from Tehran.

Saudi Arabia attracted the attention of *Amnesty International* which accused the regime of abuses against Human Rights. Its report (January 1990) alleged that over 700 political opponents of the regime, mainly Shia, were being held without trial, some since 1983, and being subjected to torture in inhumane prison conditions. This was denied by the *Saudi Press Agency*.

Egypt

Egypt saw itself as the natural leader of the Arab Nation, a status position that Saddam Hussein envied, and was hoping to assume. Egypt is a large country (some 383,000 square miles) and its population, which exceeded 54-million in 1990, was increasing at the rate of another million each year. Egypt occupies a strategically important cross-road position, having an East Mediterranean and a Red Sea coastline, and the Suez Canal which joins the two seas. Unfortunately it has difficulty in feeding its people, being dependent on food imports, reputed to cost some $4-billion annually. Despite revenue from the Suez Canal, a small oil export income, and remittances from its overseas workers, and possessing both an industrial and a military-industrial base, with low cost management and skilled workers, Egypt was a debtor country.

The International Monetary Fund (IMF) had called on Egypt to accelerate economic reforms before it would agree to reschedule its debts. The Egyptian problem, the classic dilemma of developing countries, was basically how to change an inefficient centralised system into a free market one, and at the same time not alienate sections of the population.

Egypt is perhaps the only Arab country whose nationals do not need an exit visa to leave, and accordingly up to three-million Egyptians worked abroad, sending remittances back home, which was of considerable assistance to the domestic economy. During the Iran-Iraq War over one-million Egyptians worked in Iraq, but when the war ended, and demobilised Iraqi servicemen returned to the work force, Egyptians were no longer required with a consequential detrimental effect on the Egyptian economy. Moreover, redundant Egyptian workers were shabbily treated by the Iraqi authorities in respect of contracts, payment of wages and travel home, which caused a wave of anti-Iraqi resentment in Egypt.

President Mubarak of Egypt, had pursued a slow policy of liberalism and multi-party democracy. Egypt has an elected People's Assembly, in which Mubarak's party, the National Democratic Party (NDP), held a majority of seats. There is an elected consultative council, the Majlis ash-Shura, also with a NDP majority. Mubarak has executive power, and appoints the Council of Ministers, and can dismiss them. Generally speaking the majority of Egyptians support his policies, but there are extremist elements, some violent, in opposition to him, the most prominent being Islamic Fundamentalists, who want an Islamic State.

After being ejected from the Arab League for signing a peace treaty with Israel, Egypt was reinstated at the Casablanca Summit, in May 1989, and the Arab League began to move back to its old HQ, in Cairo. That month, Egypt became a founder-member of the ACC, regarding it as an essential defensive shield against the Iranian Fundamentalist threat to the Arab Gulf region. However, despite its peace treaty, Egypt still tended to see Israel as the main military threat.

Egypt's active armed services numbered almost half-a-million men (*IISS*), but the Second Five Year Defence Plan (1988-93) catered for a reduction in strength, and to compensate for this arms and equipment were to be modernised. The USA was helping, and for example, had agreed to sell Egypt some 550 M1A1 Abrams main battle tanks and 144 US Maverick air-to-ground missiles. The Egyptian military-industrial base, which employed some 55,000 people, had concentrated upon obtaining Western technology, assembling projects under licence, and joint productions. Examples included the US TOW and the British Swingfire anti-tank missiles; the French Matra 550 Magic air-to-air missiles; and the Lynx and Gazelle helicopters.

Egypt became one of the four main states in the Middle East (with Israel, Iran and Iraq) engaged in an arms race, working to extend, and improve, its military capability, especially in the field of non-conventional weapons. One project was the Argentinian-Egyptian-Iraqi consortium to produce the Condor-II, a ballistic missile with a range of over 500 miles. Egyptian personnel were detected trying to smuggle 'prohibited material' (nose-cone material) out of the USA for the Condor-II project. The Americans eventually persuaded the Egyptians to abandon this project, and to placate them the Egyptian Defence Minister was moved sideways, to become Assistant to the President. In March 1989, the United States expressed concern that Egypt was developing a chemical warfare factory at Abu Zimbal, near Cairo, with Swiss help.

Egypt, which had experienced assassinations and violent political incidents from subversive elements, attracted the attention of *Amnesty International*, which alleged the use of torture on suspects in detention. The Egyptian government admitted, in January 1990, that it was holding '2,411 political prisoners under emergency laws', but rejected all other allegations.

Morocco

King Hassan of Morocco is a Constitutional Monarch, the elected Chamber of Representatives being the legislative authority, with a multi-party political system producing a seven-member coalition government, but behind this facade, there is no doubt the King wields executive power. Hassan was regarded as a 'moderate Ruler', and to have a pro-Western stance, which did not endear him to several member-states of the Arab League.

Morocco has a population of 24.8-million people (IISS), which is comparatively small for the size of the country (some 213,000-square miles) although much of it consists of mountainous terrain and desert tracts. With limited natural resources, and lacking a significant industrial base, Morocco has economic problems, and its international debts were considerable.

Moroccan armed forces were relatively small for such an extensive defence responsibility, consisting of just under 200,000 men, the majority of whom were engaged in the long-stalemated desert war against the Sahrawi People's Liberation Army, the military wing of the Popular Front for the Liberation of Saguia al-Hamra and Rio del Oro, backed by next door, oil-rich Algeria, which aims to establish the Saharan Arab Democratic Republic in barren Western Sahara, once Spanish colonial territory, also claimed by Morocco. Morocco has to buy in practically all its arms, obtained mainly from the USA, France and South Africa.

King Hassan gradually improved his relations with certain radical Arab States, and in February 1989, joined the five-country Arab Magreb Union (AMU), together with Algeria, Libya, Mauritania and Tunisia. That month President Chadli Bendjedid of Algeria, visited Morocco, and after encouraging talks on the mutually stalled frontier agreement (of 1972), King Hassan signed a pact to permit Algerian natural gas for Europe, to be piped across Moroccan territory. In May, Colonel Gaddafi of Libya, also visited Morocco. Just previously (January 1989), Morocco resumed diplomatic relations with Syria, which had been ruptured when King Hassan had met the Israeli Prime Minister (in July 1980).

Syria

Certain Western countries had broken off diplomatic relations with Syria, alleging that it was involved in aiding international terrorism, and that its Embassies were suspected of providing international terrorists with weapons and travel documents. Britain, for example, had severed diplomatic relations with that country in October 1986, having 'conclusive evidence' of Syrian involvement in the attempted destruction of an Israeli airliner, and kidnapping Western hostages held in Lebanon.

It was known that certain notorious terrorist leaders, and their activists, visited, passed through, or were given sanctuary or training facilities in Syria. As Syria was almost completely supplied with arms by the USSR, it was regarded as a Soviet client state. The American CIA insisted that Syrian chemical warfare development was the most advanced in the Middle East.

President Hafez Assad of Syria, leader of the Syrian faction of the Baath Party, had come to power in 1969, ruling behind the facade of an elected People's Assembly, in which the National Progressive Front (NPF), a six-party coalition dominated by the Baath Party, governed the country. In the May 1990 elections for the People's Assembly, the NPF retained its majority, and so Syria continued to be ruled by the Baathists, which in fact meant Hafez Assad.

Syria is a country of factions, shifting alliances and conflicting interests, ridden with independent intelligence agencies, that included Military Intelligence, Air Force Intelligence (Assad was an air force officer), Internal Intelligence, Ministry Intelligence, and others.

Syria is a small (about 115,000-square miles) Arab Mediterranean country with a population of about 12.3-million (IISS) people. Its economy was ailing, agriculture had been affected by drought, Arab finance was declining, World Bank loans had been suspended, and food had to be imported. The Syrian international debt was very heavy indeed. Its infant oil industry was slowly developing, producing about 300,000 bpd (in 1989), and new significant oil reserves discovered in 1989 and 1990, were expected to eventually improve the economic situation.

Syria had comparatively large armed forces for the size of its population, numbering about 400,000 (IISS), and as Syria did not have an industrial base of any significance, arms had to be obtained from the USSR, which had provided them in reasonable abundance. The Syrian military inventory, for example, included SCUD-B and SS-21 ballistic missiles, and its air force was in the process of receiving a batch of 48 MiG-29 combat aircraft. In April 1989, President Assad visited Moscow to ask for more modern arms to enable him to 'keep parity' with Israel, but was refused. Gorbachev's new policy was to allow Syria only to have 'a reasonable self-sufficiency' of arms. Assad's request for SS-23 ballistic missiles was refused. By July 1990, Syria was negotiating with China for M-9 ballistic missiles, reputed range being about 500 miles.

Syria's foreign military threat perceptions were basically two — one being Israel (Syria maintained up to 40,000 troops in Lebanon), and the other being next door Iraq, ruled by the hostile, breakaway faction of the Baath Party. Syria was the only Arab State to openly side with Iran during that country's war with Iraq. In 1989, Syria sought reconciliation, but this was rejected by Iraq. Iraq sheltered and supported exiled political groups in opposition to President Assad.

Syrian relations with Turkey, its northern neighbour, were usually strained over riparian differences. In 1975, Iraq massed troops on the Syrian Border, demanding that Syria release more water from the Assad Dam, on the Euphrates River. The demanded increase was agreed to by President Assad. Syria also accused Turkey of reducing, and regulating the river water flowing through that country after the completion of the Ataturk Dam. An unofficial agreement was made between the two countries (Turkey and Syria) for an increased volume of river water through Syria, on the condition that Syria did not harbour any Turkish Kurdish separatists, who had been operating amongst Turkish border villages for some years.

In 1988, Syria and Turkey jointly agreed to build a dam on the River Euphrates. However, relations between them deteriorated in October the following year, when the Turks alleged the Syrians were actively helping, sheltering and training Turkish Kurdish 'rebels'. Assad was also hostile to Yasir Arafat, leader of the PLO, supporting the breakaway faction of Arafat's Fatah organisation, the Palestine National Salvation Front (PNSF), led by Abu Musa, but on the other hand his visit to Cairo in May (1990), had repaired relations with Egypt.

Jordan

The small (some 61,000-square mile) Hashemite Kingdom of Jordan holds a strategic 'corridor' position between Egypt, Saudi Arabia and Iraq, and is a 'confrontation state' (having a land border with Israel). Almost completely bereft of natural resources, Jordan has survived for years as a 'remittance' state, relying mainly on subsidies from Western and Arab States, donors and amounts varying according to changing political scenarios. Jordanian relations with Saudi Arabia were satisfactory, although promised payments were invariably delayed, but paid eventually, as the Saudis saw Jordan as its convenient shielding confrontation state. Relations with Syria were more mercurial, and the two countries fought a mini-tank battle in 1970, but in recent months had been improving.

Jordan had a heavy foreign debt, and there were riots in April 1988, when the IMF imposed certain austerity measures after re-scheduling debts. Income had been received during the Iran-Iraq War, as recompense for the transit of munitions and supplies in quantity, landed at Jordan's southern port, Akaba, to be trucked to Iraq. Jordanian relations with Egypt and Iraq were good, and it was included in the ACC, mainly because it was a land corridor. Jordan relied upon Iraq for its oil imports.

The Jordanian active armed forces were small, about 82,250 (IISS), but well-trained and reasonably well-equipped by the USA, Britain and France. The army was expecting to receive about 90 Chieftain tanks, captured by Iraq from Iran, which were to be up-dated by the Egyptians, while the air force was expecting 12 French Mirage-2000 modern aircraft, to add to its some 100 combat planes, that included US F-5s and French Mirage F-1s.

In theory King Hussein is a Constitutional Monarch, who appoints a Prime Minister, who forms a government answerable to the National Assembly. There are no legal political parties in Jordan, so elections depend upon personalities with thinly disguised political affiliations or views. The last election, in November 1989, brought about a change of Prime Minister, Mudar Babran taking that Office. King Hussein exercises executive powers, but has to temper his decisions to the mood of his people.

The estimated population of Jordan is about 4.1-million, and is said to be about 60% Palestinian, or of Palestinian origin, the remainder being Bedu, or of Bedu descent, meaning desert inhabitants. The Palestinian majority often colours political decisions in Jordan. King Hussein was generally regarded by the West as a 'moderate', and by Arabs as being pro-Western.

In July 1988, King Hussein renounced all claim to the 'West Bank' (of the River Jordan), now under Israeli occupation, which had previously been included in Jordan in 1948, but was lost to the Israelis during the 1967 War. Despite this change of orientation, Hussein regarded his main perceived military threat to be from Israel, which could instantly close the Gulf of Akaba, and so throttle Jordanian maritime trade and traffic.

Gulf Co-operation Council

To quote its formal title the 'Co-operation Council for the Arab States of the Gulf', more commonly known as the Gulf Co-operation Council (GCC), consists of 'traditional' Arab States, meaning those with automatic regimes, and was formed in May 1981. The GCC included Bahrain, Kuwait, Oman, Qatar, Saudi Arabia and the United Arab Emirates (UAE). The Iran-Iraq War had been in progress for about nine months, and the dark shadow of Ayatollah Khomeini's Islamic Fundamentalist expansionist ambition loomed large on the Arab Gulf horizon.

These Arab Gulf States have small populations, and their defence capability was comparatively negligible. Bickering and insular, GCC member states have territorial claims against each other, while age-old feuds and prejudices simmer just beneath the surface. For example, the Rulers of Bahrain and Qatar were barely on speaking terms with each other, and when Qatari soldiers occupied a Coast Guard station under construction on Bahrain's Fasht al-Dibal Island, only Saudi intervention prevented armed conflict. Gulf Rulers are introvert and ostrich-like, hoping international problems would go away so they could continue uninterrupted their placid traditional way of life. The threat to their survival forced them to a common conference table.

The Supreme Council of the GCC consists of the six Rulers, and periodic Ministerial meetings are held in alternating states. The Secretary General was, Abdullah Bishara, a Kuwaiti. Ostensibly the objectives of the GCC were economic, social and cultural, but in practice it was a feeble attempt to form a defensive coalition. The word 'defence' was unwritten and unspoken, lest it arouse the wrath of Khomeini. GCC States openly backed Iraq in its war, giving some interest-free loans and other assistance. All gave lip-service to Saddam Hussein's 'Arab cause', but most had reservations. They did not know which side was going to win. For ages, most of the GCC States had traded with Iran, and had other long-time contacts and were reluctant to sever such links. Some continued covert trading across the waters of the Gulf throughout the war.

It was not until October 1983, that a timid start was made in the defence sphere, when *Exercise Peninsular Shield*, designed as a joint multi-Arab one, was held in Abu Dhabi (UAE), which turned out to be little more than a small static military show. This became an annual event, and developed slowly as individual States produced their expensive prestige weapons, such as aircraft and tanks, to give a hollow appearance of military capability in a one-up-manship manner.

Although little serious joint military training took place, a Command and Staff structure of the 'Peninsular Shield Force' appeared, heavily dominated by the Saudis, which was re-named the 'GCC Rapid Deployment Force' (GCC RDF). Located at Hafar al-Batin, in northern Saudi Arabia, it was also slow to develop. In September 1989, immediately after the Cease-Fire in the Iran-Iraq War, GCC States sought to improve relations with Iran, and to openly resume trade links, to the annoyance of Saddam Hussein.

As Kuwait and Saudi Arabia have been introduced, it may be helpful to briefly outline the other four GCC States:

Bahrain

Bahrain is a small island, of about 430-square miles, now joined by a motor-causeway to Saudi Arabia, having a population of less than half-a-million people. It is the only Arab State with a Shia majority (of about 60%), with perhaps the blurred exception of Iraq (if Kurds are excluded), although its traditional Ruler is a Sunni. An alleged Iranian-instigated plot to seize power, was unearthed and crushed in December 1981.

Bahrain has to import crude oil for its oil refinery, and has large international debts. It made contact with China, which agreed to expand Bahrain's hydrocarbon, and other, industrial projects. Bahrain's armed forces numbered about 6,000 (IISS).

Qatar

Qatar has an area of about 7,000-square miles, and a population of 335,000, of which it is thought that less than one-third are Qataris. Qatar has both oil (is a member of OPEC) and natural gas, but still has large international debts.

Between March and August 1988, Qatar was involved in controversy over its acquisition of US Stinger ground-to-air missiles, that had been destined for the Afghan Mujahideen.

Oman

Oman is a Sultanate consisting of 123,000-square miles, having both a Gulf and Arabian Sea coastline, and regards itself as the Guardian of the Gulf and the Hormuz Strait. Its population was estimated to be about 1.5-million, which included a large, but unknown, number of expatriates. Oman has special relations with Britain, as the British organised the coup in 1970, which brought the present Sultan, Qaboos bin Said, to power, who contents himself with a nominated Consultative Council. Oman is an oil-producing country, but is not a member of OPEC. It has diplomatic relations with China, and a heavy international debt.

Oman's armed forces numbered about 29,500 (IISS), which included about 4,000 expatriates. The USA refused to sell Stinger missiles to Oman in case they fell into the hands of terrorists. In May 1989, Oman cancelled its plan to buy eight Tornado combat planes, and instead opted for 12 cheaper British Hawk aircraft. With the aid of British and Iranian forces, the Sultan, had crushed his long-running insurgency in his Dhofar Province by 1973.

United Arab Emirates

The United Arab Emirates (UAE), an unintentional misnomer perhaps, has an area of less than 50,000-square miles, and a population estimated to be 1.6-million, which included over 800,000 expatriates. The UAE consists of seven Emirates, the former British Trucial (Truce) States, which were bundled hastily together, just before the British left that region. They are Abu Dhabi, Adjman, Dubai, Fujairah, Ras al-Khaimah, Sharjah and Umm al-Qaiwain. The seven Emirs are each absolute monarchs in their own Emirates, touchy, introvert and distrustful bed-fellows, plagued by territorial disputes and riddled with age-old feuds. The Emirs constitute the UAE Supreme Council, but decisions must have five supporting votes.

The UAE armed forces numbered about 44,000 (IISS), of which about 14,500 are expatriates. In view of long frontiers and small populations, it was decided that a strong air force would be the corner-stone of UAE defence. An agreement was made with France in 1989 for 36 Mirage-2000s, and when this delivery is completed, together with British Alpha Jets on order, the UAE air force would have over 150 modern aircraft, and be second only in GCC air force strength to Saudi Arabia. The UAE, an oil-producing State, is a member of OPEC, and had diplomatic relations with both the USSR and China. China agreed to construct a huge petrochemical plant in the UAE.

Turkey

Turkey does not like to be thought of as a Middle East country, although it dominates the northern fringe of that region, being Muslim with a minimum of secular leavening. Turkey is a large country, comprising some 294,500-square miles, lying mainly in Asia, with only a small part of its terrain in Europe, across the Dardanelles. It had a population (1990) of 55.8-million people, estimated to be increasing at the rate of 2.5-million annually. Undeveloped industrially, Turkey has an agrarian-based economy, and exports agricultural products. It is burdened with very heavy international debts.

Turkey received revenue for the transit of Iraqi oil through the twin pipelines to its east Mediterranean oil terminal at Yumurtalik, along which flowed some 1.6-million bpd; and although it has no oil production of its own, its refineries work to full capacity. During the Iran-Iraq War, Turkey impartially supplied both combatants with agricultural produce, and many embargo-ed items; and after the Cease-Fire its trade with these two countries increased considerably.

Turkey had large active defence forces, numbering some 650,000 men, with a reserve of over one-million, but its army was largely immobile and in need of modern equipment. It was accepted into NATO, with some reservations, as its numerous infantry battalions were essential to hold the vulnerable south-eastern front against any Soviet agression. Turkey has NATO bases on its soil, and provides officers for UNIIMOG (UN Iran–Iraq Monitoring Observer Group). It wanted to become a member of the EC, but its application to join made in December 1989, was pended by the EC until at least 1993. In short, Turkey was a valuable member of NATO, but would be a drag on the EC economy.

Turkey had internal security problems. Its estimated 12-million Kurdish minority had long been in a simmering state of insurrection, and some of its political opposition groups resorted to terrorism. At times Turkey had co-operated with both Iran and Iraq in measures against Kurdish insurgents, and in mutual frontier stretches villages had been depopulated to hinder trans-border movement of Kurdish 'rebels'. In some Western eyes, Turkey still carried the stigma of its former period of dictatorial rule, which attracted (and still did attract) the attention of *Amnesty International.*

Turkish troops invaded Greek-governed Cyprus in 1974, to 'protect' Turkish Cypriots, and had remained in occupation since, which made it unpopular in Western circles; while to its south it had differences with both Iraq and Syria over the distribution of the waters of the Euphrates and Tigris Rivers. By its geographic position, Turkey could 'regulate' the flow of these two rivers, which caused disputes over 'water allocation' — a desperately serious issue in parts of the Middle East. During the construction of the Turkish Ataturk Dam, on the Euphrates, reputed to be the largest in the world, waters of the Euphrates and Tigris were temporarily diverted, which caused alarm. Turkey was pushing for its gigantic water 'Peace Line' project, that would pump water southwards to arid countries, which had been met with caution and suspicion as it smacked of Turkish intent to re-establish its former Ottoman influence in the region.

Iran

Dominating the east side of the Gulf was Iran, a large non-Arab country, of just over one-million-square miles, recovering slowly from the traumas of the Khomeini Islamic Fundamentalist Revolution of February 1979, and the debilitating eight-year war with next-door Iraq. Although Iran, with a population of 52-million *(IISS)*, had a much larger well of manpower than Iraq, its ill-armed infantry militia had been unable to break through the linear Iraqi defences. Exhausted, Khomeini at last had to ask for a Cease-Fire (his 'cup of poison'). The Cease-Fire held, but the situation remained unstable, causing Iranians to maintain active armed forces numbering about 604,000. Neither country had the capability to continue the war, but they bickered away at each other over conditions, and a peace agreement seemed a long way away.

Major Iranian efforts concentrated upon national economic recovery, rehabilitation and reconstruction. Iran was an oil-producing country, the third largest Middle East one in OPEC. Iran had no international debts, so all means were available for a massive Five Year Plan (1990-95). The Iranian government, which had been almost completely isolated internationally during its war with Iraq, successfully sought help from certain nations.

A huge re-organisation was taking place in Iran to reform the armed forces on more conventional lines, and also to provide them with modern weaponry. In May 1989, the Ministries of Defence and the Islamic Revolutionary Guards Corps were merged into a single 'Ministry of Defence and Armed Forces Logistics'. Iran became caught up in the Middle East arms race to gain 'parity' with Israel, Iraq and Egypt, which involved striving to manufacture nuclear and chemical weapons, and also to develop short-range ballistic missiles.

In January 1990, an agreement was made with China for scientific and technological co-operation in military industries, and a similar one with Pakistan, both of which were suspected of having nuclear implications. Covert contracts were made with certain European countries for assistance in weapon production, while the USSR, Rumania and Yugoslavia promised modern aircraft, some to be partly paid for by oil deliveries.

Iraq

Back to Iraq. During the Iran-Iraq War, Iraq had been seen as the Arab 'David' struggling against the Islamic Fundamentalist Persian 'Goliath', and oil-rich Arab Gulf States had little option but to overtly support it. After the Cease-Fire and Saddam Hussein's victory boasts, danger seemed to have passed, and the attitude of the Gulf States became colder, which eventually triggered off the Rape of Kuwait.

Iraq had also been devastated by the war, but as its export oil still flowed, it being the second largest Middle East oil exporter in OPEC, and grandiose plans were made for reconstruction, and clearing away damaged buildings and slum areas and replacing them with modern structures. This included whole towns, such as Fao, which had been literally flattened. Not only was Saddam Hussein constructing improved dwellings for his people, he was also concerned with reviving glories of the ancient Mesopotamian Empires, and reproducing ancient historical cities, such as that of Babylon. The whole of Iraq seemed to be crawling with construction workers like busy armies of ants, which was another reason why few thought Saddam Hussein would take the military option against Kuwait.

Incredible though it may seem, at the same time Saddam Hussein was engaging in the Middle East arms race with energy and cunning. The French who had supplied him throughout the war, quickly re-scheduled his debt to them, and successfully sought huge arms contracts; while the Soviets, Iraq's main arms supplier since the Iraqi-Soviet Friendship and Co-operation Treaty of 1972, began to send new weaponry.

Not content to simply buy new weaponry, Saddam Hussein wanted the means to manufacture his own independently and to develop a military-industrial base, which he hoped would produce certain weapons his suppliers would not let him have. These ambitions included a nuclear weapon, a large stock of chemical warfare means, and improved longer-range ground-to-ground ballistic missiles. During the war many Western, and other, governments had turned a blind eye to export licences for 'civilian' machine tools, but since the Cease-Fire, had become more circumspect, which caused Saddam Hussein to resort to covert methods to obtain them.

Iraq sought to obtain plans for a projected, long-range 'super gun', which would be able to deliver a shell on to Israeli territory, and also hit Tehran. He had threatened to strike at Israel. The designer of this project, a Canadian (Dr. Gerald Bull) was assassinated, reputedly by the Israeli Mossad secret intelligence organisation. A huge explosion occurred on the 17th August 1989, at the al-Hillah military-industrial complex about 40 miles south of Baghdad, which caused great devastation, and cost many lives. It was believed to have involved the Condor-II project.

Saddam Hussein had established a Nuclear Research Centre, at Thuwait, near Baghdad, and with French help, and French nuclear fuel, began work to produce a nuclear warhead. This Centre was bombed by the Israelis in June 1981 (Israeli *Operation Sphinx*), but it was said that a small amount of weapon-grade plutonium was salvaged. The Iraqis continued to work on this nuclear project at other locations.

Demobilisation was slow in Iraq, partly because of the uncertain Cease-Fire situation, and partly because servicemen had to be filtered back into the work force as imported foreign labour departed. According to one authoritative source *(IISS)*, Iraqi armed forces in mid-1990, numbered just over one-million, and were backed by the 850,000-strong People's Army. The active element was deployed in seven Army Corps regions *(IISS)*. Ground troops consisted basically of seven armoured and 42 infantry divisions; the Republican Guard; and a number of Special Forces commandos. Iraqi armed forces were mainly equipped with Soviet weaponry, although items had been obtained from other countries, as and when opportunity had offered.

The People's Army, formed in the Iran-Iraq War, initially as a Baathist militia, had been expanded into a basic reserve, which was partly mobilised. Young people under 18 years, and those over 45, served in the People's Army, which had a token women's section.

The Iraqi air force had over 500 combat aircraft *(IISS)*, mostly of Soviet origin, but included were almost 100 French Mirage F-1s of various types, some with Exocet missiles, and some with in-flight re-fuelling capability. Iraq also had over 40 Chinese Sheyang J-6s (copies of the Soviet MiG-19) and over 80 Chendu J-7s (copies of the MiG-21). The Iraqi navy was very small, with just a handful of tiny craft, cooped up at its Umm Qasr naval base, in the Khor Abdullah channel, as the lower reaches of the Shatt al-Arab were still unnavigable, owing to the Iranian presence on the east bank and the Iranian refusal to allow this section to be cleared of sunken ships and debris, as that would have been of benefit to Iraq.

During the war Iraqi ground forces had become accustomed to static defence, there having been little mobile armoured combat. The Republican Guard had the best weapons and equipment available, and had come to be used as a trouble-shooting formation. Over 10,000 Soviet and 2,000 Egyptian military advisers and technicians, still worked at Iraqi defence establishments.

Compared with Iran, Iraq is a small country, of some 273,000-square miles, with a population (1989) of 19-million, of which perhaps half were Shia and nearly half Sunni, with 15% being Kurdish. The governing faction was Sunni. A General Election had been held in April 1989, which confirmed the Baath Party majority in the National Assembly.

Political opposition to Saddam Hussein was either very deep underground in Iraq, or in exile. During the war the Iranians had sponsored the Supreme Council of the Islamic Revolution of Iraq (SCIRI), consisting mainly of disaffected Iraqi Shias. Other small opposition groups, that included Communists, anti-Baathists, Kurds and the Dawa terrorist organisation, operated in exile.

The main internal security problem in Iraq was the some three-million Kurds, inhabiting the northern mountainous areas, who had been in almost continual revolt or insurrection, against the Baghdad government. During the war with Iran, certain groups of Iraqi Kurds, sponsored by the Tehran government, operated against Iraqi armed forces. Towards the end of the war (in April 1988), Saddam Hussein mounted a punitive expedition against them, in which chemical warfare means were used. The most notorious incident occurred at the small town of Halabja, when a number of Iraqi Kurds perished due to the effects of chemical warfare, including women and children. Numbers are uncertain, but most authorities quote them in four figures.

3

Operation Desert Shield

The policy of President Bush, Baker, Cheney, the Pentagon, and the small tight handful of top personalities in the US Administration and the armed forces, was to continue the Reagan Doctrine of restoring American military prestige, which after reaching a high peak of acclaim after World War II, had declined to a low trough of unpopularity during the Vietnam War, largely through self-denigration. The Vietnam experience had been a harrowing one for the American people; it was the first foreign war they had lost. The United States media had been hostile to involvement in it, which reflected on American military morale, impinging upon efficiency and effectiveness.

The run-down of self-esteem in the armed forces continued under the Carter Administration, which culminated in the seizure of American hostages in Tehran by Iranian Islamic Fundamentalist Students, who held them for 444 days. The attempted US hostage rescue mission (*Operation Eagle Claw*), on the 24th/25th April 1980, failed disastrously, and had to be aborted after eight US servicemen were killed by accident, and others injured. This rendered the USA, probably the most powerful Super Power in military projection terms, helpless, and unable to free its captive nationals.

President Reagan

When President Reagan took Office in January 1981, he brought a new attitude towards American military prestige, and set about re-arming, re-organising and re-vitalising the huge American defense establishment. The Gates Commission of 1970, had recommended that conscription, the 'draft', in force since World War II, be abandoned, in favour of voluntary recruitment, and this change-over was made during 1973, while the

Vietnam War was still in progress. In 1973, largely to save money, the US Department of Defense (DoD) adopted the concept of 'Total Force' policy, which was to integrate the active and reserve components of the US armed forces.

By May 1980, the American armed forces (IISS) were about 3.2-million strong, being in three classifications. Those on active duty numbered about two-million; those in the Selective Reserve, which included the part-time National Guard, numbered about 800,000; and the Individual Ready Reserve numbered about 400,000 — but all had manpower problems. The majority of these armed forces were stationed in Continental America, just over a quarter-of-a-million were in Europe as part of NATO defence, and the remainder were sprawled across widely-flung parts of the world, some lacking cohesion and capability. The USA had a most powerful nuclear armoury.

President Reagan managed to increase defence budgets, to initiate new weapon projects, re-vitalise some stagnant ones, and institute others more far-reaching, such as the Strategic Defense Initiative, but he did not overlook military power projection. The Pentagon was just getting over its 'short war' (with the USSR) concept, and was settling down with the 'protracted war strategy', which had a requirement to be 'credible' in Southern Asia. The US Rapid Deployment Joint Task Force (RDJTF), formed for this latter purpose, had not proved to be a satisfactory solution. In 1982, the RDJTF was transformed into the US Central Command (CENTCOM), a 'unified' one, which was expanded by elements of the army, navy, air force and marine corps. The Commander reported directly to the US Defense Secretary.

When the Israelis invaded Lebanon in June 1982, and remained in occupation, Reagan saw an opportunity to intervene in that country, and American military personnel became part of a Multi-National Force (MNF). Reagan's excuse was that 'Lebanon is now central to our credibility on a global scale'. For the Americans it was a disastrous intervention as all Lebanese factions turned against them. The worst incident occurred on the 23rd October (1983), when a suicide-driver drove his vehicle, loaded with explosives, at a building housing American Marines. The explosion killed 239 of them.

Operation Urgent Fury

Meanwhile, President Reagan had been giving attention to the Caribbean Basin area, where on the island of Grenada (133-square miles, population 110,000), in the chain of Windward Islands, there had been a left-wing coup. On the 25th October, two days after the US Marine Corps disaster in Lebanon, Reagan launched Operation Urgent Fury, the initial landings being made by 1,900 Rangers and Marines, a number that was increased to about 6,000. Greater resistance than had been expected came from the 750 para-military Cubans, who were constructing a large airstrip on Grenada. It took American troops a month to gain full control of the island.

The Pentagon had regarded *Operation Urgent Fury* as being a low-risk opportunity to demonstrate resolve in the Caribbean Basin, and indeed had persuaded tiny military elements from some of the other Caribbean countries to co-operate in this adventure. A large US naval flotilla, of 12 ships, including both an aircraft-carrier and a helicopter-carrier, with bomber aircraft, had supported the assault landing. It was certainly a sledge-hammer to crack a small nut, but Reagan was satisfied as the American media gave him a blaze of favourable publicity, over-shadowing the Lebanon disaster. The Americans claimed it as a stunning victory, which put Cuba in its place and had a good effect on American policy in Central America, which was not going particularly well at that moment.

The twist to this American adventure was that Grenada was a British Crown Colony, and the American invasion had been launched without prior British consent, or even fore-knowledge. No British troops were involved. Somehow, the claimed 'special relationship' between the USA and the UK, that blossomed under Reagan and Thatcher, solved this protocol gaffe. *Operation Urgent Fury*, which proceeded on a jerky, unco-ordinated course, made the US defence establishment feel better. The army commander for this American assault operation was General Norman Schwartzkopf.

American Military Reforms

When Reagan was re-elected for a Second Term in 1984, with George Bush as his running mate, he declared he wanted the USA "to recover her optimism, military and morale strength, and self confidence", and he pushed through certain military reforms. One of the main problems of the American armed services was that they were separate establishments, each self contained, and jealous of its own dignity and exclusiveness, making co-operation between them less than was desirable. Whenever operations were mounted, all Services demanded 'a piece of the action', thrusting their own elements into the arena, while lack of integration led to duplication and confusion. In particular, Special Forces were disinclined to integrate, each intent on 'doing its own thing'. American inter-Service one-upmanship was a major problem.

Some of the Packard Commission recommendations were implemented, one of which, in 1986, 'strengthened' the role of the Chairman of the Joint Chiefs of Staff (JCS), and created the new post of Vice-Chairman. The JCS consisted of the serving Heads of each of the Services. Unlike some national military establishments, the American JCS had no executive authority, and indeed in 1953, President Eisenhower had declared that the JCS was not a command body, but an advisory group, responsible for formulating strategic plans. It was stipulated the JCS would not operate as a European-type General Staff. The Chairman of the JCS was to deal with the President, the Defense Secretary and Congress, and although he could not 'originate' orders, he could 'transmit' commands — a blurring of power in which dominant personalities could make an impression.

Another adopted Packard Commission recommendation was to bring all Special Forces, of all four Services, under one umbrella command. This was implemented in 1987, when a Commander of US Special Forces was appointed, and given certain executive powers, to bring to heel in the USA, the collection of 'private armies' that tended to mushroom, to curb maverick tendencies, and to blend all into a common plan.

During the 1980s, four deployable Light Infantry Divisions (LIVs) were formed in the USA (the 6th, 7th, 35th, and 10th Mountain Division) to be available for 'out of area' operations, which together with the 82nd Airborne Division, the 101st Air Assault Division, and most of the Marine Corps, were earmarked to be available to CENTCOM. It was planned that LIVs would be deployed within a week, but lacking main battle tanks and heavy guns, would be vulnerable in battle against conventionally equipped troops. Tanks, anti-tank guns and heavy engineering equipment would follow, sometimes by sea.

Operation Just Cause

In January 1989, George Bush superceded President Reagan, and having been his Vice-President during Reagan's Second Term, working closely with him, was considered to be in the Reagan mould. The main overt differences between the two men were in personality and presentation. After eight years of the Reagan 'Hollywood sense of the occasion', and being four years in Reagan's shadow, at first the American media tended to see Bush as a wimp, more of a concensus man, who sought support before making decisions, rather than a bold, decisive leader.

Momentous changes were in progress in Europe. The Berlin Wall was breached in November 1989, which led to the loosening of the Communist grip on Eastern Europe, while the USSR began to experience economic and separatist problems. This left the USA on centre stage as the main active Super Power. Because of its territorial extent, huge population and nuclear arsenal, China was regarded by many as a Super Power, but after its disastrous war with Vietnam in early 1979, was thought to lack serious conventional military expeditionary capability, or power projection means.

The scene was set for President Bush to solve the vexed Panama Canal Problem. In 1903, the Americans detached a piece of Colombian territory, and called it the Panama Republic, across which they constructed the Panama Canal, which linked the Atlantic and Pacific Oceans for the first time. This was a most valuable asset, both strategically and economically, and a US military contingent was stationed in the Canal Zone to safeguard this prized American possession. Under an agreement of 1978, President Carter 'returned the Canal to the people of Panama', a process that is continuing, to be completed by the year 2000. This most controversial decision was generally unpopular in capitalist-orientated USA.

Moreover, the sitting President of Panama, General Manuel Noriega, a former employee of the American CIA, and apparently a one-time faithful American servant, had become arrogant and independent, having just ignored a general election in which he had lost power. The US Administration began to smear Noriega as a dictator and drug dealer, demanding that he step down and face justice in an American court. Noriega stood defiant.

Bush saw his chance and on the 29th December 1989, launched *Operation Just Cause,* to bring about Noriega's downfall. The Canal Zone was some 20 miles wide and 27 miles in length, with hinterlands on either side of the Canal amounting in all to over 30,000-square miles of jungle terrain. Panama's population was about two-million, and its armed forces numbered about 7,300 men. There were over 12,000 US servicemen in the Canal Zone.

The Americans mustered an invasion force of some 26,000 personnel, but it took several days to overcome Panamanian resistance, during the course of which, according to US official sources 'about 400 Panamanians died', but many think that 4,000 might be a more accurate figure. Some 13,000 Panamanians still remain homeless after American bombing raids, in which for the first time, the US F-117A (Stealth) combat aircraft came into action. Noriega took refuge in the Papal Legation, where he remained until forced out by American pressure, to be whisked off to Florida where he still languishes in jail, waiting for a show trial.

Although this was another huge sledge-hammer to crack a small nut, *Operation Just Cause* was considered to be Bush's first foreign success, and the American media trumpeted his victory over evil. Bush was no longer regarded as a wimp. The expression Pax Americana began to be used by some of his critics. It is quite probable that Bush saw himself as something of a modern Roman Emperor, sending out military commanders to extend his domain, and bring back defeated chieftains in chains for a Victory Parade. Shades of the ancient Briton, Caractus. The former Commander of CENTCOM (General Woerner), had reputedly formulated the plan for the invasion of Panama, but is said to have objected to its 'political aim', and was 'retired' before it was launched.

The Initial Bush Reaction

The scenario in Europe continued to change dramatically in 1990, and after decades of nuclear tension and threats of total annihilation in a Nuclear Winter, in July, the London Declaration pronounced the termination of the Cold War. This brought relief, relaxation and talk of the 'peace dividend'. Suddenly, the cursor of the strategic barometer moved from Europe to the Middle East, where President Saddam Hussein, who had been uttering threats against Kuwait, sprang into action and invaded that country.

Although American intervention in this region had often been unfortunate, and even disastrous, the large reservoir of cheap oil remained a magnet. Bush thought that if he could muster sufficiently large modern forces, armed with a plethora of sophisticated weaponry, that Saddam Hussein would back down, when he could be suitably rebuked, humiliated and the stamp of Pax Americana put on his forehead. The US Defense Secretary and the Pentagon prepared contingency plans, while an eager speculative media began to formulate views on 'worst case' scenarios.

Sabre-rattling was the order of the day in Washington, and on the 11th August, President Bush announced his intention to mount a naval blockade against Iraq. The previous day the first serious 'leak' was published in Washington newspapers, which stated that the Pentagon had adopted a 'contingency plan' which would involve '250,000 troops', to be used if it came to war. Some credence was given to this, when on the 22nd, Bush issued an Executive Order, calling up reservists from the Individual Ready Reserve.

To demonstrate Presidential resolve, locations of certain major ships were given, showing them all steaming towards the Gulf area. These included the *USS Kennedy* in the east Mediterranean; the *USS Eisenhower* and the *USS Saratoga* in the Red Sea; and the *USS Independence* being off Oman. On the 30th, Bush unveiled his 'Action Plan', under which he envisaged affluent Western nations and oil-rich Arab States, would contribute to the cost of *Operation Desert Shield*. By the end of August, the USA had over 40,000 troops in the Gulf area. Bush was being advised by Brent Scowcroft, US National Security Adviser, and members of the National Security Council.

Meanwhile, Bush and Baker were busy co-opting support from whichever nations could be persuaded to give it. Initially, both men concentrated on whipping in Arab States. A few background comments on certain countries may be of help and interest.

Arab and Islamic Allies

It was most important to President Bush that *Operation Desert Shield* should be seen to have as much Arab and Islamic support as possible, and such States as did support this Allied Coalition by sending military detachments were suitably, and occasionally, generously rewarded. The key Arab country was Egypt, which became a willing volunteer, as much because of Mubarak's hurt feelings at being lied to by Saddam Hussein, as for what he could obtain by way of material gain from the USA.

The Americans cancelled some of Egypt's debts to the USA, and soon the first detachment of 4,000 Egyptian troops were in Saudi Arabia in a defensive role. Also interest re-payments due in September to the USA from Egypt, which if unpaid, could have invoked the Brooke Amendment, meaning that all American aid would cease, were waived. When Egypt joined the Allied Coalition the ACC fell apart, which pleased Bush.

Other favourable American aid packages went to Egypt in appreciation of its open support for the Allied cause. In October, America wrote off more of Egypt's debts, and the German government gave Egypt economic aid to the value of about $300-million; while Japan gave that country $400-million, being part of a promised $2-billion economic package in which Jordan and Turkey also shared.

The general mood of the Egyptian people remained 'anti-Iraqi', owing to poor treatment of their nationals, and most went along comfortably with President Mubarak's decision to become part of the Allied Coalition. But this was not without pain, as the Islamic Fundamentalists became more active and violent, their demonstrations condemning this course. These culminated (2nd October) with the assassination of the Speaker of the People's Assembly. The government blamed the al-Jihad organisation, and mass arrests followed.

Considered to be a friend of the West, as expected, King Hassan of Morocco, was quick to rally to the American call, obviously in anticipation of remission of debts and further American aid.

The Americans expected that it might be hard to persuade Syria to join the Allied Coalition, despite the long-time animosity between Presidents Assad and Saddam Hussein, and also hard for Western Allies to accept, but it was eminently desirable that Syria should support the Western cause. On the 10th August, President Bush made the first move, and put through a personal telephone call to Assad. Horse trading was done, and Syria came into the Alliance. Syria sought Western recognition, Western acceptance and Western financial and economic aid. A hard bargain was struck. Diplomatic relations were restored between the USA and Syria, and Britain followed suit, but there was some internal opposition to Assad's sudden and unexpected decision, which he handled in a firm manner.

GCC Arab States were 'captive allies', having little option but to go along with the American-led and organised *Operation Desert Shield,* as they knew Saddam Hussein's sights were on their oil wells. The multi-state GCC RDF, still with a nominal strength of 20,000, was still based at Hafar al-Batin. Saudi Arabia claimed over-optimistically that it had 40,000 troops opposite the Kuwait frontier, which obviously included its GCC RDF contingent, while those of the remaining GCC States (Bahrain, Oman, Qatar and the UAE) in that area numbered about 3,000. Escaping Kuwaiti armed forces personnel re-assembled in Saudi Arabia, and volunteers were called for.

GCC States (less the unfortunate Kuwait) opened their main air bases to Allied aircraft, which included those at Hufuf and Muharraq (in Bahrain); Thrumrayt and Seeb (in Oman); Dhahran, Jabayl, Khamis Mushayt, Riyadh, Tabuk and Taif (in Saudi Arabia); and Abu Dhabi, Doha and Dubai (in the UAE).

That three major Arab countries had been persuaded to join the Allied Coalition, together with the dragooned GCC States, gladdened the hearts of Bush and Baker. It was quite an achievement. Remaining Arab States (except Yemen) all denounced Saddam Hussein's occupation of Kuwait, but few were prepared to go any further, most distrusting and disliking the USA, basically because it so ardently supported Israel, and was consequently seen as an enemy of the Arabs. Most were reluctant to fight brother Arabs, many thought that this Arab problem should be solved by Arabs, and others stood aside, watching in dismay as Western infidels disembarked on to sacred Saudi soil.

Non-Arab Member States of the Islamic Conference Organisation expressed similar views. They condemned the invasion of Kuwait, considered it to be an Arab problem, and expressed distaste at the thought of infidel soldiers on Saudi soil. Generally, non-Arab Islamic States stood aside, but there were exceptions.

One exception was Pakistan, which provided a military contingent. It was not unusual for one or more Pakistani brigades to be in Saudi Arabia, as the House of Saud hired them as fall-back security forces in case of internal upheavals, but they kept a very low profile. Relations between the USA and Pakistan were moderately good, but were fast faltering owing to the suspicion that the Pakistan government was working to produce a nuclear weapon. American aid packages were coming under threat, and Pakistan obviously had material reward in mind.

The other main exception was Bangladesh, a country plagued with natural disasters, poverty and corrupt rule, which was quick to espouse the Western cause in the hope it too, could attract more Western aid and assistance. Both the Pakistan and Bangladesh military detachments were in a defensive role only in Saudi Arabia. The West African states of Senegal and Niger were persuaded to each provide an infantry battalion, also in a defensive role.

Jordan

It was generally thought that Jordan would have rushed forward to support the USA, which in the past had provided, and was indeed still providing, military and economic assistance, but this did not happen. King Hussein of Jordan, hesitated, and tried to remain as a neutral peace-maker, advocating that the problem was an Arab one. Baker was disappointed. No one with a cause loves a neutral. Baker did not want a peace-maker, he wanted unquestioning, unswerving support.

King Hussein's position was a very invidious one as the PLO, led by Yasir Arafat, had openly opted to side with Saddam Hussein, and if street demonstrations were any guide, the majority of Jordanians were in favour of Iraq, and against the American-led Allied Coalition that was emerging. A flood of refugees from Kuwait and Iraq, passed through Jordan on their way home, and had to be accommodated in makeshift camps until they could be checked through. It was officially stated in Amman that between the 2nd August and the 7th September, over 600,000 passed through these Jordanian camps.

Although overtly agreeing to comply with UN Resolutions, in practice he prevaricated. Some 90% of Jordan's oil had been supplied by Iraq, and Hussein said he could not implement an economic blockade against Iraq until he found an alternative source of supply. Saudi Arabia stepped in and began sending oil to Jordan, but it is doubtful whether King Hussein ever really stopped the flow of goods, destined for Iraq, being landed at Akaba.

European Support

President Bush's two main European Allies were Britain and France. On the 3rd August, the British naval 'Armilla Patrol' in the Gulf, which had done sterling work during the Iran-Iraq War on 'sanctions busting', was re-constituted with two frigates and a destroyer, which were soon joined by three minesweepers. The first British military contingent to arrive in Saudi Arabia was a communications unit, and on the 9th, it was announced that a British Tornado squadron was being sent to that country also, and a Jaguar squadron to Bahrain.

At her first Press Conference on the Kuwait Crisis (21st August), Prime Minister Thatcher stated that "The purpose of sending British troops is to get the invaders out of Kuwait". Later that month, at the Helsinki Summit, she openly criticised the "patchy and disappointing response from other European countries", excepting France from her comment. On the 15th September, a British armoured brigade, stationed in Germany, was ordered to move to the Gulf area.

It was not true to say that France hesitated to join the American-dominated *Operation Desert Shield*, forming up in the Gulf region, but France had no desire to be seen to be slavishly following on British heels. On the 6th August, the French announced that its aircraft-carrier, *Clemenceau*, a cruiser and other naval craft, were being sent to the Gulf. France had supplied quantities of munitions to Iraq during, and since, the Iran-Iraq War, but this decision swept away doubts about what attitude it would take over the Kuwait Crisis.

France also said it would send military instructors to Saudi Arabia, and ground reconnaissance units to the UAE. However, the French Defence Minister, Jean-Pierre Chevenement, who was suspected of being less than whole-hearted about the project, said there were no plans for French contingents to join up with either American or British troops in the Gulf area, or for any joint chain of command. Command of all French military personnel was to remain firmly in French hands. The French as usual were standing resolutely on their dignity. Chevenement was a founder-member of the Franco-Iraqi Friendship Society, and the reputed architect of massive French arms sales to Iraq.

Apart from Britain and France, despite Secretary Baker's many lobbying visits to leaders of European States, and numerous telephone chats with Foreign Ministers, there was a distinct lack of enthusiasm for sending military personnel to the Gulf to increase the size and weight of Bush's 'big stick', with which to threaten Saddam Hussein. West Germany said its Constitution prevented it from sending its troops abroad, while some NATO member-states pointed out that Kuwait was well 'out of area'.

EC meetings (of the 4th, 10th and 21st August) agreed to condemn Saddam Hussein, to enforce economic sanctions against Iraq, freeze Iraqi and Kuwaiti assets, and to suspend arms sales, but were reluctant to go any further despite pressure from Bush and Baker. On the 10th August, NATO Foreign Ministers, meeting at Brussels, decided there would be no formal NATO response as such, but that member-states should contribute each in its own way; although if Turkey were attacked, that would be a different matter, and would draw 'a corresponding response from the Alliance as a whole'; but did give 'strong support' to the USA; and endorsed the decisions of Italy, Portugal and Spain to provide air base facilities. As far as NATO was concerned the problem was thrown back to individual member-states to do something, or nothing, as they pleased.

But a trickle of support was forthcoming. France, always uneasy as a NATO member, having long since quit its military framework, began to push the older Western European Union (WEU) (of Belgium, Britain, France, Italy, Luxembourg, the Netherlands, Portugal, Spain and West Germany), founded in 1948, and enlarged in 1954. The Kuwait Crisis was discussed at a WEU meeting held in Paris, on the 21st August, with Observers from Denmark, Greece and Turkey. Some of the member-states confirmed they would contribute to *Operation Desert Shield* — but not all. Greece had already said it would send a frigate to the Gulf; and both Belgium and Italy, on the 25th, indicated they would also send naval craft there.

Plainly Bush was disappointed by the poor European response, and on the 9th September, Secretary Baker addressed a NATO meeting, at which he plaintively called on member-states to contribute more to "responsibility sharing", not only by helping to transport troops by air and sea, but by committing their own armed forces, "should countries see fit, even if these were only symbolic", he pleaded. But it seemed that Baker's appeal aroused little enthusiasm.

On the 14th September, Italy stated it would add another frigate and eight Tornado aircraft; Belgium offered the use of four military transport aircraft and a frigate; and on the 18th, the Netherlands said it would send a squadron of F-16s to Turkey, but in a NATO context, meaning only for the defence of that country. Italy, the current holder of the EC Presidency, argued for a European-led military contribution, but this was not quite what Bush and Baker had in mind, nor was it responded to positively by EC member-states. From Eastern Europe came a Czechoslovakian offer to provide a Chemical Defence Unit.

Meanwhile, Baker lobbied far and wide outside Europe, and attracted a few disparate countries to join the American-led military coalition. These included Argentina (two frigates and a transport military aircraft); Australia (two frigates and a supply ship); and Canada (a destroyer and a supply ship). Japan blandly replied that its Constitution (imposed on it by the Americans after World War II), prevented it from sending troops abroad, but it did offer large financial contributions to the Bush Plan for sharing financial costs. By the 5th October, Secretary Baker boasted that over 25 nations had produced, or promised, military support in the Gulf. Just previously, on the 23rd September, the French aircraft-carrier, *Clemenceau*, arrived at Yanbu port (Saudi Arabia), disembarked 500 troops and 42 helicopters, and returned to France.

Turkey

At first President Bush was a little anxious about Turkey, and what stance it might take, but he need not have worried, as reputedly President Turgut Ozal stated on the day Saddam Hussein marched into Kuwait, that "However this Gulf Crisis resolves itself the map of the Middle East will be re-arranged, and I want to have a say in that re-arrangement". Perhaps he had an eye on the northern Iraqi oil-fields.

Turkey was the paid host to some 20 NATO (USA-run) installations on its territory, with American officers in charge, and a Turkish officer nominally in command, some being quite small for intelligence-gathering purposes, but others were quite large.

Larger ones included the naval bases at Istanbul, Izmir, Iskenderun and Karates; and air bases at Ankara, Incirlik and Gigli, all of which had considerable repair and re-fuelling facilities. NATO's 6th Tactical Air Force was at Incirlik, and its combat aircraft included 30 F-16s and F-111s, the latter just re-positioned from Britain. Soon US F-117A (Stealth) aircraft were arriving, and the air bases, and certain naval ones, filled with US aircraft and ships, crammed with American troops and stores, on their way to Saudi Arabia.

Over-night, Turkey became a 'front-line' state, and Baker paid an early visit. Ozal told him he would co-operate, but would expect to be well rewarded. In particular, Ozal wanted preferential access to EC markets for Turkish textiles, and to US home markets for other Turkish products; but this was beyond Baker's influence. On the 7th August, the day after UN Resolution 661 was approved, Ozal closed his frontier with Iraq, severed all connection with that country, and closed down the twin oil pipelines. This meant a considerable loss to Turkey in oil transit dues, and of oil for its refineries, as well as an end to the prosperous trade with Iraq in food and agricultural produce that had developed since the Cease-Fire. Financial recompense did not flow to Turkey in sufficient amounts to satisfy Ozal, although Saudi Arabia sent him oil for his refineries, and he received compensatory grants and aid from the EC, and the Gulf Financial Co-ordination Group (formed in October). In mid-September, he appealed unsuccessfully to the IMF for loans, calculating his losses for 1990 would be about $5-billion.

On the 12th August, the Turkish National Assembly had granted 'war powers' to Ozal. At first Ozal had talked vaguely and loosely of mustering a brigade of troops and some naval craft, ready for any proposed joint action, but he soon had second thoughts, and decided against taking part in *Operation Desert Shield*, although he did increase the number of Turkish troops near the Iraqi border to about 90,000. Ozal's excuse was that as the former colonial power in the days of the Ottoman Empire, Turkish troops, even though they were Muslim, would not be exactly welcome in Saudi Arabia. This would have been true, but a few days earlier, neither would American, British nor French soldiers have been welcomed. Circumstances had dramatically and conveniently changed attitudes in the Gulf area.

Soviet Reaction

Now the Cold War was over, neither President Bush nor Secretary Baker knew exactly how to take President Gorbachev. Would he co-operate with them, would he become an active Ally in *Operation Desert Shield*, would he be obstructionist, and most important, would he survive in power?

These and other doubts were to the forefront of the minds of these two men. They need not have worried unduly as Gorbachev desperately wanted something the Americans could give him — massive credits and economic aid — to prevent the USSR from devolving into economic chaos and unrest. To obtain this it seemed that Gorbachev set out to show himself as 'Mr. Nice Guy'.

Baker had pressured Shevardnadze into initially supporting an arms embargo against Iraq, a long-time Soviet investment and power projection means into the Middle East. The question was would the Soviets really abandon Iraq, just to please the Americans, until recently their hard-line, deadly rivals for global power? It seemed they would, as President Bush was the Soviet key to badly needed assistance.

The Soviets assured Baker they had stopped sending arms to Iraq, but this may have only been partly true. In answer to Baker's questions about Soviet military advisers and technicians working in Iraq, he was told there were "only 150, who will return when their contracts expire". This was also taken with a pinch of salt. Baker noted the Soviets had not expelled the small Iraqi naval contingent training at Riga, but this was ejected on the 2nd November, by a Latvian Assembly decision.

On the 25th August, the UN Security Council approved Resolution 665 (Cuba and Yemen abstaining), the Soviets voting in favour. This authorised member-nations 'to use measures commensurate to the specific circumstances', which were taken to include military action, to enforce the economic embargo against Iraq. The following day, Shevardnadze stated that the Soviets had "no plans to use force, or take part in this operation, but would not object to the USA, or others, using force to implement the embargo".

At the Helsinki Summit, Gorbachev said he was in favour of a political solution to the Kuwait Crisis, and as Bush and Baker were ostensibly seeking the same course, they could not complain, although they would have liked a more whole-hearted response. Soviet policy was to give economic sanctions full opportunity to see if they would be effective. Gorbachev said the problem was an Arab one, and one the Arabs themselves should solve, which did not please the Americans.

Chinese Reaction

Remote and enigmatic, China voted with the USA in the UN Security Council, but said little. There had been American anxiety in case the Chinese veto-ed American-brokered Resolutions, but so far they had not done so. Reputed secret negotiations between the USA and China were in progress, in which China was trying to obtain 'high-tech' expertise in return for its support in the Kuwait Crisis. On the other hand the Americans strove to give only a bare minimum of expertise, just sufficient to keep the Chinese overtly on their side. In fact, the Chinese had not changed their spots at all, and continued, as usual, to supply arms to any Middle East state, or indeed practically any other country, that could pay hard cash, while blandly denying it was doing so.

General Norman Schwartzkopf

Meanwhile on to the Middle East scene came a huge (six feet four inches tall) burly, larger than life, extrovert figure, who through the medium of the TV, and his own efforts, came to be known universally as 'Storming Norman'. He was General Norman Schwartzkopf, who had been appointed to command *Operation Desert Shield* because he was Commander of the US Central Command (CENTCOM), and the Middle East was part of his geographical remit. In keeping with the new US military doctrine, Schwartzkopf was given executive power, and it was his task not only to persuade elements, of all four US Services to work together, but also to co-ordinate the several multi-national military detachments. His task was to command *Operation Desert Shield*, within the parameters laid down by the US President, Secretary of Defense and the Chairman of the JCS.

Of German immigrant descent, aged 56, and a product of the West Point Military Academy, Schwartzkopf was an airborne infantryman, who had been Advisor to a Vietnamese Airborne Division, and then commanded an American infantry battalion in Vietnam. In the course of his successful military career, it was claimed he had become an expert in desert warfare. Little known outside his profession, Schwartzkopf was known to his contemporaries as the 'Bear', because of his physical bulk. US Military Public Relations staff, aided by the US media, set to work to present him as a competent, formidable General, who would over-awe Saddam Hussein.

He was well briefed for his task, as according to one source *(Cohen & Gatti)* only a few days before the 2nd August, CENTCOM had concluded a War Game *("Internal Look 90")*, based on a supposed Iraqi invasion of Kuwait, and he also had visited Saudi Arabia (15th-17th July), to discuss such a contingency with senior Saudi military personnel.

By early September, some 150,000 American and Allied troops had assembled in the Gulf area, mainly in northern Saudi Arabia. Excitement ran high. If it came to war, a quick victory was anticipated. These high hopes were somewhat dampened, when on the 9th September, General Schwartzkopf openly expressed the opinion he would need another two months to bring his force up to strength. This led to the belief that he was planning a mid-November deadline to attack the Iraqis in Kuwait. It also became known that Schwartzkopf was stock-piling for a 60-day operation.

President Bush's Speech to Congress

On the 11th September, President Bush outlined his objectives to Congress, as being:–

1 — Unconditional Iraqi withdrawal from Kuwait;

2 — Restoration of Kuwait's legitimate government;

3 — Assurance of stability and security in the Gulf; and

4 — The protection of American citizens.

Bush emphasised "This is not as Saddam Hussein would have it — the United States against Iraq. It is Iraq against the world". He wanted to persuade everyone he was not just a lone voice. Bush pointed out that Iraq controlled some "10% of the world's proven oil reserves, and with those of Kuwait, controls twice that percentage". He declared "We cannot permit a resource so vital to be dominated by one so ruthless".

In the same speech to Congress, Bush said "Out of these troubled times, our fifth objective — that of a 'New World Order' — can emerge a new era, free from the threat of terror, stronger in the pursuit of justice, and more secure in the quest for peace. An era in which the nations of the world, East and West, North and South, can prosper and live in harmony. . . .This is the vision I shared with President Gorbachev at Helsinki". It must be doubted whether Gorbachev quite saw the vision the American way. Bush was specifying his own version of Pax Americana. His expression "New World Order", disturbed some of America's Allies, and gave propaganda fuel to its enemies. It was later exorcised from the US Administration's vocabulary.

Although Bush's speech seemed pointed enough, it had a deeper meaning, which became known as the 'hidden agenda'. In reality this meant the removal of Saddam Hussein, and the neutralisation of Iraq's suspected nuclear and chemical warfare establishments, which although implied, was never voiced, and in fact, was vigorously denied whenever mentioned. Somehow it was assumed that Saddam Hussein could not last the course, would back down at the last minute in the face of American military might, and that in defeat his own officer corps would topple him from power. President Bush anticipated being able to dictate his own terms to a compliant and docile successor. This American fantasy endured, being one the US Administration was loathe to let die.

Dismissal of General Dugan

There arose considerable controversy, both within the US JCS and the Pentagon between the 'wings' who felt that air power alone could win a war for the Allies, and that a ground operation would be superfluous, and the 'legs' (the army) who insisted that ground combat troops were essential. Worried about heavy casualties it thought would be inevitable in any hard-fought ground battle against Iraq's reputed large, battle-hardened army, the Pentagon veered towards the 'air power' theory and discussed whether a US Air Force General should be appointed to command any extension of *Operation Desert Shield*. Commonsense prevailed and General Schwartzkopf retained his command throughout the war.

On the 17th September, General Michael Dugan, Air Force Chief of Staff, who had only held his appointment for about three months, carelessly (or perhaps deliberately) revealed what was assumed by some to be the plan the Pentagon was working on. He told media reporters that if war broke out the United States would bomb Baghdad, and that such an attack would target Saddam Hussein himself. Dugan suggested that air power was the only way of forcing Saddam Hussein out from Kuwait, and that a massive air campaign had been planned that would 'decapitate' the Iraqi leadership by targeting Saddam Hussein, his family and senior Iraqi commanders.

General Dugan said, "If push comes to shove, the cutting edge would be in down-town Baghdad. This would be nibbling at the edges. If I want to hurt you, it would be at home, and when we choose violence he ought to be the focus of our efforts. I don't see us making a big invasion. To try to beat Iraq on the ground risks destroying Kuwait in order to save it".

General Dugan was instantly 're-assigned' by the Secretary of Defense, the reason given being that he had violated Standing Orders on public discussions on military operations, and 'had showed poor judgement at a sensitive time'. To illustrate strong feelings held by the 'air power' lobby, Edward Luttwak, an acknowledged military expert, when asked why military commanders had felt it necessary to have so many ground troops in Saudi Arabia, replied *(AFJI)* "Because the President picked a bunch of gardeners to do his cooking". Rivalry between the 'wings' and the 'legs' was a left-over from Vietnam days. Certainly, some advocated the Commander of *Operation Desert Shield* should have been an Air Force General.

4

Strategic Defiance

Meanwhile in Baghdad, President Saddam Hussein was operating a policy of Strategic Defiance in what seemed to develop into an eye-ball to eye-ball confrontation with President Bush, neither daring blink in case it revealed a vital weakness. A prolonged period of 'brinkmanship' followed in which Bush became more angry and threatening, while Saddam Hussein stone-walled. Bush was convinced that at some stage Saddam Hussein would back down, while on the other hand Saddam Hussein was convinced that Bush would not resort to the military option. It took some time for the misbeliefs of these two Presidents to turn into reality.

Bush was continually increasing the size of his 'big stick', and waving it at Saddam Hussein in a threatening manner, only to be met by a cold response. The struggle became personalised between these two Presidents, although Bush was quick to deny this and spoke in generalities, but the media was always ready to emphasise this aspect. Saddam Hussein was certainly very pointed in his views on Bush. Both had much at stake, as Bush's reputation depended upon bringing Saddam Hussein to heel, while Saddam Hussein knew he was in a 'survival situation', but each felt the other was the weaker.

The Human Shield

On the 16th August, all American and British nationals in Kuwait had been ordered to 'surrender themselves' to the authorities, and already they had been 'assembled' in hotels in Kuwait City, from where a few of them had been moved into Iraq. Some had already been positioned adjacent to potential military targets, such as airfields or oil installations. On the 17th, the Speaker of the Iraqi National Assembly announced that citizens of 'aggressive countries' would not be released until the threat of war against Iraq ended.

Saddam Hussein took to calling the American and British detainees 'guests' and nationals of countries that contributed to the Allied military coalition, also became 'guests'. On the 19th, he said "Their presence, along with Iraqi families, may prevent military aggression".

The following day he stated that the foreign 'guests' would be freed when American troops were withdrawn from the Gulf area; when the economic blockade against Iraq was lifted; and when President Bush gave a written assurance that the USA would not attack Iraq. On the 23rd, President Bush for the first time referred to detained nationals as 'hostages'. That day Saddam Hussein was shown on Baghdad TV chatting affably to groups of hostages. The following day, all foreign Embassies in Kuwait were closed, being surrounded by security forces, but no attempt was made to forcibly enter them. On the 28th, it was announced that women and children would be allowed to leave, and were flown out in batches in succeeding days.

The Iraqi Ambassador to the USA, on the 31st, suggested that male Western 'guests' could be released if the USA guaranteed not to attack Iraq. This offer was rejected by the US State Department, which while emphasising that American armed forces were in Saudi Arabia for 'defensive purposes only', would not consider conditions at all. Previously, Saddam Hussein had suggested a TV discussion with President Bush and Prime Minister Thatcher, but their governments rejected the idea.

Foreign nationals in Kuwait, whose governments had not signified any intention to contribute military detachments to the Allied coalition in the Gulf were not formally detained, and by the end of the month almost 600 of them had been able to leave.

On the 25th August, by a Baghdad Decree Kuwait became the '19th Governate of Iraq', which was divided into three districts, of Kadhima (Kuwait City), Jahra and al-Nida. Another decree extended the border of the Basra Governate south into Kuwait, creating the new province of Saddamiya al-Mitlaa.

Sanctions

UN Resolution 661 had authorised the imposition of an economic blockade against Iraq, but the question arose as to whether these sanctions could be imposed by force. The USA was of the opinion that a legal right to do so was inherent in the UN Charter, but Perez de Cuellar, the UN Secretary General disassociated himself from this view, which caused some to hesitate. However, the Americans went ahead, and on the 17th August, US naval vessels intercepted two Iraqi coastal craft in the

Gulf, but allowed them to continue when found to have no cargo aboard; and the following day, warning shots were fired across the bows of two Iraqi oil-tankers in the Gulf of Oman.

At this stage the Americans did not use the expression 'blockade', but instead used 'interdiction of sanction-breaking'. Bush worked to legalise the use of force by UN Resolution, putting forward a Draft Resolution containing the words 'use of such minimum force as may be necessary', but this had to be changed at Chinese insistence to read 'measures commensurate to the specific circumstances'. China had a veto right in the Security Council, and so its view had to be respected.

The US DoD later stated (27th November) that to date a total of 4,162 ship-interceptions had been carried out, which included 500 boardings and 19 ship diversions; adding that US forces had carried out 320 of the boardings, Allied forces 162, and combined US-Allied forces 18. All US warships in the Gulf region were connected by radio-telephone to CENTCOM HQ Operation Centre at Tampa, Florida (USA). The Commander, or his staff officers, could talk directly to the Captain of any USN ship involved in any incident, even while the incident was in progress.

Iran-Iraq Peace Accord

Suddenly, Saddam Hussein turned his attention to Iran, with which country he had fought an eight-year long war. A Cease-Fire had come into effect on the 20th August 1988, but as mutual relations between the two countries remained poor, little progress had been made towards a formal peace treaty. On the 14th August, Saddam Hussein made overtures to the Iranian President, Ali Akbar Hashemi Rafsanjani, who on the following day accepted Iraq's proposals for a peace accord. Main concessions included Iraqi withdrawal from about 1,625-square miles of alleged Iranian territory, and the repatriation of some 30,000 Iranian POWs, a process which had been halted due to friction.

The Baghdad government stated that its troop withdrawals had been completed by the 21st, and that the exchange of POWs was in progress. Some 70,000-100,000 Iraq POWs were also involved in the exchange. As a gesture of goodwill towards Iran, Saddam Hussein allowed 'thousands' of Iranians to leave Kuwait by crossing over the Shatt al-Arab waterway to their own country. The real reason for Saddam Hussein concluding a peace accord with Iran was two-fold; first being able to redeploy his notional '23 divisions' positioned along the Iraqi frontier facing Iran, and second to eliminate the potential Iranian opportunity attack-threat on his own country.

Hiccups soom occurred over the POW exchange. By mid-September, Iran halted the process as it was claimed Iraq additionally held about

20,000 more Iranians than were registered by the International Committee of the Red Cross (ICRC). Iraq insisted the ICRC numbers were correct, but did state that the RCC had decided to pardon all Iranian POWs, either convicted of offences, or whose cases were pending. Ali Akbar Velayati, the Iranian Foreign Minister, visited Iraq in mid-November, when it was announced that the POW exchange would be resumed.

Palestine Liberation Organisation

The Palestine Liberation Organisation, an umbrella one for several Palestinian groups, some of which are patently terrorist ones, is dedicated to the establishment of a sovereign Arab Palestine State, and had come into the Kuwait Crisis scenario when Saddam Hussein (12th August) had mentioned 'linkage' for the first time. The PLO has been at long-time odds with Israel, which is still occupying territory captured in the 1967 War, which the Palestinians claim is theirs. The 'Occupied Territories', as these disputed areas are known, are administered by Israel, in which the Intifada (Uprising) had been in progress since December 1987, but had generally been contained.

Yasir Arafat, Chairman of the PLO, who is also leader of Fatah, the largest group within the Organisation, has the nominal support of Arab League countries, but in practice this is uncertain and unreliable. Arafat had been recently experiencing a spasm of low fortune, his ever-mercurial relations with some Heads of Arab States had deteriorated, and America's dialogue with the PLO had been broken off in June, as the Chairman would not condemn a sea-borne terrorist attack on Israel (30th May 1990) by the Palestine Liberation Front (PLF), a constituent member of the PLO. Arafat was also in open dispute with President Assad, who had expelled him from Syria, and who was supporting a Fatah breakaway faction, led by Abu Musa.

The PLO obtained funds from several sources, including considerable sums from Kuwait and Saudi Arabia. For some time before the 2nd August, Arafat had been making overtures to Saddam Hussein, as he felt he was the only Arab leader standing up to the USA, and making viable threats against Israel. When Saddam Hussein marched into Kuwait, Arafat refused to condemn his action and openly gave him full support. In this respect, Palestinians generally followed suit, which annoyed Arab members of the Allied coalition, which withdrew their financial support from the PLO. Arafat visited Saddam Hussein, and other Arab Heads of State, several times, endeavouring to become a negotiator, but was rejected because Palestinians had suddenly become unpopular. Palestinian demonstrations in Jordan caused King Hussein to walk very carefully.

The Conference of Arab Popular Forces, a gathering of pro-Iraqi radical Arab factions, organised by the Jordanian National Democratic Alliance, an umbrella organisation, established in 1989, took place in Amman (17th-19th September), attended by over 120 'representatives', which supported Saddam Hussein against 'Imperialists' and 'linked' the Kuwait Problem with that of the Palestinians'. Two notorious Palestinian terrorist leaders, who had been barred from Jordan since the Jordanian-PLO clashes in 1970, were allowed back into the country, and both were received by King Hussein. They were George Habash, of the Popular Front for the Liberation of Palestine (PFLP), and Nayef Hawatmeh, of the Democratic Front for the Liberation of Palestine (DFLP).

International Terrorism

Saddam Hussein added the threat of international terrorism to those of non-conventional weapons, should he be attacked by the US-led Allied military coalition forces. Several terrorist groups in the world operated on an international basis, meaning in more than one country, taking advantage of international barriers and the tight insularity of national security forces. Three were notorious Palestinian ones, all very effective and very deadly, whose leaders and activists had been periodically employed, often on a mercenary basis, and sheltered in turn by Libya, South Yemen, Syria and Iraq, migrating from one to the other depending upon rewards, moods and pet requirements of respective Rulers. A few months before the 2nd August, they moved from Syria to Baghdad, where there were reputed sightings of notorious activists from time to time. After that date, visits of terrorist leaders to Baghdad became more frequent.

One group was the Popular Front for the Liberation of Palestine – General Command (PFLP – GC), a breakaway faction from the main organisation, led by Ahmad Jabril, who was suspected of implication in the 'Lockerbie' air disaster (21st December 1988). Another was the Palestine Liberation Front (PLF), led by Abu Abbas, allegedly responsible for hijacking the Italian cruise liner, *Achille Lauro*, (7th October 1985); and the third was Fatah-Revolutionary Council (Fatah-RC), a breakaway from Fatah, led by the notorious Abu Nidal, which had carried out a series of deadly attacks against international airports and international airliners. In September, President Bush placed Iraq in the US List of Countries Sponsoring Terrorism.

The Peace-Makers

The latter part of 1990 was mainly taken up with increasing the strength of *Operation Desert Shield* forces, and President Bush's threats to Saddam

Hussein, while Saddam Hussein, with his captive foreign nationals, maintained his Strategic Defiance. During this period several Heads of State, Foreign Ministers, Special Envoys, the UN Secretary General and humanitarian-motivated VIPs, shuttled between Capitals in America, Europe, the USSR and the Arab world, endeavouring to bring about a peeaceful solution to the Kuwait Crisis, and above all to gain the release of the hostages.

Reciprocal expulsions between Iraq and other countries, of diplomats and diplomatic staffs took place. Some hostages were deployed near potential military targets, and some still remained in hiding from the Iraqi authorities. In a letter, made public by the Americans on the 26th September, from Saddam Hussein to the US Ambassador in Baghdad, he warned that people without diplomatic immunity taking refuge in an Embassy would be hanged.

Food rationing was introduced in Iraq in early September, and allegations surfaced that 'humanitarian' aid sent to Iraq was not reaching intended destinations, but was being syphoned off by the military. In September, Presidents Bush and Saddam Hussein exchanged TV appearances on the other's channel to state their respective cases, but this only increased the verbal abuse log-jam. Nationals of countries that had not contributed to the Allied military coalition, and who wished to leave Iraq, were eventually granted exit visas.

Saddam Hussein did, however, allow small numbers of his 'guests' to be released, such as the sick and elderly, and also a few as a humanitarian publicity gesture whenever foreign VIPs came to visit him in Baghdad. Examples included, in August, Chancellor Waldheim of Austria, who returned with 80 of his countrymen; in October, a French Delegation obtained the release of nine French hostages; and the same month Edward Heath, a former British Prime Minister, returned with 40 hostages. Heath had a long personal interview with Saddam Hussein, and when asked why the hostages could not all be released, was told that "I have to rely upon the hostages, my ballistic missiles and chemical warheads, as they are my only deterrents against an American attack".

Suddenly, on the 6th December, the Iraqi RCC announced that all 'foreign guests' would start to be released on the 25th December, and that unless something occurred to disturb the peace process, all would be repatriated within three months. Two days previously, Iraqi authorities had announced that '3,232 Soviet citizens would be allowed to leave, even if they had not completed their contracts', but on the 17th, a spokesman at the Soviet Embassy in Baghdad, said that exit visas were being refused to Soviet nationals whose contracts had not expired.

Conflicting estimates of numbers of hostages by nationality tended to confuse the situation. This was partly because there was no independent co-ordinating centre with authority to consolidate data, and partly because a number still remained in hiding. One source (*Washington Post: 11th December*) gave the total number of hostages held as '3,400', which included 580 detained at strategic military and civilian sites; being '1,175 British, 900 Americans, 197 Japanese and 180 Italians' (i.e. only 2,452), but it was said that about 1,000 had chosen to remain in Iraq. Suddenly, Saddam Hussein decided to release all the hostages in the Human Shield immediately, and by the 12th December, most had left Iraq.

Several VIPs, including King Hassan of Morocco, and Yasir Arafat of the PLO, claimed a share in persuading Saddam Hussein to take this momentous decision. One source (*John Simpson*) credits Arafat, whom he says was engaged in secret diplomacy, for making it plain to Saddam Hussein that he had nothing to gain from continuing to hold the hostages. Saddam Hussein declared it was a humanitarian issue, that the "guests had given a great service to peace", and that he had been encouraged by the attitude of the American Democratic Party, and an EC invitation to hear a dialogue from the Iraqi Foreign Minister. He also said that "The liberation of the 'guests'" would lead to a wider dialogue. This time Saddam Hussein had badly miscalculated as President Bush had already made up his mind to take military action, and was unstoppable. The last barrier was removed.

Iraqi Deployment

Saddam Hussein had made a bellicose speech on the 23rd September, threatening all-out war against the Allied multi-national force, and also threatening to strike at Israel, and Middle East oil-fields. On the 9th October, he claimed he had a missile capable of reaching Israel and Saudi Arabia, but this was dismissed by most Western analysts.

After concluding the Peace Accord with Iran in August (1990), Saddam Hussein was able to withdraw some of the Pentagon-estimated '23 divisions' from his Eastern Front. The Pentagon calculated the Iraqis had '42 divisions' of all types, based on satellite reconnaissance, although it was admitted that many were under-strength. The Iraqi mobilised strength was quoted as being between one-million and 1.2-million men.

Three of these very much under-strength divisions (about 11,000 men) were redeployed to the Syrian Front, and a similar number to the Turkish Front, while about 100,000 troops, in five divisions, were sent south to the Kuwait area (JDW). Republican Guard divisions that had spear-headed the occupation of Kuwait, were being withdrawn to form both a tactical reserve near Kuwait City, and a strategic one in the Basra area. Ten divisions already in Kuwait, included three armoured, two mechanised, four infantry and one commando one. On the 5th October, Defense Secretary Cheney over-stated that the Iraqis had about 350,000 troops deployed in the Basra-Kuwait Region, and that the Iraqis were constructing strong defences in southern Kuwait, facing the Saudi border. On the 30th, Iraqi armed forces were placed on a General Alert.

Kuwait-in-Exile

On the 27th September, the Emir of Kuwait had addressed the UN General Assembly to plead for immediate action to be taken to restore his country to him. There was little compassion in his speech, only a harsh note of urgency to the Allies to hurry up and liberate his country for him, which in practice could mean completely destroying it, and probably killing half-a-million people (a Pentagon estimate).

Over 1,000 exiled Kuwaitis, who included members of the Ruling Sabah family, the government and opposition leaders, met together at a Popular Congress, at Jedda (13th-15th October), to see if unity in exile could be achieved. The Kuwaiti opposition was encouraged to be bolder in speech by awakening American awareness of the type of autocracy the Emir headed, and wanted to perpetuate, and their disapproval of it. Joint Presidents of the Popular Congress were the Emir and his Crown Prince, the Emir promising vaguely and uncertainly elections for the National Assembly when he was restored to power back in his own country again.

The Saudi Hiccup

When President Mubarak visited Saudi Arabia, on the 22nd October, it was suggested, and repeated by the Saudi Defence Minister (Prince Sultan ibn Abdul Aziz) that Iraq might be allowed to negotiate an advantageous re-alignment of its border with Kuwait, in return for evacuating its troops from Kuwait. This idea had been floated before by other peace-makers, and involved Iraq being allowed to retain Bubiyan and Warba Islands, and a small piece of adjacent Kuwaiti territory. This suggestion upset President Bush, who was firmly against granting any concessions at all, and was quietly, but firmly crushed. This basically was the Arab solution, and had it been accepted many lives might have been saved.

Allied Build-Up

On the Allied side, naval craft were converging towards the Gulf in number, and on the 11th September, a conference was held by Arab, American and other naval commanders, and officials of 20 nations, to co-ordinate their activities in enforcing sanctions against Iraq. In early

October, Allied reinforcements began to arrive in Saudi Arabia, including Egyptian, Syrian, and others, by the hundreds and then by the thousands. The US ground contingent soon reached a strength of some 230,000, but even so on the 25th, a Pentagon spokesman stated that it might be necessary to send up to another 100,000 troops, and many hundreds more main battle tanks.

As weeks passed by without any sign of military action, and with General Schwartzkopf continually calling for more troops before he could be ready to move, boredom began to set in. No General in any war ever has enough troops. Within the US contingent there came to be talk, and hope, that a system of rotation of personnel would be introduced, or if not, at least a short-period of local leave on the lines of the 'R & R' (Rest and Recreation) of Vietnam days, to give personnel a break from spartan life under desert conditions. The Pentagon opposed both these ideas, as both would require extra personnel to cover change-overs or local leave, which would involve calling up more reservists. It would also mean admitting the war was not going to be a short one.

The Military Option

Probably it was about mid-October when President Bush realised that Saddam Hussein's Strategic Defiance could continue indefinitely, and the military option would have to be resorted to. The current argument in defence circles was 'give sanctions time to work', but Bush, angry and impatient, was no longer sure they would, at least not quickly enough, and feared there was a limit to the time he could keep the fragile Allied multi-national coalition intact and docile.

Some time that month, Bush asked General Schwartzkopf for a briefing on how an offensive military operation against Iraqi occupation of Kuwait should be conducted. Apparently, Schwartzkopf was taken by surprise, no doubt working on Bush's statement (of the 8th August) that "The mission for our troops is wholly defensive". It seemed as if Schwartzkopf had thought that was that. In any event, he did not seem to have a battle plan ready, and had to 'work 20 hours a day' in his Tampa Command Centre to produce one.

One source (Bob Woodward) wrote "Schwartzkopf was furious. He (the President) had to be kidding. He was not ready to present such a plan. He had no warning". On the theory that where there is smoke there must be some fire, it seems there might have been lack of foresight and flexibility on Schwartzkopf's part. Some authorities, who claim to have inside information, say that General Powell wanted sanctions to be given a longer trial period to see if they would have the desired effect on Saddam Hussein, but as Powell was not regarded as one of Bush's 'insider team', little notice was taken of such views.

In preparation for the military option, and not forgetting the Hidden Agenda, on the 25th October, William Webster, Director of the CIA, stated that the Iraqi arsenal must also be destroyed to keep the region secure. In Saudi Arabia, on the 5th November, it was agreed on the diplomatic front that all American, and other Allied, troops would come under command of a Saudi General, Prince Khaled bin Sultan (Commander of the Saudi Air Force), but once off Saudi territory would revert to US military command. This was a face-saving agreement for the Saudis, who as the hosts, had to be placated, but in practice meant very little.

President Bush made his 'military option' speech on the 8th November, prefacing it by saying he preferred a "peaceful solution". Sweeping aside all argument over troop rotation, he announced that a further 200,000 US military personnel would be deployed in the Gulf, as he needed to make *Operation Desert Shield* credible. Schwartzkopf had assessed the existing potential of his command as having only "the capacity to defend successfully".

This new deployment, due to be completed in January 1991, would bring the US military contribution up to the 430,000 mark, which was quoted (*Pentagon* figures) as being '34% of the total strength of the US Army'. These reinforcements were to include three tank divisions from Germany, doubling the US Marine contingent to bring it up to a strength of 90,000, three more aircraft-carrier groups, and a second battleship, the *USS Missouri*. The call-up of Marine reservists had begun, and the army followed suit.

There was domestic opposition to this overt change of policy by Bush towards the Kuwait Crisis, voiced by Claiborne Pell, Chairman of the US Senate Foreign Relations Committee, who warned the President that he "would be badly advised to go to war without a clear prior expression of Congressional support", and should not "establish an offensive capacity in advance of a UN Resolution authorising offensive action". Secretary Baker was sent off to lobby for such a Resolution. When Bush visited US troops in the field in Saudi Arabia on Thanksgiving (28th November), he found a degree of reservation amongst them and some lack of enthusiasm, not entirely masked by the Public Relations facade.

Growing domestic concern at the prospect of a military offensive in the Gulf caused apprehension, but moves to have Congress specially recalled for a full debate on the issue, failed. On the 27th, the US Senate Armed Services Committee opened hearings on the Administration's management of the Kuwait Crisis. Opposition certainly worried Bush, he did not like to stand alone, but Baker saved the day for him.

An Appointment for War

The UN Security Council approved Resolution 667, on the 29th November 1990, unanimously by 12 votes to nil, with China, Cuba and Yemen abstaining. This Resolution virtually authorised the use of 'all necessary means' to ensure Iraq's complete withdrawal from Kuwait by the 15th January 1991. China had been unsuccessfully lobbied by Baker for its fuller support, but as a reward for not using its veto, diplomatic relations with the USA, having been broken off due to the 'Tienanmen Square Affair' of June 1989, were resumed. This was the first occasion during the Kuwait Crisis that the five permanent members had not voted in unison.

UN Resolution 667 was not only a declaration of war against Saddam Hussein, but it also gave a deadline for battle, which invoked the since often used expression 'an appointment for war'. Baker, who had busily shuttled from one Security Council member to another, wheeling, dealing and promising, declared it to be the Security Council's "most important meeting ever". For Bush and Baker it probably was. The following day the Chairmanship of the Security Council, by rotation passed from the USA, the holder, to Yemen.

The Extra Mile for Peace

Warning signs were now switched on, which alerted and also alarmed many people, who had never seriously anticipated the military option would be chosen. It was suggested that the American Secretary of State should visit the Iraqi President, and that the Iraqi Foreign Minister should visit President Bush, to see if a peaceful solution could be found. With reluctance, Bush declared he would "go this extra mile for peace", but his inflexible attitude did not inspire confidence.

This turned into a snappy, bad tempered inability to match convenient dates. The US suggested the 17th December for Tariq Aziz to meet Bush in Washington, but this was rejected by Baghdad. The Iraqi suggested that James Baker should meet Saddam Hussein on the 12th January, but this was turned down by the Americans, as being too close to the deadline (of the 15th). However, Baker and Tariq Aziz, did finally meet at Geneva on the 9th January, the day Saddam Hussein warned that the US forces would "swim in blood if they attack my country".

The latter part of December had seen a posture of studied inflexibility between the two opposing Presidents. On the 20th, Bush said "Saddam Hussein has got to be kicked"; and on the 21st, Saddam Hussein said he would not quit Kuwait, and accused Bush of planning war against him; and on the 27th, Bush replied that "US forces are now ready to engage in combat in the Gulf".

Iraqi Reaction

Saddam Hussein's reaction to Bush's threats had been to re-shuffle some of his Top Brass. On the 14th November, he had replaced General Ali Hassan al-Majid, Governor of Kuwait, with Aziz Saleh al-Nouman, a former Minister and senior Baath Party official. The Kuwaiti Ambassador to the UN alleged the Iraqis had confiscated all 'ID Cards' (Identity documents) in Kuwait, and burned the State archives and population statistics, but boasted the "Population Register was smuggled out on the 2nd August", and had been given to the UN Secretary General for safe-keeping.

Also, in November, Saddam Hussein appointed General Hussein Rashid (a son-in-law), former Deputy Chief of Staff for Operations, and Commander of the Republican Guard (JDW), to be Chief of Staff of the Armed Forces, in place of General Nazir al-Khazraji, whom it was rumoured had incurred displeasure being blamed for allowing the Kuwaiti Ruling Family to escape during the occupation of Kuwait. That month it was alleged (Kurdish sources) that 20 Iraqi officers, most of General rank, had been purged, of whom six were executed, including General Thablet Sultan, commanding the 2nd Army Corps area, for plotting against the regime.

In mid-December, the Defence Minister, the elderly General Abdul Jaber Khalil Shamshal, who had been appointed to that post after the mysterious death of General Adnan Khairallah, a relative of Saddam Hussein, who had died in a helicopter crash in May 1989, was removed, and General Saadi Tuma Abbas, Inspector General of the Iraqi Armed Forces, became Defence Minister. Previously, General Abbas had been Deputy Chief of Staff, a successful Commander of the 3rd Army Corps in the Iran-Iraq War, and was also credited with constructing the formidable defences shielding Basra from Iranian offensives.

Rumours indicated that an unnamed Air Force General had been arbitrarily executed, being blamed for a leak to the media that Saddam Hussein kept two fully fuelled aircraft at the Baghdad International Airport ready to fly him and his family out of the country in case of an Allied attack. Such rumours, and worse, were rife about senior Iraqi military officers, usually initiated by opposition sources. They were impossible to substantiate, or disprove, as Iraq was not a country conducive to investigative journalism. Changes were certainly made in higher military echelons, new command appointments were made, and there were dismissals, reduction in rank, imprisonment, and even perhaps executions. One did not come to know, except sometimes by chance, what really happened to missing individuals, and how many were really simply living in quiet retirement.

Saddam Hussein also gave attention to Civil Defence, especially in Baghdad, a city of probably four-million people, and where it was reported that some '370 civil defence posts' had been established. Instructions in Civil Defence were shown on TV each evening, it being explained how everyone should react to enemy raids, how to take shelter, how to adjust gas-masks and how to render First Aid. Citizens were urged to stock-pile fuel, cooking fuel and food. On the 22nd-23rd December, there was a massive Civil Defence evacuation exercise, involving hundreds of thousands of inhabitants to camps a few miles outside the city. On the last day of the year (1990) Saddam Hussein received a piece of good news — it was that Iran had decided to remain neutral in any conflict between Iraq and the Allies.

Crescendo to Conflict

On the 6th January 1991, Saddam Hussein promised the "Mother of all Battles" if war broke out; on the 9th, President Bush ordered the 'mobilisation of resources in the interests of national security'; and on the 12th, US Congress authorised the use of force against Saddam Hussein. Bush breathed more easily. However, there was a sizable minority against the military option, voting being 52-47 in favour in the US Senate, and 250-183 in favour in the House of Representatives. The disputed constitutionality of the War Powers Act of 1973, dogged Bush almost to the deadline.

On the 14th, the Iraqi National Assembly voted unanimously to support Saddam Hussein and fight to retain Kuwait, last minute French peace proposals to the UN, being blocked, and the UN Secretary General, after meeting Saddam Hussein, said "There is little hope for diplomacy". On the 15th, a White House spokesman forecast military action "sooner rather than later". In the Gulf area over a million-and-a-quarter troops were tensely poised for battle, there being (*Pentagon* figures) '680,000 Allied troops against 545,000 Iraqi troops', with another 500,000 Iraqi military personnel as back-up in Iraq proper.

5

The Air War

At 0200-hours (local time), on the 17th January 1991, *Operation Desert Shield* was superseded by *Operation Desert Storm*, which began with a long, intensive Allied air campaign against Iraqi and Kuwaiti targets, that lasted for about six weeks (or 40 days, or 1,000 hours in round figures for the publicity-minded), during which over 50,000-tons of High Explosive munitions were dropped, causing untold damage, and (as belatedly admitted by the US Pentagon) probably caused over 400,000 Iraqi casualties, that included Servicemen, civilians, women and children, of whom probably a quarter were killed — no one knows exactly as yet. Very 'high-tech' sophisticated 'stand-off' and 'laser-guided' weapons were used, some for the first time in combat. A small number (about 2% of the sorties: *General Horner*) could strike their targets with astounding accuracy, but in this cold, computer-controlled air war, most of the remaining 98% used less modern munitions. The Iraqis were taken by surprise.

Credit for the first Allied aircraft strike into Iraqi air space was officially given to the US 101st Aviation Brigade *(ADJ)*, when eight of the US Army's AH-64 Apache armed helicopters, carrying Hellfire laser-guided missiles, attacked and destroyed key Iraqi Early Warning and Control posts, power generators and communication facilities, to cut a swath to form a 'radar-black corridor' through which Allied aircraft could fly.

High altitude F-117A (Stealth) aircraft, subsonic and ungainly, made precision strikes against Command and Communication buildings, and other strategic targets, using a claimed capability to deliver a laser-guided 2,000-lb bomb to within two feet of its target. Each plane carried two GBU-27 'Smart' bombs with an encased penetration warhead, or the GBU-27/109, which had a delayed fuse. This plane was designated 'Stealth' as its silhouette and composition reflected a very low radar profile.

Undetected by Iraqi radar, at 0230-hours on the 17th, one F-117A (Stealth) locked its laser-designator on to the flat roof of the main Communication Centre building in Baghdad. Moments later one of its laser-guided bombs, with pin-point accuracy hit the top of the vertical ventilation shaft, to disappear down within it, to explode inside the building. In Baghdad all TV and radio transmissions were abruptly cut off. An official video, taken of this exploit, was shown at media briefings on several occasions, and repeated countless times on world TV networks, which deeply impressed viewers of the fine accuracy of American precision weapons.

The F-117A (Stealth) had taken off from the Turkish/NATO air base at Incirlik, near Adana, where the Turkish government later that day gave permission for the USA to position '96 war planes', in addition to those already there in a NATO role.

As the F-117A (Stealth) aircraft turned away from Baghdad, the first of a barrage of over 100 Tomahawk cruise missiles, launched from US warships, sped towards their targets, which in Baghdad included the Ministry of Defence Building, the Baath Party HQ, and one of Saddam Hussein's palaces. Low-flying (50-300 feet) Tomahawk (MGM-109), multi-role cruise missiles, with 1,000-lb warheads, were launched against a wide spread of targets, not only to destroy them if possible, but also to induce emission from Iraqi defence and guidance radars to enable the Allies to locate them. Tomahawks have a 'terrain contour-matching guidance system', which was pre-set. Western journalists on the roofs of hotels in Baghdad were able to watch Tomahawk cruise missiles approaching, following the wide street avenues, before turning off suddenly to engage their targets.

A wide variety of Allied aircraft were brought into action against various targets. For example, the EF-111A, EA-6B and EC-130H aircraft, packed with surveillance radars, jammed communications between Iraqi ground controllers and their fighter aircraft, guidance systems of SAMs (Surface-to-Air Missiles) and radars carried by Iraqi interceptor aircraft. F-111E/F, F-15E, A-6, and F-4G aircraft concentrated upon attacking ground air defences; Tornados attacked airfield runways; and the F-15C/D and Tornado F-3 aircraft (designed with the Soviet bomber threat in mind) flew protective sweeps and patrols around attacking bomber aircraft.

The USN EA-6 (Prowlers) (NATO designations) and USAF EF-111A (Ravens) had flown off half-an-hour ahead of the main waves of Allied aircraft, using their tactical jamming systems to neutralise Iraqi Early Warning and ground interceptor radars. Iraqi radar operators knew that Allied aircraft were overhead, but were unable to ascertain their altitude or direction. E-3A AWACS aircraft, with a 200-mile radar vision, flying in Saudi air space, were able to look deep into Iraq, and inform Allied aircraft flying over that country, or Kuwait, of any hostile fighter planes in their vicinity.

Also, heavy B-52 bombers were involved, some flying the five-hour journey from their base in Diego Garcia, in the Indian Ocean, and others making even longer journeys, navigating with the aid of GPS (Global Positioning Systems). Weather conditions on the night of the 16th/17th were clear, but dark, with a new moon, which was ideal for the FLIR (Forward Looking Infra-Red) night vision system in use on Allied bombers.

There was euphoria in General Schwartzkopf's Command Centre (CENTCOM FORWARD) in the depths of the Saudi Ministry of Defence building in Riyadh, over the results of the first day of the air campaign. It was announced that 'during the first 14 hours, over 1,300 sorties had been flown', and claimed that about 80% of the mission objectives had been achieved, in that air crews had identified their targets, and released their munitions. The 20% failure was put down to 'service difficulties en route', meaning either bad weather, ground mist or inability to positively identify targets, when aircrews had been ordered not to release their bombs to minimise civilian casualties.

US Decision to Fight

The ultimate decision to launch *Operation Desert Storm* was taken by President Bush about 1100-hours, on the 15th January, the day of the deadline *(Washington Post)*, at a meeting of his National Security advisers. All present were in agreement, and Bush signed the Presidential Directive authorising the attack on the Iraqis, provided 'there was no last minute evidence of a diplomatic break-through'.

Air Tasking Officer

In keeping with the principle of centralised command, of integrating US Services, and remembering the chaotic situation in Vietnam when each Service air element had acted independently, General Charles Horner, Commander of the Air Component Command of CENTCOM, was appointed Air Tasking Officer (ATO), which meant he had control of all Allied aircraft in the Gulf area. The French hesitated for a while, but eventually agreed to co-operate.

Horner was responsible for tasking and controlling all Allied air sorties and missions, designating air corridors, IFF (Identification – Friend or Foe) codes, and other details essential to co-relate and co-ordinate almost 2,000 Allied aircraft of several nationalities. General Horner's multi-page Daily Task Plan of detailed orders and current information were master-pieces of organisation and deployment that should long be studied at Defence Colleges and similar institutions. Any hold-ups in this relentless and continuous air campaign were due to bad weather which unusually plagued this part of the Middle East at this time of year, rather than Iraqi opposition, which soon sank to negligible.

Brigadier General C. Glosson, commanding the US 14th Air Division, became the principal target planner for CENTCOM. Horner and Glosson worked well together, both were extremely efficient, and professionally both deserved more praise than has been accorded to them, being overshadowed by the extrovert personality of the Commander of CENTCOM.

Intelligence Gathering

The previous five months of *Operation Desert Shield* had been spent in obtaining intelligence data about Iraq, upon which to form the Air Plan. Comprehensive information was obtained about vital targets until about 400 *(Washington Post)* were selected for special attention, the intelligence acquired being stored in the US Air Force computer, which became known as its 'Bombing Encyclopaedia'. Both electronic and human (HUMINT) methods were used.

High-flying US TR-1 aircraft (a successor to the U-2) produced photographs of everything for 35 miles on either side of its flight path, by means of its ASARS (Advanced Synthetic Aperture Radar System). In the latter weeks of 1990, Allied aircraft persistently probed Iraqi air defences in Kuwait, using F-15s, F/A-18s (Hornets), and Tornados, to fly at speed towards them, and then to swerve away at the last moment, while overhead RC-135 reconnaissance aircraft monitored radar responses. This happened so frequently, that in frustration the Iraqis took to switching off their Early Warning radars for long periods at a time. Indeed, it seems that many of them were switched off when the Allied air offensive began.

The USA had four KH-11 satellites covering the Middle East region (amongst many others of different types) that produced visual and thermal Infra-Red digital imagery, but tended to be impeded by cloud; and also a Lacrosse radar satellite that could track surface movement, but could not produce minute detail. High-flying aircraft such as the TR-1, were similarly handicapped, which placed a heavy burden on the ageing RF-4Cs, and the recently operational Tornado GR-1A. RF-4Cs could not relay imagery in 'real time', that is directly without going through a central control HQ, but the two E-8 J-STARS aircraft did provide valuable radar-based imagery of the Iraqi ground forces, despite not being fully operational.

The J-STARS is a side-looking phased radar mounted on a Boeing 707 aircraft, claimed to be a 'day and night, all weather system' designed to 'acquire and transmit real time data' on moving and stationary ground targets.

US satellite surveillance capability was enhanced, on the 12th November, when a Titan-4 rocket lifted into geo-stationary position (some 22,000 miles above the earth) an improved Lacrosse-type satellite, which improved Infra-Red monitoring of the Gulf region, and could operate 24-hours a day. It was reputed to be able to identify vehicles and weapons on the ground, but the claim that it could 'read vehicle number plates' seemed to be over-optimistic. Additionally, the Allies (meaning the Americans and the Saudis) had a total of 13 AWACS aircraft, and over 60 other aircraft carrying electronic surveillance equipment.

Human intelligence meant obtaining information from individuals who had recently been working, or visiting, Iraq or Kuwait, refugees, POWs, businessmen and academics who had studied these two countries.

Satellite information aids must be briefly mentioned as Allied aircraft relied upon them considerably. One was the GPS (Global Positioning System), which provided for '20-hours a day' two-dimensional navigation information. Another was the MSP (Meteorological Satellite Programme) constellations which gave details and forecast the weather over Kuwait and Iraq, which was far more turbulent and changeable than had been expected.

Iraqis had no access to satellite intelligence, but did possess electronic and listening devices, which were not quite in the same class of technology as those possessed by the Allies, nor were they so numerous. They had hundreds, perhaps thousands, of small GCI (Ground Control Interceptor) radars, some of which 'have already jammed AWACS aircraft' (*Washington Times*). The Iraqis had produced their own version of the US AWACS, known as the 'Adnan', based on the Soviet Ilyushin-76 aircraft, with a mixture of Soviet and West European electronic equipment. Three Adnans had been produced.

Allied Air Plan

From intelligence obtained, and taking into account resources available, the Allied Air Plan was produced by Generals Horner and Glosson, which laid down priorities. These were:–

— destruction of Iraq's Command and Control systems;

— nuclear, chemical and biological establishments;

— military installations; and

— military-industrial infrastructure.

Over-lapping aims were:–

— progressive destruction of Iraqi air defences;

— interdiction of supply routes; and

— destruction of bridges.

In addition, it was anticipated that massive air-to-ground support would be required for the land battle in the final phase of *Operation Desert Storm*.

The whole Allied Air Plan was based on the NATO Air-Land Battle 2000 strategy the US had been forging, with its NATO Allies, in the Cold War in Europe to counter Soviet superiority in troops and equipment, relying on very 'high-tech' weaponry to neutralise enemy air capability, in conjunction with rapidly advancing ground troops, some in helicopters, under cover of NATO air support and heavy artillery and missile barrages. This was modified for the Gulf campaign to the extent that *Operation Desert Storm* was to be in two phases, the first being the air campaign, and the second being the ground assault to force the Iraqis out of Kuwait (if they had not already withdrawn or surrendered), which would not commence until the Allies had achieved 'air supremacy', as President Bush was desperately anxious to avoid incurring American casualties.

The original Pentagon-estimated time-frame for *Operation Desert Storm* had been that it would only take three days to destroy the Iraqi Air Force (IAF), render all runways inoperative, and to incapacitate all defensive radars. It was thought at first that if all 'went according to plan', the whole operation could be over in about ten days for the cost of as 'few as 100 Allied casualties'. The Pentagon expected, however, the Iraqis to incur 'thousands of casualties' *(USA Today)*. Many analysts thought this to be much too optimistic, and were soon proved correct, as military spokesmen began speaking of 'days rather than weeks' and then of 'weeks rather than months'.

Accordingly, the Allied Air Plan had to be an over-lapping and multi-stage one. As the air campaign unfolded and more vital targets were located and identified, intelligence gained about them was fed into the Bombing Encyclopedia.

The Iraqi Air Force

The fact that air forces had played a comparatively minor role in the Iran-Iraq War probably caused the Pentagon assessment of the IAF to be a low one, it being thought to have poor leadership, indifferent pilot skills and an unreliable maintenance record. After the invasion of Kuwait by Iraqi troops the Pentagon had to dig deeper to re-assess the IAF, and as the Bombing Encyclopedia was steadily compiled, its assessment began to rise. US planners began to talk of the IAF being the 'sixth largest' air force in the world.

Pentagon estimates tended to vary, but seemed to settle down as accrediting the IAF with having about 700 combat aircraft, of which up to 500 were modern sophisticated ones. The majority were of Soviet origin, but some were of French and Chinese manufacture, and included:–

— 50 MiG-29s,

— 25 MiG-25s,

— 70 MiG-23s,

— 60 SU-25s, and

— 24 SU-24s; and about

— 100 French Mirage F-1s of different versions.

The remainder were of an older generation, and included Soviet MiG-21s and Chinese J-6s.

Serious opposition was anticipated by Allied pilots from the French Mirages, and the Soviet MiG-29s. The capabilities of the Mirages had been demonstrated at successive Paris Air Shows, but the MiG-29 fighter/ ground attack version, was seen for the first time by the West at the Farnborough Air Show in 1988. The MiG-25 had a formidable reputation and was regarded by some analysts as being more than a match for the US F-15 and F-16. The SU-24 ground attack plane was also regarded with some apprehension as it had the range to strike into both Israel and Saudi Arabia. However, it was suspected the MiG-29s did not yet have all their avionics, and the SU-24s had yet to be fully integrated into the IAF.

Aircraft-carried missiles were mainly of Soviet and French origin. Soviet ones included the AS-10 and AS-14, both 'stand-off' munitions; and the AA-6 and AA-7 air-to-air missiles; while French ones included the Exocet, R-530 and R-550 Magic, which were heat-seeking and laser-guided.

Iraqi Air Defence

Iraq had an extensive spread of airfields, which included over 20 main air bases, each with several long concrete runways, and HAS (Hardened Air Shelters) for individual aircraft; and over 50 more airfields able to cope with combat aircraft landing, taking-off and refuelling. It was estimated that Iraq had about 600 HAS, and it was known that some 300 of them had been constructed by Western firms (IISS Survival). The HAS were strongly built of steel and concrete, and were reputed to be resistant to normal HE bombs.

Iraqi ground defence consisted of missiles, guns and GCIs, and included high-altitude Soviet SAM-2s and SAM-3s, medium and low-level SAM-6s, SAM-8s and SAM-9s, and also the French Roland system. Iraq had over 4,000 anti-aircraft guns, mainly of Soviet origin, that included ZSU-23 x 4s, ZSU-57 x 2s, and others varying in calibre from 85mm to 130mm. The GCIs were linked to a Control HQ in Baghdad by duplicated voice and digital communications.

A review of the IAF potential and the Iraqi ground defence lay-out, led Allied airmen to anticipate an initial grand air battle. From November onwards the USAF had been selectively probing, spoofing and jamming Iraqi radars and communications to try to establish their pattern of resistance, in preparation for the air campaign.

First Air Losses

On the 18th January, the second day of the air war, it was announced that the Allies had brought down eight Iraqi planes, for the loss of only seven of their own. Allied losses were quoted as being — one USAF F-15E; one USN A-6 and one F/A-18; two British Tornados; one Italian Tornado; and one Kuwaiti A-4 (Skyhawk). It seemed that the grand air battle was just warming up.

IAF Reaction

Since the early part, of *Operation Desert Shield* Iraqi combat aircraft had generally remained in their dispersed and camouflaged HAS, avoiding runways and aprons unless actually using them for taking-off or landing. Out-numbered and out-weaponed, Saddam Hussein decided his air force should remain grounded in their HAS, to avoid clashing with Allied planes. It seems this instruction was not rigidly complied with by certain Iraqi pilots, who flew *(ADJ)* about 70-80 sorties on the first day, and a rapidly declining number on eight succeeding days, after which offensive action ceased entirely. The Iraqis later admitted that ten of their major airfields had been put out of action, mainly by low-flying Tornados. E-3A aircraft patrolling along the Saudi-Iraqi border 'saw many IAF interceptors, but their pilots were in effect blind and deaf because of the absolute Allied mastery of electronic combat' *(Survival)*.

The first Allied misconception was that there would be an initial gigantic trial of aerial strength between opposing air forces. This did not happen, but was daily expected, the Allies assuming Saddam Hussein was simply waiting for an opportune moment. At a CENTCOM briefing on the 24th, it was claimed that Iraq had lost '38 aircraft', most during the early hours of the air offensive, after which there was less co-ordinated Iraqi air movement as Iraqi HQs lost contact with their airfields due to Allied interdiction of communications.

On the 20th January, seven Allied captured pilots and aircrew had appeared on Baghdad TV, being four Americans, two British (Peters and Nichols) and one Italian. They gave their names, messages to their families and made a brief statement on the war. Some of them (especially

Peters) showed signs of what might have been rough handling by his captors, but this was explained for the moment that this could have been caused when ejecting from cockpits. Two days later, two more Allied POWs were shown on Baghdad TV. It was not until early August (1991) that it was openly admitted by the American and British governments that their POWs had been subjected to torture and psychological abuse while in Iraqi captivity.

RAF Tornados

The initial British air contribution to *Operation Desert Storm* included '42 Tornado GR-1s and six Tornado GR-1As' *(ADJ)*, some of whose pilots had been trained to fly very low, at heights of 200 feet or less, to attack enemy runways with free-fall JP-233 'cratering' and BL-755 'cluster' bombs. These low-flying tactics had been developed in the European Theatre, which was subject to low cloud and ground mist conditions, where in a war-time scenario NATO aircraft attacking airfields would have faced a proliferation of over-lapping ground-based guns and missiles, and enemy interceptor aircraft, which would make medium altitude flying very hazardous.

Although very successful in their 400 low-level missions to disrupt Iraqi runways, the British lost four Tornados. It was pointed out by CENTCOM that these losses only represented a '1% loss', when a 5% one could have been expected in a similar European situation. A later RAF study produced information that losses did not occur when Tornados flew without protective escort or surveillance planes, which prematurely alerted Iraqi defences, as they flew so fast and low they took the defenders completely by surprise. The British senior RAF officer at CENTCOM, had a power of veto over certain targets, and exercised it twice when 'severe collateral damage would have resulted from any weapon system mal-function' *(Operation Granby Report)*, in other words when the missions might have caused excessive civilian casualties.

It was said the RAF had not brought their Jaguar aircraft, which had laser-guidance systems, with them to fly at medium height, as this would have meant 'duplication', as the USAF already had that capability. The USAF did not carry out any low-level bombing of Iraqi airfields, and one wonders why the task was given to RAF Tornados. Later, the British Defence Minister (Tom King) stated that "These low-flying missions had been explicitly requested" *(AP)*. The USAF already had the French 'Durandal' bomb for cratering runways, but which had to be dropped from about 500-feet to obtain optimum results.

After these initial British losses RAF Tornados were re-tasked to medium altitude missions, and eventually ageing British Buccaneer attack-aircraft were sent out to the Gulf as laser-designators. The RAF obtained Rockeye cluster bombs from the USAF to replace their BL-755 free-fall ones. Some electronic equipment had to be rushed out to the Gulf, including the TIALD (Thermal Imagery And Laser Designation) system, and the LANTIRN (Low Altitude Navigation and Targeting Infra-Red at Night) system. British Tornados carried out in all 4,000 combat sorties, in the course of which two more Tornados were lost, bringing the total up to six (Operation Granby Report).

Force Packages

The F-117A (Stealth) aircraft, using heat-seeking Infra-Red sensors capable of seeking out targets not normally detectable by other aircraft, which it could bomb with precision, was used for high-level missions. At one CENTCOM briefing, spokesmen claimed that in the first three days of the air war F-117A (Stealth) planes destroyed "two out of every five" of their targets, which brought a comment from a journalist present that this must mean that "on three out of every five occasions these aircraft missed their targets".

The Allies had a good 'mix' of aircraft and weapons available, and General Horner weaved them into effective teams, which became known as 'Force Packages'. These contained several types of aircraft, all given the same set of targets, and included 'jammers', defence suppression planes, air-to-air fighters, and bomber aircraft, which set off from different bases, at different times, and flew at different heights and speeds to successively strike at their targets. Bombing missions were usually carried out by US F-15Es and F-16s, delivering 'smart' bombs from altitudes about 2,000-feet, priority being given to Command and Control facilities, aircraft in the open and fuel dumps.

Up to half the Force Package sorties were support missions, and EC-130s and EF-111As were used in electronic suppression tasks. After land-based aircraft in the Force Package had completed their missions and were returning to base, carrier-based aircraft would follow through to take advantage of the support element. These Force Packages became masterpieces of air integration and timing. General Horner said that he had planned the air campaign from the "bottom up", with squadron commanders' 'input'. One Marine pilot said "We didn't fly a single mission over Iraq or Kuwait during the first week of the air war that had not been previously rehearsed by flying a comparable mission profile".

Nuclear Targets

Nuclear establishments had a high priority, and it was announced that four Iraqi nuclear reactors had been hit by Allied bombers, two being identified at the Tuwaitha nuclear complex, near Baghdad. CENTCOM stated that "The Soviet-built one was heavily damaged, and the French one less damaged". At his daily conference (on the 21st) General Schwartzkopf said "I have very high confidence that those two nuclear reactors have been thoroughly damaged and will not be effective for quite some number of years".

After the war, Saddam Hussein admitted to the UN that '18 out of 24 nuclear sites were destroyed'. The Iraqi nuclear weapon programme was obviously far more advanced than the Allies realised at the time. Later, General Horner, in an article (*Air Force Magazine*), excused himself, saying that "These were the only four we knew about then", which gives a poor impression of the quality of Allied intelligence gathering. Schwartzkopf also later (when the war was over) complained that he had been getting little confirmatory feed-back intelligence on damage caused by Allied bombing.

However, for the moment Schwartzkopf was well pleased with himself, and again showed video footage of the successful F-117A (Stealth) precision attack on the Baghdad main Communications Centre building. B-52 heavy bombers, flying at high altitudes, continued free-fall bombing, without improving their poor record of accuracy.

General Powell Explains

A progress report on the war was given by General Powell at the Pentagon, on the 23rd January, in which he claimed the Allies had 'achieved general air superiority'; that the Iraqi nuclear reactors were 'finished'; that Iraqi aircraft could only operate from 'five out of 66 airfields'; and that Iraqi radar defences had been reduced by 95%. He confirmed that after 10,000 Allied sorties that '41 Iraqi aircraft' had been destroyed (a figure that had to be later re-adjusted), and admitted that Iraqi Generals still retained command and control of their divisions. He stated the air campaign would continue for a considerable period before the ground assault could begin.

As regards future strategy, General Powell said "First we are going to cut it off (referring to the entrenched Iraqi defences in southern Kuwait that had developed), then we are going to kill it. As we get into the process of cutting it off we will also step up the process of killing it by going after his stockpiles, ammunition, food, stripping away their gun air defence, using air tactics. And if it becomes necessary, we are assembling a fairly sizable ground force that can finish off the job, should that be necessary". In answer to a question on suspected inflated Allied claims, he replied "Trust me".

A Saudi Double Kill

On the 24th January, Allied warships in the Gulf detected three Iraqi Mirage aircraft moving southwards, presumably to attack either them or other shipping in the area. This information was passed to a Saudi patrol of two F-15s, which engaged the IAF aircraft, one Saudi pilot (Captain Ayhed Sallah al-Shamrani) shooting down two Mirages. This was the first, and only, 'double kill' in the air war. The pilot said "I just rolled in behind them and shot them down. It was very easy. It was my day". These IAF sorties were amongst the last aggressive ones launched against the Allies.

SCUDs

Meanwhile, Saddam Hussein had put into effect one of his major threats, that of bombarding Israeli and Saudi territory with SCUD short-range, ballistic missiles, which disrupted the Allied air campaign for three weeks at least, as about one-third of its resources were diverted to seek out their launching sites to destroy them. It also caused a profound strategical sea-change to the doctrine of 'secure land boundaries' in the Middle East.

The first SCUD attack was launched on the evening of the 18th January, when eight missiles were fired from mobile launchers in Western Iraq, aimed at Tel Aviv and Haifa, of which five were destroyed in flight, and three missed their targets. A ninth SCUD was fired at Dhahran, which was destroyed in mid-air.

The following night (19th-20th January) four more SCUDs were launched at Israel, of which two were destroyed, the other two missing their target, which had been Tel Aviv. The next evening (20th-21st), ten SCUDs were launched against Saudi Arabia, targets being Riyadh, Dhahran and Hafar al-Batin, of which nine were destroyed by the Allies; while the tenth fell into the Gulf waters. SCUDs were launched under cover of darkness, when Iraqis brought the missiles and mobile launchers out from hiding, set them up, fired them and hurriedly returned the mobile launchers to secure shelter. It took just over an hour to make a SCUD missile ready for firing, but its state of readiness was of limited duration owing to fuel deterioration.

Allied E-3A AWACS aircraft were used extensively to 'Hunt the SCUD', their multi-layered radar being expected to be able to detect missile-launchers, and to direct fighter-bombers to destroy them. Also used were

E-8 JSTARS AWACS, whose highly-advanced 'ground-sweeping' radar could detect SCUD firing emissions, and guide bomber planes against them in 'real time'.

The Allies had a problem — they did not know how many SCUDs the Iraqis possessed. US Intelligence Agencies estimated that between 1,600 and 2,000 had been obtained from the USSR in the 1980s, and also a few from North Korea, but it was not known how many had been fired in the Iran-Iraq War. Guesstimates were that the Iraqis had about 400 SCUDs, and it was known they were producing their own mobile-launchers, in that they were carried on elongated trailers, and firing them either from these trailers, or from fixed concrete bases (JDW). Elimination of these SCUDs and their launchers became high priority tasks.

First deployed in 1965, the Soviet SCUD-B (SS-1c) was later phased out and replaced in the Soviet inventory by the SS-23. A short-range ballistic missile, the SCUD had a range of about 180 miles (300-kms), and could carry a HE (or chemical or nuclear) warhead of up to 2,000-lbs. By reducing the weight of the warhead and adding boosters to the rocket, Iraqis achieved greater ranges, producing two 'stretched' models. One was the 'al-Hussein', with a reputed range of 350 miles, and the other the 'al-Abbas', with a reputed range of 500 miles. These weapons brought the cities of Tel Aviv and Riyadh within Iraqi reach. It was thought that it took three SCUDs to produce two 'extended' ones.

The HE warheads were so reduced in weight, and consequently lethality, that they caused relatively little damage, as compared with the effect of a 2,000-lb HE bomb, but their psychological impact on the people in Israel, and to a lesser extent in Saudi Arabia, was dramatic. One US munitions technician described them derisively as 'little more than a gas-tank with a grenade at the end', an under-statement, but one which gave a fair idea of their relativity in the scale of munition capability. At a media briefing (23rd) General Schwartzkopf asserted the SCUD was "a terrorist weapon, and had no military and little political significance", but this was before the al-Khobar incident.

Lightly constructed houses and buildings in Israel, for example, suffered devastation from SCUD strikes, which caused many injuries, but in ratio there were comparatively few deaths. The worst SCUD raid on Israel occurred on the night of the 22nd, when two fell near Tel Aviv, injuring 96 people, while three elderly people died of suffocation as they had failed to remove filter caps from their gas masks.

Lacking accuracy, SCUDs were an area weapon, rather than a precision one. The most lethal SCUD attack occurred on the 25th January, when one struck the al-Khobar 'barracks' (an unoccupied group of apartments that had been allocated to US armed forces) near Dhahran, killing 29 troops and injuring about 90. Later, this disaster was put down to a faulty radar in the US Patriot anti-missile missile that should have brought the SCUD down before it reached its target area. Iraqi 'stretched' SCUDs began to fall apart during the downward trajectory of their flight, which caused 'multiple target tracks' on radar screens.

The US Patriot

The Allied (American) response to SCUD attacks, which had been anticipated, was the US Patriot (MIM-104) anti-missile missile, originally designed to intercept low-flying aircraft, which had an uncertain development period with 'suspect' computer systems, before being taken on to the US inventory in 1984. Its present role was not determined until after successful competitive tests in 1986.

The Patriot missile can fly for a maximum of ten seconds, over a 105-mile span, before it 'senses' the target, when the proximity fuse explodes its warhead as it rapidly nears an incoming SCUD in mid-air. If the Patriot flight was less than ten seconds it would simply crash into the SCUD to destroy it by impact, or by explosion. As the weight of a Patriot and a SCUD combined exceed 4,500-lbs, if the explosion occurred over an inhabited area there was danger below from lumps of descending red-hot metal. Patriot antenna picks out the reflected radar beam given out by a SCUD on launch, relays it back to the ground computer, commands then being relayed back to the Patriot's guidance system.

Each Patriot unit consists of four pre-packed missiles, a radar unit, a computer control centre, and an independent mobile power generator. Six Patriot units form a battery, and eight batteries form a Patriot battalion, enabling the computer to select from 192 missiles available, the one most suitably placed to destroy the incoming SCUD. It is claimed a Patriot battalion can track 125 targets simultaneously, and guide nine missiles to their targets. On the 22nd, a Patriot missile was launched by mistake at the Incirlik air base, which caused alarm in nearby Adana.

Two Missile Warning spacecraft of the USAF Space Command Defense Support Program (DSP) had been moved into geo-synchronous orbit (over the Equator) in early August (1990). Each DSP was equipped with Infra-Red telescopes that swept the SCUD launching areas in Western Iraq every 12 seconds, to detect SCUD ignitions, or the SCUD's 'plumes' during trajectory. The DSP had picked up at least two SCUD test-firings in Iraq in October. Comparison with known SCUD data determined the approximate target area and launch points within two minutes, but a further five minutes were required to pass the information from the US-based DSP to the Gulf area. The average flight-time of SCUDs was between 7 and 10 minutes. This meant there was less than three minutes available in the Gulf for Early Warning purposes. A data-link between the DSP satellites and Patriot batteries was established, which increased SCUD 'warning time'.

Israeli Reaction

Saddam Hussein's prime objective in launching SCUDs into Israel was to rouse that country into retaliatory action, and by entering the war on the Allied side, destabilise the coalition. His hope was that Arab Allies would object to becoming comrades-in-arms with Israelis in a fight against an Arab State, and perhaps withdraw from the Alliance, leaving it to be seen as a struggle with Israel and the USA both pitched against Iraq. Israel had been dreading SCUD attacks, especially if they had chemical warheads, and alerted by Saddam Hussein's previous threats, had conducted (9th August) a well-publicised maiden flight of the Arrow, a joint venture with the USA to produce a next generation anti-missile missile.

As the first SCUDs fell on Israeli territory, a demand went up in Israel for IDF bomber-aircraft to strike back at Iraq. The mood of the Israeli government was in favour of taking the military option against Saddam Hussein. Fully realising the difficulties that would arise should Israel become involved in the Gulf fighting, and the effect such action would have on the shaky multi-national coalition, the Americans sought strongly to dissuade the Israeli government from any such course.

The Israelis demanded to be allocated an 'air route' to Iraq, and the necessary IFF and other codes, but this was refused. Israelis then threatened to attack Jordanian US HAWK anti-aircraft missile sites, should SCUDs over-fly Jordan. One can only speculate whether it would have been possible for the Israeli air force to 'go unilateral'. This is doubtful, as General Horner kept his air space under tight control, and any aircraft failing to respond with the correct IFF procedure would have been shot down. According to one source (New York Times) the Israelis planned a lightning invasion of Western Iraq, using strike aircraft, helicopters and commando teams, to wipe out SCUD launcher sites. The Israeli idea was to establish a defended base in Iraqi territory for this purpose.

During the early SCUD raids, Israelis had been advised to wear their gas-masks, as the authorities feared that chemical warheads might be used, and to sit in 'sealed rooms' they had been advised to prepare on top floors of their homes. Palestinians in the Occupied Territories complained that gas-masks had only been issued to Israelis, and none to them, and that there were no air raid warning sirens in the Occupied Territories, except in Jewish Settlements. On the 14th January, a Palestinian took legal action, and an Israeli High Court Judge found this to be 'blatant discrimination', ordering the distribution of gas-masks to Palestinians, but by the end of that month, only about 30,000 had been issued.

Using political bribery and promises of loans and arms, the Americans were able to persuade the Israeli government not to take the military option, and to leave it all to the Americans. The US Deputy Secretary of State (Lawrence Eagleburger) is credited with persuading the Israelis to stay out of the conflict. A Patriot anti-missile missile battery had been in Israel for 12 months for evaluation (*Survival*), but was not operational. Patriots were rushed to Israel, and Israelis who had been training on Patriots in the USA, hurried home. US military specialists were sent to Israel to train Patriot crews, and according to some sources, also operated Patriots against incoming SCUDs.

The Flight of IAF Aircraft

As IAF combat aircraft remained snugly in their HAS, showing little intention of coming out to fight in the air, on the 25th January, the Allies began a 'shelter-busting' onslaught against these sturdy constructions. Contractors' blue-prints were examined to find weak spots on which to focus laser-guided precision weapons. Taking advantage of diversions of Allied air resources to counter the SCUD threat, and the switch of some Allied sorties to bombing Iraqi Republican Guard formations, and logistic routes in southern Iraq, certain Iraqi aircraft began to decamp to Iran. A few planes had already fled to that country, the first detected escaping on the 20th. This exodus increased in volume, until by the end of the month, it was reported (*Daily Telegraph*) that 'of the 96 Iraqi planes to reach Iran 36 were combat ones'.

At first Iranians appeared to be surprised to receive these Iraqi aircraft, some of which it was said were flown by inexperienced pilots, as a few crash-landed. It was later said that about '115 Iraqi combat planes' were flown to Iran (*IISS*), and included:–

— 4 MiG-29s;

— 12 MiG-23s;

— 7 SU-25s;

— 24 SU-24s;

— 40 SU-22s;

— 4 SU-20s;

— 1 Adnan AWACS; and

— 24 French Mirages.

On the 29th January, CENTCOM issued revised figures of air casualties, claiming that in all '26 Iraqi aircraft have been brought down and 23 more destroyed on the ground'. This still left quite a number of Iraqi combat aircraft secure in their HAS. The following day, General Schwartzkopf stated that "complete air superiority has been gained", but that the air campaign would continue against Iraqi ground forces.

The precise reason for the unexpected flight of Iraqi combat aircraft and the Adnan AWACS, was something of a mystery. CENTCOM claimed it was because all communications between Iraqi HQs and airfields had been disrupted by Allied air action, and that the IAF 'was falling to pieces in panic'. There had been a precedent in 1980, as when Saddam Hussein went to war with Iran, he initially dispersed numbers of his aircraft to havens in friendly Arab countries to prevent them from being destroyed by enemy action. The dispersed aircraft returned to Iraq when it was safe to do so.

Allied 'shelter-busting' continued against Iraqi HAS, and although Iraqi air defences had been almost completely smothered, with seemingly little success. One US pilot is quoted as saying (ADJ) "It's like being in the Super Bowl, but the other team didn't show up".

Censorship

By this time there was some discontent amongst the several hundred media persons of many different nationalities assembled in Saudi Arabia to cover the war, over restrictions on reporting, and in particular being unable to obtain certain information, particularly about Iraqi casualties caused by the air campaign. The media generally blamed the US military authorities, believing they still thought the media had lost them the support of the American people in the Vietnam War, and were determined that this should not happen again. The US military had studied how the British had handled the media in their Falklands Campaign (1982), with some admiration. Certainly, officialdom blanketed journalists' desire to roam at will and seek exclusive stories.

On the 14th January 1991, the US DoD had issued media 'guidelines', which had been agreed at various Washington political levels. About 60 or so journalists from the assembled hundreds accredited to cover the war, were selected to form a 'News Pool', which would be given facilities to see what was happening, but their reports would be 'pooled', and the material made available to all others. Sharing news is an anathema to all newsmen, and particularly to American ones weaned on 'exclusives'. News Pool Journalists were formed into small 'Media Response Teams', and deployed to military formations in the combat zones. Local commanders would strongly discourage journalists travelling independently, who became known in the jargon as 'unilaterals'.

Material for publication, or transmission, would be 'reviewed before release' in the field by local commanders and military Information Officers, to determine whether it contained any sensitive matter. If agreement could not be reached on disputed text it would be sent to the 'joint Information Bureau' in Dhahran. If still unresolved at that point, it would go to the Assistant Secretary of Defense responsible for Public Affairs. Officialdom's best weapon was delay. American officials stressed this was not censorship, as they insisted the ultimate decision to publish, or screen, should remain with the journalists' news organisation, although media personnel on the ground could not be convinced on that point.

US military authorities apparently had wanted to prohibit journalists approaching local commanders and officials unannounced, and to ban the dissemination of pictures of troops (and the enemy) in agony or shock, which they more or less managed to do, as they wanted the folks back home in the USA to see the war as a clean, clinical one, without pain or anguish. Most US news agencies accepted the 'guidelines', but journalists themselves were unhappy, and in particular expressed concern at being prevented from showing the real horrors of war, and restrictions relating to the transmission of visual material.

When journalists over-stepped the mark, or refused to accept censorship, they were passed over to the Saudi authorities, all having first had to obtain a Saudi visa to be in the country anyway, to be 'dealt with', meaning deported. Neither the USA, nor Saudi Arabia, wanted the responsibility for deporting journalists, some with powerful news agencies behind them, and it is thought that only one was actually expelled.

These guidelines were American ones, and each of the other combatant countries had their own media rules, which were broadly on the same lines. Most Arab States were already under forms of censorship. BBC authorities stressed the need to observe advice from military authorities 'unless there were strong reasons' for not doing so, and also cautioned on the need to be 'circumspect' in showing pictures of death or injury of soldiers or civilians. The war was to be like a video game. The US military wanted to give the impression that 'high-tech' precision weapons were simply demolishing buildings and military targets, with hardly any mention of what was, or might be, happening to Iraqi civilians, unfortunate enough to be in, or near them.

Iraqi Censorship

Strict internal censorship was in force in Iraq, where Saddam Hussein had given orders that while pictures of damaged buildings could be shown (he wanted to enlist Islamic and Arab sympathy) there was to be no mention, or pictures of, Iraqi civilian casualties, as he did not want to undermine the morale of his people.

On the 18th January, most western journalists were expelled from Iraq, leaving through Jordan. Until that moment most had been reporting, almost without censorship, within the scope of limited movement, covering for example, the initial bombardment of Baghdad 'live' as it happened. The only western TV team remaining in Baghdad was that of the American-based CNN, which was allowed to remain and continue reporting, and although under the watchful eye of a 'minder' transmitted 'live' coverage with few inconveniences. All non-official communications out from Iraq had been severed.

Previously, the CNN team had persuaded Saddam Hussein to allow it to use the then fairly uncommon portable 'satellite transmitting dish', that could be set up in a few minutes almost anywhere. It was an apparatus that looked like, and folded and unfolded like, an umbrella, and was the state-of-the-art satellite communication technology. All that was required was a video camera, a TV monitor and the transmission equipment. Pictures were relayed by a telephone link, the so-called 'four wire' apparatus in the jargon. CNN was able to use an official Iraqi 'four-wire' communication line to Amman (Jordan), from where its pictures were beamed out 'as they happened' via satellite to Atlanta (USA), the CNN home base, and so into living rooms worldwide. It was said that the CNN concession was obtained from Saddam Hussein on the 'flyaway' condition, that it left its portable satellite apparatus behind when it departed. It was very 'high-tech' equipment the Iraqis did not then possess.

6

The Obstacle Belt

As the Human Shield scenario stumbled through its various stages, and against a background of intense diplomatic activity, American, British, French and other ground forces arrived in northern Saudi Arabia, and began to expand in strength as quickly as they were able. Swift and monumental though this was, President Bush still wanted to gild the lily. In military theory 'rapid deployment' means to move with alacrity, but in practice this is seldom possible, especially when large numbers of troops have to rely upon whatever air-lift or sea-lift facilities are available; how close any pre-positioned troops and equipment may be to the theatre of operations; and how quickly they can be mustered and dispatched with a full complement of weaponry, equipment and logistic back-up.

Allied resources in this respect were not unlimited, and so the media was fed with misleading reports of the rapid Allied build-up in the Gulf region, of thousands of troops and thousands of tons of stores pouring into northern Saudi Arabia. This deception policy was designed both to over-awe Saddam Hussein, and also to disguise the fact that this was not actually the case. It was reckoned the USAF could quickly deploy limited forces to the region from either Continental America or Europe, which could become active 'within days', as invariably aircraft and personnel landed on established, well equipped, friendly airbases, where there was accommodation, fuel and maintenance facilities.

It was also reckoned that US warships, with their support vessels, having integral mobility, could deploy to active service stations in the Gulf region 'within weeks'. To a certain extent US Marines, with equipment, could also arrive 'within weeks'. But it was soon realised that it took American ground formations, with all their weapons and equipment 'some months' to move from the USA to Saudi Arabia, and be ready for action. Their main problem was lifting tanks and heavy equipment, which generally had to be transported along slow sea routes.

The Pentagon's transportation problem was compounded by its experience in the Vietnam War, when American build-up and reinforcement had invariably been too little and too late, to be really effective at vital moments. Determined not to repeat this folly, right from the start the Pentagon decided upon a massive troop reinforcement programme, so that ample military strength would be in position on the ground, should the military option be chosen.

US Military Air-Lift Command had '85 C-5s, 195 C-141s and 410 C-130s' (*Survival*). The C-5 (Galaxy) was the only transport aircraft that could lift an Abrams main battle tank, and then only one at a time, making a four-day round trip from the USA. US transport aircraft were able to carry large numbers of military personnel, although not as many as the media would have the Iraqis, and indeed the American public, believe.

The first US army formations to reach Saudi Arabia were airborne or light infantry ones, with some assault helicopters. A few main battle tanks were air-lifted by C-5s for the 24th Mechanised Division when it arrived, but that was all. The large majority of the '928 tanks' (*AFJI*) actually in Saudi Arabia prior to the 8th November, had arrived by sea.

The 40 merchant ships chartered by the US Military Sea-Lift Command in early August, were insufficient to keep pace with the desired rate of troop reinforcement, and another 15 had to be chartered in November, when it was decided to send further reinforcements to Saudi Arabia, to carry the heavy weaponry and equipment from Europe. William Taft, US Ambassador to NATO, had to request his NATO European Allies to provide both air and sea-lift facilities from Germany to the Gulf. In fact, the full complement of tanks for some US armoured formations had not reached them by the 15th January (1991) (*AFJI*). US armoured divisions had a complement of 324 tanks, and mechanised ones 280 tanks.

The first US ground formations to arrive in Saudi Arabia were the:–

— 82nd Airborne Division;

— 101st Airborne (Air Assault) Division;

— 11th Air Defense Artillery Brigade; and

— 1st Marine Expeditionary Force (elements).

These were followed by the 24th Mechanised Division, less its tanks, which were mostly brought over by sea.

It was not until early October, by which time elements of the US 1st Cavalry Division and the US 2nd Armored Division had begun to arrive in Saudi Arabia, that General Schwartzkopf began to breathe a little more easily, as at least he became confident that his ground forces could hold any Iraqi armoured thrust southwards. Schwartzkopf later admitted (*CBS*) that this waiting period had been "my worst nightmare". A US staff officer reportedly summed up the situation in his vernacular, saying that if Iraqi armour had moved against them "They could have cleaned our clocks".

President Bush's speech of the 8th November, changed the situation for the ground forces. It was still thought by many that Saddam Hussein would crack at the last moment, and that *Operation Desert Shield* forces would have to stay in position until he did so. Bush's massive reinforcement plan, for another 200,000 US military personnel to be sent to the Gulf area, gave some indication of his early determination to use the military option if he had to.

On 14th November, Defense Secretary Cheney announced that 125,000 US reservists would be called up, and on the 1st December, he increased that number to 188,000. US formations in the second wave of reinforcements included armoured divisions. Once in northern Saudi Arabia they were formed into two army corps — the 18th (XVIII) Airborne Corps, consisting of four divisions; and the 7th (VII) Army Corps, consisting of three armoured divisions. Additionally, there were three US Marine 'divisions'.

It was calculated that when these formations were in position, with their inventories completed, they would have '1,200 M1A1 tanks and over 200 assault helicopters'. US Marines had brought in from their pre-position base at Diego Garcia '450 tanks, 300 assault amphibious vehicles, 90 light armoured vehicles, 120 howitzers (155mm) and 1,500 trucks' *(Survival)*.

American and other Allied contingents were deployed in northern Saudi Arabia westwards from the Gulf coast, a few miles south, both out of sight and out of artillery range, of Iraqi troops massed along the southern Kuwaiti border. It was a very wide spread indeed, as a massive logistic framework of motorable tracks, and a maze of fuel and water pipelines appeared. Tented camps, field hospitals, logistic bases, landing strips and other facilities sprang up in this vast, seeming endless wilderness. Thousands of troops adapted themselves, their vehicles and weapons, to arid desert conditions, carrying out training exercises, while hundreds of helicopters and thousands of vehicles scurried to and fro.

Testifying before the US Senate Armed Services Committee (3rd December), General Powell boasted of the gigantic US air-lift of personnel, weapons and stores, over a distance of 8,000 miles. He said "By the sixth week of *Operation Desert Shield* we had already moved by air the equivalent of the entire Berlin Airlift, an operation that took place over 65 weeks. As of today we have airlifted enough cargo to equal 2½ Berlin Airlifts". DoD figures for the 31st December 1990, showed there were 425,000 US armed forces personnel in the Gulf area, of whom approximately 15% were recalled reservists, this being '20.7%', of the total mustered active strength. US military retirements and discharges were pended.

General Powell also spoke of maritime interception of ships in the Gulf, saying "Over 100 warships of 14 different navies are involved. To date, more than 4,200 ships have been intercepted by USN and Allied ships".

The British Contingent

The first British ground forces contingent *(Operation Granby)*, the 7th Armoured Brigade, from Germany, of about 6,000 men and 120 Challenger tanks, had arrived in the Gulf in October, being placed under CENTCOM, and positioned in the eastern part of the vague Allied 'front line', in support of US Marine formations. Known as the 'Desert Rats', this formation had gained fame in the Western Desert in World War II, and has as its symbol the desert gerbil.

In late November, the British government decided to send another formation, the 4th Armoured Brigade, also from Germany, and also equipped with Challenger tanks. These two armoured brigades, with some supporting elements, came together to form the British 1st Armoured Division. The British ground contingent had a notional strength of 30,000 men, although on the 15th January, it only numbered about 25,000 men, with 170 tanks and 84 guns.

General Sir Peter de la Billiere was appointed to command all British ground forces in the Gulf, and had direct access to General Schwartzkopf, attending his daily meetings, and later claimed to have had some influence on strategy and planning the ground campaign. De la Billiere had a distinguished career in the British SAS.

The French Contingent

The initial French contingent *(Operation Daguet)* expanded into the 6th (Daguet) Light Armoured Division, with a notional strength of about 9,000 troops, as personnel, weapons and equipment were drawn from the French Force d'Action Rapide, concentrating in the Hafar al-Batin area. This French division was 'on wheels, rather than tracks', and its 72 light armoured wheeled vehicles included the GIAT-10, with a high-velocity 105mm gun (claimed to be able to pierce all known armour); and the Panhard ERC-90. Both vehicles were amphibious, NBC-proofed (Nuclear, Biological and Chemical Warfare) and extremely mobile across country, but did have to stop to fire their guns, as vehicle turrets were not stabilised. French infantry were carried in Renault VAB vehicles. These vehicles could be lifted by C-130s.

The French commander was General Michel Roquejoeffre, who 'liaised' with General Schwartzkopf, and attended his joint conferences, but insisted that he only took orders from his own C-in-C, President Mitterrand. The French were anxious to 'have a piece of any action' that was going, having in mind the value of 'combat-proven' weaponry when it came to international arms and equipment sales, but were less anxious to be tied down under American command.

In early November, a French officer and two soldiers, on a forward reconnaissance probe, suffered the indignity of being captured by the Iraqis. They were duly returned home from Baghdad by Saddam Hussein, as a 'gesture of good will towards the French'. The following month the French division was withdrawn southwards for a few miles to make way for the Syrian contingent, which wished to be in the 'front line', and was later redeployed westwards to Rafha to become responsible for the security of the western end of the Iraqi 'Obstacle Belt'. By the end of November, the French contribution amounted to '13,000 troops, 14 warships and 100 helicopters' *(Daily Telegraph)*. One source *(Cohen & Gatti)* suggested that the French contingent was ready in their new flanking positions by the 17th January (1991).

On the 29th January, Jean-Pierre Chevenement, the French Defence Minister, resigned, dissatisfied over the course the war was taking. He stated that the French involvement in the Gulf conflict, was "avoidably unnecessary and harmful to the prospects of peace in the Middle East", and added "to say nothing of the danger to French contacts there".

Egyptian and Syrian Contingents

By the end of 1990, the Egyptian ground contingent, commanded by General M Halaby, amounted to about 35,000 men, and consisted of the 3rd Mechanised Division and the 4th Armoured Division, the latter with 300 M-60 tanks.

The Syrian military contingent, commanded by General A Habib, had increased to about 12,000 men by mid-January, and consisted basically of the 9th Armoured Division, with 270 Soviet T-72 tanks, and detachments of Special Forces.

The Saudi Contingent

Less precise details are available about the ground force contingents from the GCC States. CENTCOM figures indicate the Saudis produced about 40,000 troops for *Operation Desert Shield*, which amounted to four armoured, or mechanised, brigades, with a total of about 200 tanks, but it is thought that only a proportion were in the 'forward area'. The Saudi regime had a potential internal security problem to take care of which they would be unlikely to neglect.

The Kuwaiti Contingent

The strength of the Kuwaiti ground force contingent was vague, and lacking in detail, it being assumed that it might have been about 3,000 strong, or even a thousand or so more. The Kuwait government-in-exile claimed it was over 7,000 strong, being boosted up to this figure by Kuwait volunteers. Certainly two brigades were being formed, or re-formed, one in a camp in Saudi Arabia, and the other in the UAE, where volunteers were given a one-month training course by US Special Forces.

One of these formations, quoted by one authority (JDW), was the '35th Armoured Brigade', which had withdrawn from Kuwait with '22 Chieftain tanks', and was said to be in the process of being re-equipped with Chieftains. Also, the Kuwaitis were receiving 80 Yugoslav M-84 tanks (Yugoslav assembled Soviet T-72s), long on order.

The GCC Rapid Deployment Force

Even less is known precisely about the size, composition or state of the GCC Rapid Deployment Force, CENTCOM giving its strength as being about 10,000, with 50 tanks. It is assumed that only about 3,000 or so, were from the four GCC States of Bahrain, Oman, Qatar and the UAE, with Saudi Arabia making up this number.

Of the other national ground force contributions, Pakistan produced an infantry detachment that eventually totalled 10,000 troops; Bangladesh one of about 5,000, and Morocco one of about 2,000 men, the latter including a Special Forces detachment. Few integral details have been released about these three detachments.

The Lack of Intelligence

The bogy of lack of intelligence continually haunted the Allies, and despite US wealth of highly sophisticated satellite and electronic intelligence-gathering equipment, CENTCOM was poorly informed about the strength and dispositions of the Iraqi ground forces. General Schwartzkopf received reports from the US Defense Intelligence Agency (DIA), which obtained information from satellite surveillance, and the CIA. There also seemed to be distribution and co-ordination problems, and for example, the US Army and US Navy could not share intelligence data as their computers were not compatible.

CENTCOM worked on the premise the Iraqis had '41 or 42 divisions' available, eight of which were elite Republican Guard ones, having the best morale, weaponry and mobility. Pentagon estimates (15th December) were that there were 28-29 Iraqi divisions of the '3rd and 4th Army Corps' in the Basra-Kuwait area, of which 14-15 were in the Kuwait Theatre of Operations (KTO), with '1,750 tanks and 1,450 other armoured vehicles'. Two Iraqi Special Forces units were believed to be in Kuwait City. A few days later, General Powell gave out 'new estimates' of Iraqi strength, saying there were about '480,000 Iraqi troops' in the Basra-KTO area, some 30,000 more than in the previous month, with '4,000 tanks, 2,500 armoured vehicles and 2,700 guns'. All over-estimates as was later revealed.

Not only was CENTCOM not exactly sure how many mustered Iraqi divisions there were, or where they were, it did not seem to know how Saddam Hussein was likely to react. Neither the Pentagon, nor any of the US intelligence-gathering agencies, seemed to be able to read his mind, nor penetrate his public 'inscrutable' image. The reason for this was because there were hardly any reliable 'psychological' (Human) intelligence coming out from Iraq. In this respect, Iraq was a closed country, and so Allied assessments were largely 'guesstimates'.

A great deal of psychological intelligence can be obtained about an individual by 'tapping' his telephone conversations, to determine his mood, attitude, doubts, fears and hopes, and to assess whether he is confident, depressed, undecided, or is becoming desperate. Human spies can detect attitudes and moods of leaders and populations, to find out how much, or how little, support a national leader may have, and something of the aspirations and fears of his people. Even Western hostages returning from Iraq, including those who had been held at, or near, potential military targets, as part of the Human Shield, seemed unable to glean, or provide any worthwhile information. The Pentagon admitted that Saddam Hussein no longer used his radio-telephone to talk to his field commanders, as he was aware this was monitored by US surveillance systems.

It was reported (NCB) that the US *Voice of America* radio station operated throughout the Kuwait Crisis, and that the CIA operated a number of anti-Saddam Hussein clandestine radio stations beaming into Iraq. The BBC Monitoring Service in the UK, monitored all broadcasts of *Radio Baghdad* and other government transmissions.

The Iraqi Obstacle Belt

Meanwhile the Iraqis were constructing seemingly strong, impregnable, static defences in the Kuwait Theatre of Operations (KTO), which became known in Allied jargon as the 'Obstacle Belt'. This extended from the shore of the Gulf waters, along the southern Kuwaiti border, a mere 'line in the sand', an east-west, 'dog-leg' rather than a straight one (the sharp bend in the Kuwaiti-Saudi frontier became known as the 'elbow'), for about 120 miles westwards to the Wadi al-Batin, a wide, dry water course.

The Obstacle Belt varied in depth from 1,000 to 3,000 yards or more. Its southern-most edge consisted of a strip of anti-personnel mines to deter Allied probes, and to take a toll of any infantry raids or patrols. This was backed by huge sand ramparts, known as 'berms', which would cause advancing Allied tanks to expose their 'soft under-bellies' when surmounting them. A broad and deep anti-tank ditch lay behind the berms, backed up by an area littered with anti-tank and anti-personnel mines, barbed wire fencing and entanglements.

Behind the Obstacle Belt were 11-12 Iraqi infantry divisions in entrenched defensive positions, with guns, mortars and missiles, and with T-55 tanks sunk into the sand to give direct fire support. At intervals were pools of oil ready to be ignited, to engulf attackers in flames. The Iraqis had been influenced by Soviet military doctrine, which in defence was to rely upon strong continuous frontal linear positions, but to leave flanks to be covered by natural obstacles. In the east the Iraqi Obstacle Belt was covered by the Gulf, and in the west by wild desert terrain, which while not entirely impassable to vehicles, to the Iraqis at least, did not seem to lend itself to a major flanking movement by heavy armoured forces, but only to light reconnaissance movement. Iraqi shortage of mobile manpower was probably really the deciding factor in the decision to leave this flank weak, and practically uncovered.

Six Iraqi infantry divisions manned the coastal defensive entrenched line which was protected by sea-mines, land-mines, barbed wire and booby traps. These Iraqi defences, especially the coastal ones, were later found to be much weaker than envisaged, being poorly positioned and constructed.

Some five miles to the rear of the Obstacle Belt was the Iraqi tactical reserve, of two-three armoured or mechanised divisions; and farther to the rear still on the Kuwait-Iraq border was the strategic reserve, of 'eight Republican Guard armoured divisions, with probably 150,000 men and 750 Soviet T-72 tanks' (the Pentagon estimate).

The Obstacle Belt was portrayed in graphic detail by the Allied media, causing speculation on what the human cost might be to successfully break through it. Assault engineers with modern equipment and techniques, would be required to clear preliminary paths for attacking troops to move through. Accordingly, dummy lay-outs of the Iraqi Obstacle Belt were constructed in rear areas to practise on.

Schwartzkopf's Deception Plan

By this time General Schwartzkopf had decided (if indeed, the decision was left to him) that, if and when, it came to launching the ground campaign, he would feint towards the eastern end of the Obstacle Belt, and create amphibious activity in the coastal area of the KTO, under cover of which he would mount a massive wide-sweeping, west-flanking armoured assault to encircle the defenders to roll them up from the west. What other course could a prudent, sensible General take? (When interviewed on *CNN*, on the 31st January, I explained that this was the only feasible plan possible under the circumstances.) Correctly, Schwartzkopf was giving the Iraqis the impression he was preparing for a head-on frontal assault against the forward Iraqi defences in the KTO, in conjunction with amphibious landings. One source *(Cohen & Gatti)* suggests that Schwartzkopf unveiled his 'deception plan' as early as the 10th November.

Misleading Allied media reports over-emphasised amphibious activities in the northern Gulf area, and for example, in November, Allied *Exercise Imminent Thunder,* a large amphibious one, was given publicity, even though it actually had to be terminated due to 'high winds and rough seas', which made it impossible for hovercraft, upon which the exercise largely depended, to operate. Also, misleading reports were given out that a large US Marine Task Force, having completed practice landings on the southern Arabian coastline, was steaming northwards. Journalists were discouraged from wandering too far westwards in Allied assembly areas, but were able to write about the enormous Allied ground build-up opposite the eastern end of the Obstacle Belt.

Special Forces

Coincidental with conventional activities, it was hinted that a covert war was in progress against the Iraqis by Allied Special Forces troops, about which in fact little was known. American and British Special Forces were certainly operative, and used, for example, Chinook helicopters, fitted with in-flight re-fuelling facilities, sound-proof engine mountings and muffled exhausts; and 'dune buggies', with reputed amazing cross-country performance, relying upon satellite navigation systems for direction. Allied media reported, on the 7th January, that 'six Iraqi helicopters had landed in eastern Saudi Arabia, carrying Iraqi defectors'. This was good for Allied morale, but was not true — they were carrying Special Forces personnel returning from a mission.

US Special Operations Command (SOCOM), had been formed in 1987, prior to which each of the US armed services had their own covert programmes, usually devoid of inter-service liaison and co-operation. SOCOM was responsible for developing Special Operations doctrine, strategies and tactics, and for equipment requirements. Its elements could be deployed anywhere in the world, and would supply Special Forces requirements for other US Commands. It was also responsible for preparation of special, psychological and civil affairs programmes in support of national interests, across a spectrum of conflict, from high to low intensity.

US SOCOM Special Forces in the Gulf area included about 2,000 Delta Force personnel, and three USN SEAL teams, while the British provided about 200 SAS and naval Special Boat Squadron (SBS) personnel.

The Iraqi Game Plan

The commencement of the Allied air campaign on the 16th/17th January, brought high expectation that soon Allied ground troops would be committed to battle. This did not happen for a while, and American, British and French troops, all with a known offensive role, uneasily shuffled their feet as they were held back, while media attention focused on aerial activity.

Saddam Hussein believed the Allied deception plan, because he wanted to. During the Iran-Iraq War on several occasions Iraqis had successfully drawn Iranian forces into selected 'killing grounds', and he was planning a similar trap for Allied formations. His game plan was to sit tight in his hedgehog-like defences, keeping his out-numbered combat aircraft in their HAS, and enduring whatever aerial bombing the Allies would subject him to, until they were ready to launch their ground attack.

Saddam Hussein hoped the anticipated ground battle would result in initial heavy Allied casualties, which would alarm the American people, and weaken Bush's resolve. At the best Saddam Hussein hoped there would be an automatic pause for breath after a few hours' combat, in which negotiations could re-commence. He thought that time was on his side, hoping the Americans would impatiently rush into battle before the fragile Allied coalition began to crack. But the Allies seemed to be in no hurry, and continued their relentless aerial bombing programme, under which Iraqi troops in the KTO soon lost their mobility as vehicles sank deeper into the sand, and they fatalistically dug-in for the 'duration'.

Capture of Qarah Island

For almost a week (after the 16th January) while the Allied air campaign continued overhead, all was seemingly quiet on the ground, and it was not until the 23rd, that reports were heard of artillery duels and patrol activity in the vicinity of the Obstacle Belt. The following day an Iraqi anti-aircraft detachment, positioned on Qarah Island, an uninhabited rocky protrusion, with a navigation beacon on it, about 20 miles off-shore from the Kuwaiti coast, fired on Allied aircraft. In response, the aircraft attacked the Iraqi gun position. After several Iraqis had been killed, the other '29 members' of the gun-crew surrendered. Allied forces landed by sea and took possession of Qarah Island and the adjacent uninhabited tiny Umm al-Maradim Island. These were the first pieces of occupied Kuwaiti 'real estate' recovered from the Iraqis (although both in fact, were claimed by Saudi Arabia).

The Oil Slick

Two days previously (22nd) it was alleged the Iraqis began pumping oil into the Gulf from Kuwaiti storage tanks, through the Sea Island loading terminal, and a huge oil-slick began to form, eventually extending to some '55 miles in length and over 25 miles in width' (estimates of its extent vary), and to drift southwards with some of the surface oil burning. Iraqis claimed the oil had been released when Allied planes hit and damaged oil storage tanks.

Oil spillage was estimated to be in the order of 5-10-billion barrels, and was regarded by the West as the worst such disaster since that of the *Exxon Valdez* (March 1989). It deeply affected marine life, sea birds and threatened Kuwait's oyster-beds and the livelihood of local fishermen. Western media had previously reported one or two tiny oil-slicks in the area, allegedly having been caused by Iraqi shelling of Saudi oil storage tanks at Khafji and Mishab.

An interesting point is that this huge oil-slick does not seem to have been detected by the Allies until the 25th, and it was not until the 26th and 27th, that US F-111 aircraft, using laser-guided bombs, succeeded in knocking out the two 'manifold oil-pressure controls' at the Mina al-Ahmadi oil storage facility, which fed the Sea Island terminal. By the end of January, the still slowly drifting oil-slick had not touched the Saudi shore. Skimmer vessels, protective booms and chemical dispersants were used to deal with breakaway patches that neared land. The main oil-slick, left to the natural process of evaporation and break-down of marine bacteria, eventually disappeared.

The assumed reasons for releasing oil into the Gulf (if indeed this is what they had done) would have been to impede Allied amphibious operations and naval mine clearing in the area, to choke up Saudi desalination plants, and to provoke the Allies into a premature ground offensive.

President Bush said this act "has no military advantage for the Iraqis", something he could not really mean, while the US DoD accused Saddam Hussein of 'environmental terrorism'. Soon Allied naval divers were complaining that oil-contamination was hampering the remote-control devices used to explode under-water mines, causing divers to resort to 'finger-tip searches'.

The oil-slick secretly worried General Schwartzkopf in case it foiled his deception plan. Despite the President's comment it was obvious that if the oil-slick came ashore in the KTO, successful amphibious operations and mine clearing would become almost out of the question, which might allow Saddam Hussein to move some of his coastal divisions to the largely undefended western end of the Obstacle Belt. A few oil wells in Kuwait had been deliberately set on fire by the Iraqis, the black billowing smoke adversely affecting visibility and radar functioning.

The Battle for Khafji

On the early morning of the 29th January, the Iraqis launched two small separate, southward thrusts from the Obstacle Belt in the vicinity of al-Wafra, but these were beaten back by Allied air and armoured forces. Considered by General Schwartzkopf to have the intention of provoking a premature ground offensive, few details of these two Iraqi forays were released by CENTCOM.

On the early morning of the following day (30th) an Iraqi assault force of two armoured battalions, with a total of about 90 armoured vehicles and some 3,000 men, moved out from the Obstacle Belt southwards along the coastal road leading to the small Saudi oil town of Khafji, about 12 miles distant. The civilian population of Khafji had been evacuated and the town was held by a detachment of Saudi and Qatari troops.

Leading Iraqi tanks approached Khafji with their gun turrets 'reversed', the usual sign of surrender, and so the garrison was taken by surprise, and overwhelmed. Allied Early Warning systems had failed. That day, when sounds of gunfire were heard by the Allies, a staff officer used the still functioning telephone to Khafji's only hotel, to ask "Who is in charge?" He was told by an answering Iraqi officer "We are".

The Allies re-acted with force, and on the 31st, the town was re-occupied, it being emphasised this had been accomplished by Saudi troops, but without considerable Allied air and artillery support, and US Marine assault troops, it would not have been re-taken. Iraqi attackers were driven from Khafji, but withdrew in formation after putting up a very determined resistance. It was not until the 2nd February, that all Iraqi pockets had been eliminated. The Iraqis left behind '30 dead and 42 armoured vehicles, and over 300 were taken prisoner' by the Allies (CENTCOM). Allied casualties, as initially announced, were '12 US Marines and 19 Saudi soldiers killed, and 31 US personnel unaccounted for, one being a US woman officer'.

Technically, this was an Iraqi defeat, but the ability to mount this attack in spite of Allied air supremacy, and their tenacity, shook the complacency of CENTCOM, and belied the growing conviction that Iraqi morale and effectiveness were declining. A few Iraqi deserters who had come over to the Allied side, or who had been snatched by Special Forces, had told of poor Iraqi morale, lack of food and a general desire to surrender at the first opportunity. It was suspected now that some of the Iraqi 'deserters' may have been deliberately 'planted' to lull the Allies into complacency.

Cheney and Powell Visit the Gulf

On the 8th February, Defense Secretary Cheney and General Powell visited the Gulf on a fact-finding tour, and Bush later admitted this mission was to discover if air power alone could force an Iraqi withdrawal from Kuwait. Some within Congress were impressed by the very low casualty rate amongst US personnel so far, and wanted the air campaign to continue for a while longer to see 'if it would get the job done' (New York Times).

Cheney indicated that General Schwartzkopf did not ask for permission to launch the ground offensive, in fact, on the contrary, he pointed out that some of the newly arrived units in the last wave of reinforcements were not yet up to their full complement of weaponry. Schwartzkopf boasted that a very significant part of the "world's fourth largest army" had been destroyed. Current CENTCOM estimates were that '750 Iraqi tanks, 650 guns, and 600 armoured personnel carriers' had been destroyed, although proof-positive seemed lacking. Agreeing with Schwartzkopf, Cheney said there is "no magic trigger" to start off the ground assault, and that the "capacity of the United States to do damage to Saddam Hussein's forces is still crucial". On this occasion Cheney omitted to mention the contribution of other Allies.

On the same day (8th), the Iraqi deputy Prime Minister, Saadoum Hamadi, visited Tehran, and while there gave his estimate of Iraqi casualties caused by Allied air activity, as being "20,000 killed and 60,000 injured in the first 26 days of the war' (IRNA).

Ground skirmishing seemed to continue against the Obstacle Belt, but at a low level, only one US raid of any note being picked up by the media. On the 20th February, US AH-64 Apache and CH-58 helicopters carried out an incursion into Iraqi-held territory on a 'bunker complex', at an undisclosed location, when '471 Iraqi prisoners' were flown back to Saudi Arabia. This was the first admitted occasion when American troops had attacked Iraqi ground units. The number of prisoners captured fuelled the belief that the protracted air campaign was seriously eroding the morale of Iraqi ground forces.

Allied Bombing Mishaps

The Allied air campaign continued relentlessly, and was beginning to cause some political concern about the effect it might be having on Iraqi civilians, especially women and children, CENTCOM being studiously vague on this aspect of the war. In fact, CENTCOM did not know what Iraqi civilian casualties were, and this evasion was generally duplicated by Saddam Hussein who did not want his own people to hear such bad news, fearful that it might erode resistance morale. Hamadi's figures were dismissed as being wildly exaggerated.

A few tragic Allied miscalculations did occur which Saddam Hussein exploited for propaganda purposes, as they indicated that despite US claims of pin-point accuracy of weaponry, sometimes bombs and missiles missed their targets and caused civilian casualties. On the 23rd January, the Allies bombed what they thought was a factory producing biological weapons, which caused civilian casualties. Iraqis insisted, probably correctly, that the factory produced 'powdered baby milk'.

On the 6th February, when an air-raid shelter full of civilians at Almiriya, a district of Baghdad, was hit by an Allied bomb, the CNN team was rushed to the scene to record the disaster, and film some of the '300 bodies recovered, of which 91 were of children' (INA). This was an Iraqi propaganda coup. CENTCOM insisted the building was a 'command and control centre', and the air-raid shelter was for service personnel and not civilians, but not very convincingly. Allied intelligence had been faulty.

The British RAF was involved in one such disaster, when a laser-guided 'glide-bomb' went out of control, and struck an apartment building, instead of a bridge over the Euphrates River, in the Iraqi town of Faluja, when '130 people were killed and another 78 injured' (INA). This incident, said to have occurred on the 13th/14th February, was not admitted by CENTCOM until the 17th, an unaccountable three-day delay.

Was Saddam Hussein an Air Target?

CENTCOM briefings frequently mentioned air attacks on 'Iraqi leadership and control communications', meaning the web of telephones, radio-telephones, and other micro-wave apparatus, which linked Saddam Hussein to his army and air force HQs, and field commanders, but it was constantly denied that Saddam Hussein himself was a specific target. However, according to one source (Newsday) this was not the case, and it quotes an unnamed General who said "We really went after him".

Apparently, Saddam Hussein spent most of his time in a green 'mobile home' (caravan-type vehicle), being constantly on the move to avoid bombs and missiles, knowing he was a top priority American target. It was said he had several narrow escapes, and that on one occasion two US F-16 combat aircraft attacked a convoy of vehicles moving from Baghdad to Basra, one of which was Saddam Hussein's mobile home, but the pilots missed their target.

Allied Naval Situation

By this time the small Iraqi navy had all but ceased to exist, most craft having either been destroyed, fled to Iran, or was skulking in Iraqi coastal bases, while Allied warships sailed the waters of the Gulf, the Red Sea and the Arabian Sea, with impunity, apart from the danger of mines, enforcing the UN authorised economic blockade against Iraq. On the 18th February, two US warships were damaged by mines, but this was a comparatively uncommon event.

The USS Missouri, which had frequently fired Tomahawk cruise missiles at Iraqi targets, also fired its 16-inch guns (projecting a 2,700-lb shell up to 23 miles), an elderly relic of an older generation of naval weaponry, at coastal targets, which added little to the devastation already caused by aerial bombing and missiles, but was a naval prestige boost, perhaps even a grandiose swan song, or even a means of conveniently disposing of surplus ammunition unlikely ever to be required in any future conflict.

Last Minute Diplomacy

World statesmen tried to intervene with last minute diplomacy to save Kuwait from inseparable destruction and liberation by military force. One was President Rafsanjani of Iran, who on the 4th February, offered to mediate, but on the 10th, this was rejected by Saddam Hussein. On the 15th, Saddam Hussein offered to withdraw his troops from Kuwait and to comply with UN Resolution 660, but linked it to Israeli withdrawal from 'all Occupied Territories'. President Bush rejected this offer, demanding that the Iraqi leader immediately comply with all UN Resolutions that had been approved relating to the Kuwait Crisis.

President Gorbachev of the USSR, also tried to cool the situation, sending his Personal Envoy, Yevgeny Primakov, to Baghdad on the 18th, with an 'Eight Point Peace Plan', which it is said that Saddam Hussein accepted on the 19th. It was also said that Gorbachev had obtained the secret Pentagon date for the commencement of the ground campaign, by Soviet counter-intelligence means. Gorbachev's plan was immediately stymied by Bush on the 22nd, who demanded that Iraqi troops begin withdrawing from Kuwait on the 23rd, to be completely clear within seven days.

7

Operation Desert Sabre

The Allied ground offensive, known as *Operation Desert Sabre*, was launched at 0400-hours (Local Time), on Sunday, 24th February, and consisted initially of a series of feints and attacks on the eastern part of the Obstacle Belt, followed by wide west-flanking movements intended to trap and destroy Iraqi armed forces in the KTO. General Schwartzkopf's Deception Plan was successful, and Saddam Hussein was indeed taken by surprise. Instead of drawing Allied attacking ground forces into a 'killing ground' of his own choosing, and the anticipated bloody 'Mother of all Battles', Allied ground forces moved to draw a noose around Iraqi troops in the KTO.

The Deception Plan

The Deception Plan was carried through so well that not only did it deceive the Iraqis, but also Allied accredited media personnel, who incidentally gave the overall impression when it was revealed, that the US 7th and 18th Army Corps had moved almost overnight from their eastern assembly areas hundreds of miles to their 'start lines' in the western Rafha and Hafar Sectors, while most of those formations had already been secretly pre-positioned there. Bereft of satellite and aerial intelligence, the Iraqis, having to rely much upon Western media for information about unseen Allied dispositions, had no inkling of this massive covert re-deployment, which had been in progress for some weeks. These formations moving by night, resorting to good camouflage by day, had maintained 'radio silence'.

The Deception Plan had been effective enough to cause the Iraqis not to bother to continue their Obstacle Belt any further westwards than the 'Tri-point', near the cross-tracks oasis of Ruqi (where the Kuwaiti-Saudi-Iraqi frontiers touched), near the Wadi al-Batin. West of the Tri-point the desert wastes were only occasionally traversed by small groups of nomads seeking grazing for their camels. The Saudi-Iraqi frontier to the west of the Tri-point was marked by little more than a furrow-like straight line in the sand. The only defences were occasional patchy mine-fields where nomad trails traversed the frontier. There were few Iraqi military posts, and little patrolling, in this arid desert region south of the Euphrates Valley.

According to one source (Cohen & Gatti) Schwartzkopf's Deception Plan began to be put into effect on the 12th January, when he established a deception base, code-named 'AO Kelty', designed to make the Iraqis think the US 18th Army Corps was still opposite the 'Elbow', in the Obstacle Belt, when some 150 personnel constantly deployed and redeployed inflatable tanks and helicopters, and kept up a barrage of radio traffic, for Iraqi monitors to pick up, to maintain the illusion, and emphasise the Allied intent to use its heavy armour in a frontal assault.

On the night of the 16th January, when the Allied air campaign began, which attracted the focus of Iraqi attention, the first elements of the 7th Army Corps began to move to the Hafar Sector, some 80 miles west of the Tri-point, and elements of the 18th Army Corps to the Rafha Sector, another 100 miles farther westwards. Some of Schwartzkopf's Commanders and senior staff officers, aware of the Deception Plan, became anxious that the 7th Army Corps (140,000 troops and 1,200 tanks) and the 18th Army Corps (120,000 troops) would not reach their positions and be ready for battle in time.

Knowing just how long it would take these formations, with 60 days' supplies of fuel, water, ammunition and food, to reach their positions, they had tried to persuade Schwartzkopf to commence this massive, ponderous movement much earlier. "For example, it takes 18 hours for a single US division, of 16,000 troops, to cross a road" (Cohen & Gatti). Schwartzkopf was adamant. He did not want to risk Iraqi Intelligence discovering any Allied troops west of the Tri-point.

Schwartzkopf had calculated he would need 14 clear days from the commencement of the air campaign, to make ready for the ground flanking movements, which some of his staff again doubted was sufficient, bearing in mind that some units, and their vehicles, would have to travel long distances, and those from the Dhahran area, for example, would have to make a 500 mile journey.

Count-Down Begins

On the 11th January Schwartzkopf's Deception Plan was ready for implementation; on the 12th the US Congress authorised war; and on the 15th, Bush signed the National Security Directive, authorising military action. On the 16th, as the five-week air campaign began the Deception Plan was put into motion, and the French (Daguet) Light Armoured Division led the way from the Elbow area to the Rafha Sector, to act as a screen between the major Allied ground move, and Iraqi defences and terrain.

CENTCOM soon stated that in the first phase of the Allied bombing of Iraq, supply routes had been heavily damaged, that '30 bridges had been destroyed', and that Iraqi daily supplies for the front-line troops in the KTO had been sharply reduced from 20,000 tons a day, down to about 2,000 tons. After two weeks of Allied air action against the Iraqis, Schwartzkopf was still calling for more reinforcements.

On the 2nd February, General Schwartzkopf took a trip to the Rafha Sector, where the 18th Army Corps was assembling, to find out how quickly it could swing into action. He was told that it required seven days notice, during which a series of 'deep operations' would be undertaken in preparation. These were to include '16 Special Forces missions' to destroy SCUD launching sites, artillery attacks on border posts, helicopter strikes against scattered Iraqi positions lying back from the frontier, and detailed air reconnaissance of terrain over which it was proposed to drive. 18th Army Corps commanders were concerned mainly about probable Chemical Warfare attacks by SCUDS, armoured groups being bogged down in minefields, or held up by terrain impassable to tracks or wheels. 18th Army Corps anticipated 'at least 5,400 casualties' (Cohen & Gatti).

Despite pressure from Washington, which felt the air campaign had been in progress long enough, Schwartzkopf still hesitated, explaining that the "Iraqis were not yet sufficiently diminished". This negative attitude brought about the Cheney-Powell visit to Schwartzkopf on the 8th February. The under-lying purpose was to demand the ground offensive start fairly soon. Cheney and Powell talked to senior Allied Commanders, who reckoned that the ground fighting, once it began, would last from about 10 to 30 days.

As by this time almost all Allied troops to be involved in the massive westward flanking movement were in their starting positions, it was agreed that 'G-Day' (Ground Attack) would be on the 22nd February, and that the 'count-down' would begin on the 15th February.

During the count-down period bombing of Iraqi formations and positions in the KTO would be increased, especially by the B-52s; Special Forces elements inside Iraq would be activated; engineers would begin to clear paths through minefields; and helicopters would fly on terrain reconnaissance missions up to 100 miles inside Iraq. The Allies seem to have had little knowledge of this desert corner of south-west Iraq, in which there were a few scattered frontier posts and isolated military camps. It was a deserted stretch of wild desert terrain.

The Bush Ultimatum

When President Gorbachev put forward his Eight Point Peace Plan, involving the complete and unconditional Iraqi withdrawal from Kuwait within 21 days, Tariq Aziz, the Iraqi Foreign Minister, was sent (on the 18th) to Moscow, and the following day Saddam Hussein indicated he would accept it. The Allied count-down was pended. But Bush was having none of this, his mind was made up, and he gave his 'final ultimatum' to the Iraqi President, one it was not possible for Saddam Hussein to comply with. The count-down was resumed, G-Day being put forward two days to the 24th February.

Keyed up, ready and waiting, Allied ground troops were given their medical antidotes against the anticipated CW threat, and also against the possibility of anthrax being released against them; all having protective 'chemical suits' to wear. American and European troops especially had taken full advantage of the lengthy waiting period to acclimatise themselves to desert conditions, modify their weapons, vehicles and systems to withstand local temperatures, fit filters against fine grain sand, and cope with other local problems. The 7th and 18th Army Corps continued to maintain radio silence.

The Allied Ground Line-Up

Allied ground forces were now lined up facing northwards in five separate groups, some considerable distances from each other. In the east on the coastal edge of the line, facing Kuwait City was the Saudi Group, consisting of two Saudi Task Forces and a Kuwait brigade. Next to it, on its western flank, was the US Marine Contingent, now formed into two divisions, centred on the Elbow. To the west of the US Marines was the Pan-Arab Contingent, consisting of two Egyptian divisions, a Saudi brigade, and other Arab units, facing the Tri-point area. These three groups were tasked to attack, or feint towards, the Obstacle Belt.

Further to the west, about 80 miles from the Tri-point, was the 7th Army Corps, in the Hafar Sector, near Ruqi; and another 100 miles westwards still, in the Rafha Sector, facing the Iraqi frontier (whose straight-line border changed to a north-west directional angle), near the cross-tracks oasis of Ash Shubah, was the 18th Army Corps. General Schwartzkopf did not intend to commit these two Army Corps to battle on the first day, the exception being the French division, which had a protective flank screening task.

G-Day

At 0300 hours, the Allies put down a very heavy artillery barrage on located Iraqi artillery positions about five miles in rear of the Obstacle Belt, expecting a counter-barrage to result, when precision aircraft bombing could take over to give an impression of a World War II D-Day Landing, to shatter enemy morale. At 0400 hours (H Hour), Allied troops of the three 'eastern groups', with direct artillery and helicopter-gunship support, advanced through gaps in the berms that 'had been made by engineer explosions, and along paths marked out across the outer minefields' (CENTCOM). Although this assault was intended to be in the nature of a feint and a distraction away from the planned major western flanking attack, the troops had been ordered to exploit, that is move forward, as and when, they could in any favourable situation. There were no amphibious landings, but enemy coastal defences were bombarded by Allied naval vessels (CENTCOM).

This was part of the story as told by CENTCOM, whose accounts of the ground campaign were very broad-brush in outline and lacking in verifiable detail. An example of absence of detail, although the omission is difficult to understand in this case, unless it was an 'unauthorised' operation, was that the US Marines had 'jumped the gun', when a group of some 4,000 of them crossed the protective Iraqi berms in the Obstacle Belt a full 48 hours before the Allied ground assault began.

In doing so, while crossing minefields Marines 'hopped from one anti-tank mine to another', claiming to be the only Allied troops to take such a personal risk in the campaign. This was later reluctantly confirmed by the Pentagon. It is true that anti-tank mines require considerable pressure, such as that of a 50-ton battle tank, to detonate them, and can usually withstand the weight of a single soldier without incident. What these US Marines accomplished was not stated by the Pentagon, but presumably they detected, and marked out routes through minefields for ground forces to follow in their attack and subsequent advance.

There was little resistance from Iraqis holding the forward positions in the Obstacle Belt, and as Allied troops approached many of them emerged, hands in the air, to surrender. That was the CENTCOM account. An American periodical (Newsweek), tells a different story, later (12th September) confirmed by the Pentagon, recounting how leading US assault forces advanced with their tanks pushing huge, wide earth-levelling apparatus, that tore up and levelled the sandy terrain, filling in the defensive trenches in the process. It estimated there were about '8,000 Iraqis defending some 70 miles' of front-line trenches. The first 2,000 Iraqis in the first line of trenches, managed to jump up out of them as the bull-dozing equipment neared them to hastily surrender. The remainder were not so fortunate, and some 6,000 Iraqi soldiers were buried alive in their own trenches.

Vehicles following leading Allied tanks, dragged heavy harrows that up-rooted, dislodged and exposed mines, and so formed 'mine-free' routes about 100 yards wide, for follow-up advancing Allied forces to move along. The authority identified the US formations involved, and their US home bases.

By mid-day the Obstacle Belt had been penetrated, but the Allied advance came to a stop, clogged by thousands of POWs, who co-operated with the Allies, pointing out the minefields and their extent, and giving other information. Coils of 'concertina' barbed wire were unrolled to form temporary make-shift 'POW concentration areas' to contain them. Another cause for Allied delay was having to wait for follow-up fuel supplies to reach them.

There seemed to be little fight left in the Iraqi defenders, nor any sign of any counter-attack from either the tactical or strategic enemy reserve. Allies found the Obstacle Belt defences to be extensive, more extensive than their Intelligence had forecast, but they were poorly constructed, and poorly sited, especially along its coastal stretch.

The West Flanking Movement

In the far West of the theatre the leading elements of the French military contingent moved northwards across the Saudi border into Iraqi terrain. In the words of Pierre Joxe, the new French Defence Minister "The Daguet Division took off like a high-speed train at 0430 hours on the 24th." By mid-morning it had advanced about 35 miles when it bumped into an Iraqi brigade position. The French halted and replied with mortar fire.

In view of having light armoured wheeled vehicles, the Divisional Commander opted against a frontal armoured charge, and instead co-ordinated a 'triple manoeuvre', when his units, under cover of an artillery barrage and helicopter gunship support, closed in on three sides. As the French moved into the attack, the Iraqi garrison surrendered. The cost to the French was one wounded soldier. Later, when asked what happened to the '5,000 men of the Iraqi brigade', he replied vaguely "They just went home". Certainly the Iraqi military homeward movement was gaining momentum.

The following day (25th) the Daguet Division advanced towards as-Salman, its next objective, where there was a military encampment, an air base, a desert fort, and a tiny village, arriving in the late afternoon to find it practically deserted. Elements of 101st Airborne Division were flown over to assist the French occupy this complex. Only 15 Iraqi soldiers remained, who were taken prisoner, the few civilians in the village were detained, and by evening the air base had been secured. One French soldier was wounded in this operation. The French were less fortunate the following day (26th) when they lost two soldiers killed and 25 injured in mine clearing.

It had been General Schwartzkopf's intention not to move the 7th Army Corps and the 18th Army Corps until the second day of the ground offensive, so as not to distract Iraqi attention from the KTO. By mid-day (24th) he began to realise that Iraqi military morale was snapping, that '5,500 Iraqi POWs' (CENTCOM) had been taken, and that thousands more Iraqi soldiers were either surrendering or fleeing. He realised that if he delayed his west-flank operation too long it might be too late to entrap the Iraqi Republican Guard divisions. Accordingly, he advanced the schedule for his two Army Corps by one day, both being ordered to commence moving northwards late on the 24th. Schwartzkopf was not averse to his formations becoming involved in a grand armoured battle.

The 7th Army Corps, with its heavy concentration of armour was to be the decisive striking force against the vaunted Republican Guard armoured divisions. The British 1st Armoured Division was the right flank formation in this Army Corps advance, and was scheduled to cross the Saudi border, advance northwards for a few miles, and then turn eastwards to cross the Wadi al-Batin to engage the Iraqi tactical reserve in the KTO. Other divisions of this Army Corps were to move even further north before turning eastward to attack the Iraqi strategic reserve calculated to be somewhere between Kuwait City and Basra.

Despite ample linear space along the Start-line in which to deploy formations and units, they tended to be delayed due to bottle-neck traffic problems at the few selected crossing points over the frontier, and once across were retarded owing to the constant need to refuel tanks. The speed of movement of the 7th Army Corps was governed by the rapidity of the refuelling process. By the end of the second day (25th) the major part of this Army Corps was on Iraqi terrain.

On the 25th, the weather changed drastically for the worse, and there followed two whole days of exceptionally heavy rain, high winds and stormy conditions, which made navigation difficult and hampered mobility. On that day, the leading brigade of the British 1st Armoured Division, moving according to plan, reached Wadi al-Batin, where it was ordered to halt for several hours 'due to directional errors', to avoid collision with other divisional columns within the Army Corps.

The Commander of the British 7th Armoured Brigade obtained an Iraqi 'battle map', which indicated that an Allied ground thrust had been expected northwards along the Wadi al-Batin. He noted that several delaying positions had been constructed in the Wadi, together with decoy guns and aluminium reflectors, the latter to confuse Allied radars. He said (RUSI Lecture) "If they had chosen to resist, the Iraqis had the means to prosecute a long delaying action".

The 18th Army Corps, scheduled to make a wider western sweep, moved towards Nasiriya, in the Euphrates Valley, some 120 miles north of the Saudi border, to be ready to turn eastwards to cut off the escape of

Republican Guard divisions, after their anticipated defeat in battle by the 7th Army Corps. The first stage was to establish an 'Air Head', to use the jargon, at Tallil, which was about ten miles south of Nasiriya, to be a re-fuelling, provisioning and maintenance base for the Corps. The 101st Airborne Division flew 2,000 military personnel, in one single flight of '400 Blackhawk and Huey helicopters', claimed to be the biggest helicopter lift in military history.

By the end of the second day forward elements of the 18th Army Corps were in position on the watershed overlooking Nasiriya, having progressed far more rapidly than expected. That evening General Schwartzkopf spoke to the Corps Commander by radio, and was pleasantly surprised by the good news. He asked how many casualties had been incurred, and the reply was 'one wounded soldier only'. At the end of the second day of the ground offensive, CENTCOM claimed the Allies had taken over 20,000 POWs, and destroyed over 270 tanks.

Iraqi Withdrawal Ordered

On the 26th February, Saddam Hussein ordered his armed forces to withdraw from Kuwait, although this was merely confirming what was beyond his control. He stated to his people "You have faced the whole world: you are victorious", but added that Kuwait was now no longer part of Iraq. President Bush scorned Saddam Hussein's order as a move to gain time to re-group his forces, to counter-attack, declaring that the Allies "would fight on with undiminished intensity". He emphasised that fighting could only stop if Iraqi troops "would lay down their arms".

That same evening, CENTCOM claimed the Allies had taken over '30,000 POWs and destroyed over 2,000 enemy tanks'. Mention was made that Iraqi resistance appeared to be collapsing, and that only the Republican Guard divisions were standing firm in the area of the Kuwait-Iraq border.

By this time Allied 'Psy-Ops' (Psychological Warfare Operations) came into the picture, and thousands of leaflets were dropped from aircraft on to groups of Iraqi troops, urging them to surrender, and explaining they should abandon their arms, and take the leaflet to the nearest Allied soldiers. Psy-Ops teams, with loud-hailers, broadcast on the battlefields instructions to Iraqis on how to surrender. Whenever possible, most ignored these instructions, and made for home. Despite the fact that Iraqi resistance was negligible, the several Allied columns made disjointed, and somewhat spasmodic advances, owing to frequent halts for refuelling, and having to detach men to marshal and guard hordes of POWs. Personnel were beginning to feel the effects of lack of sleep.

Kuwait Re-Captured

Meanwhile, in and around Kuwait City, on the evening of the 25th February, Iraqi troops began withdrawing in disarray, although some Iraqi resistance points remained active until well into the following day. By the evening of the 26th, Kuwaiti 'Resistance Forces' claimed to be in control of Kuwait City, and reports indicated that both American and Saudi Special Forces personnel had penetrated that city.

During the final days of the occupation it was alleged the Iraqis perpetrated a reign of terror within the city, indulging in both vengeance and random killings, looting, rape and destruction of some buildings. More oil wells were ignited, and more oil installations damaged, causing a perpetual twilight haze of oil-smog to descend on Kuwait City and its environs. On pulling out, Iraqis took with them many Kuwaiti hostages.

It is said that the '6th Kuwaiti Brigade' had been given the honour of formally liberating Kuwait City, and was rapidly approaching northwards along the main road, when it was halted on CENTCOM orders. It was feared that Kuwaiti troops, with vengeance in their hearts, might be tempted to indulge in reprisals on suspected collaborators, and any remaining Iraqis. Accordingly, Saudi troops took the lead, and entered Kuwait City on the 27th. By this time there was little evidence of any central control, but plenty of violent activity by disparate minor groups. However, a TV journalist *(Bob McKeown)* claimed he entered Kuwait City ahead of any Allied troops, where he met up with two American Marines, who told him they had just 'secured the American Embassy'.

General Schwartzkopf's Press Conference

On the morning of the 27th, both the 7th and 18th Army Corps were ordered to halt where they were. That morning at 0900 hours (dawn in Washington) General Schwartzkopf gave a Press Conference, which he referred to as the 'Mother of all Briefings'. It was a slick, public relations presentation to the media by a victorious General as a record for posterity. Extracts included:–

— To accomplish the mission I have been given, I have to make sure the Republican Guard is rendered incapable . . . and put out of business;

— out of 42 Iraqi divisions, more than 29 have been rendered completely ineffective; and

— more than 3,700 Iraqi tanks have been destroyed, and more than 50,000 POWs taken.

He went on to explain that the destruction of bridges across the Euphrates and Tigris Rivers, together with the 'extraordinary movement of 18th Army Corps' meant that the 'gate' was shut against Iraqi armour or artillery attempting to leave the KTO. He confirmed that Iraq had been effectively disarmed as a military power, and was left with an army composed of infantry, that could not constitute a threat to neighbouring States in the immediate future.

General Schwartzkopf then denigrated Saddam Hussein's claim of victory, and the man, saying "As for Saddam Hussein being a great military strategist, he is neither a strategist, nor is he schooled in the operational arts, nor is he a tactician, nor is he a General, nor is he a soldier. Other than that he is a great military man". It was certainly Schwartzkopf's moment to crow, but there was no trace of the Churchillian dictum of 'Magnanimity in Victory' in his presentation.

Some previous intelligence estimates and faulty assessments had to be amended. For example, the original figure of over '300,000 Iraqi troops in the KTO' had to be reduced to less than 200,000, while units in the Obstacle Belt were undermanned as replacement reinforcements for the normal drain on manpower due to leave, sickness and casualties, never arrived. When a journalist suggested to Schwartzkopf that this meant that Saddam Hussein still had a massive military force remaining intact, the General replied, "That is ridiculous".

Suspended Hostilities

On the evening of the 27th February, President Bush made a nation-wide TV address from his Oval Office, in the White House, to announce 'The suspension of Allied military action as from midnight' (0900 hours — local time on the 28th). He said "Kuwait has been liberated, and the Iraqi army defeated, and our military objectives are met". He added "This is not a time for euphoria, certainly not a time to gloat, but it is a time of pride. This is a victory for all mankind, and the rule of law".

He did not mention the future of Saddam Hussein, but did re-state an earlier assertion that the war had not been conducted against the Iraqi people as a whole. Bush said his statement did not constitute a formal cease-fire, insisting that one could only be achieved when Iraq agreed to surrender all Allied and Kuwaiti prisoners, provide maps of the minefields, and accept all relevant UN Resolutions without reservation.

Prior to the Bush announcement, General Powell telephoned General Schwartzkopf to discuss the situation and whether the fighting should be stopped or allowed to continue. According to one source (Cohen & Gatti), Schwartzkopf replied "I am prepared to stop, but with time I could do more", going on to express a preference for continuing the fighting, but after some further discussion with Powell, agreed to stop. Later, in an interview (Frost Report), when questioned on this issue, said "Frankly, my recommendation had been, you know, to continue the march". Afterwards, embarrassed because he had appeared to differ with President Bush, he retracted, and apologised for "my poor choice of words". The Pentagon came into the timing of the suspension of hostilities, being attracted to the expression 'The 100-Hours War', which accounts for the slightly unusual time-set.

The Turkey Shoot

Meanwhile, an exodus of Iraqi troops from the KTO was taking place, at the same time as elements of the Allied ground forces, anticipating a battle with Iraqi Republican Guard divisions, were still moving to close the 'gate', which Schwartzkopf had prematurely claimed was already shut.

The main mass of Iraqi ground forces was withdrawing along the six-lane Express Highway No. 1, which ran northwards from Kuwait City to the border town of Safwan, and thence to Basra. By the 27th, huge traffic jams on this roadway were forming and long tail-backs building up, as Iraqi vehicles jostled desperately to escape homewards.

The main 20-mile bottleneck was loosely referred to as the Mutla Pass, just south of Safwan, where the Express Highway ran between raised ground on its western side, and marshy ground bordering the Gulf waters on its eastern side. On the 27th, forward elements of Allied ground troops had edged towards the raised ground overlooking the Mutla Pass sector, and so withdrawing Iraqis were almost trapped in an ambush situation. General Schwartzkopf had stated that if Iraqi troops abandoned their tanks and heavy mobile equipment, they would not be attacked, but urged them to surrender. In the mad rush to quit the KTO, Iraqis had indeed abandoned their tanks, generally taking only lighter vehicles on to which scrambled hordes of Iraqi soldiers. Thousands of tanks were left behind, but they were mainly older ones such as T-55s and T-64s: there is no record of any of the more modern T-72s being seized by the Allies, or even of any certainty that any were committed as far south as Kuwait.

Despite General Schwartzkopf's promise, on the early morning of the 28th (some reports indicate a little earlier), Allied air forces launched a mass attack, using cluster bombs and napalm, on the stalled vehicle chaos in the Mutla Pass, that continued 'for several hours'. There is still official silence on how many Iraqis were killed in this massacre at Mutla Pass, or even why it was necessary to mount such a merciless and deadly operation, as trapped Iraqi troops were virtually defenceless and disorganised. Allied pilots came to call this operation the 'Turkey Shoot'.

However, numbers of trapped Iraqis did manage to escape northwards, and many others had made a deviation westwards before reaching the Mutla Pass sector, along a two-lane track that ran through patches of desert and scrub to reach the border town of Jahra. Both Safwan and Jahra were heavily bombed by Allied aircraft.

Further — Allied aircraft pursued retreating Iraqi soldiers to the banks of the Shatt al-Arab, where many were queuing up to cross the few remaining pontoon foot-bridges across that waterway, or to cross on make-shift rafts. Watching from their sector on the lower part of the Shatt al-Arab, Iranians called it a 'Rat Shoot'. Such was the Allied retributive *coup de gras* to end their campaign for the Liberation of Kuwait.

Throughout the ground campaign, CENTCOM briefings and communiques were aggressively boastful, but lacking in confirmed detail, and often scarred with omissions, several of the latter being grudgingly confirmed later by a reluctant Pentagon, thus leaving much scope for individual formations and units to sketch in, or embroider details to their own activities to their own advantage.

8

Praise and Appraisal

Across the USA there was joy and jubilation on the 1st March 1991, at least on the surface, a mood 'hyped up' by the media, and all who had initially been in favour of taking military action to liberate Kuwait loudly applauded. One cannot argue with success, especially in capitalist-orientated America. The US Administration was also jubilant as the diversely fragile Allied Coalition had held together, Allied casualties had been incredibly low, and Iraqi occupying troops had been driven from Kuwait, thus fulfilling the conditions of the American-brokered UN Resolution 678.

Vastly relieved, the US military establishment was lifted from the psychological depression that had haunted it since Vietnam days, as sun-like rays of popular approbation shone on it almost as brightly as they had done during World War II. The Total Force concept had been tested and found to be sound and practical, while the authority of a single US Commander in the field, with all elements of the four Services under his command, had proved to be workable and profitable, and the enhanced status of the US Chairman of the Joint Chiefs of Staff had been advantageous. The result was the Iraqi armed forces had been hammered well into the ground. There was also an euphoria of victory in other nations of the Alliance, which varied in intensity, expression and manifestation, generally being more moderate and restrained than that of the USA.

The Allies, meaning predominantly the Americans, had evicted Iraqi troops from Kuwait with a spectacular show of modern 'high-tech' weaponry, but both the USA and Britain had to employ a major part of their military resources to accomplish this. Had there been a coincidal major military emergency in any other part of the world, both countries would have faced priority problems. Practically all expeditionary capability was drained off towards the Gulf, and both the USA and Britain had to raid their NATO arms inventories in Europe for weaponry, and especially for laser-guided munitions.

One official report (British *House of Commons Defence Committee Report*: 9th August 1991) stated that 'Operation *Granby* had stretched the country's military resources to the extent that its operational capability in Germany had effectively been destroyed'.

The US military doctrine of preparing for a 'war and a half' found the Gulf conflict developing into the 'war', absorbing major attention, leaving scant little available for any 'half war' that might erupt anywhere else in the world. Clearly, another major military emergency would have meant not only reviewing military priorities, but scraping the bottom of the barrel for resources. Despite major American achievements in moving huge numbers of troops and thousands of tons of material some 8,000 miles, the USA had a sea-lift shortage, insufficient air-refuelling facilities and inadequate pre-positioned troops and equipment.

On the other hand, the USA was fortunate in being able to use a score of so well-equipped air-fields, and also to call upon Saudi back-up facilities immediately. It was said the Saudis always over-ordered aircraft spares, without which the USAF would not have been able to operate in the Gulf area so promptly and continually until US air-lift traffic became regularised. Facilities at air bases in Egypt, Turkey and GCC States contributed greatly to the initial instant combat-readiness of the USAF. Fortune also smiled on the Allies in that the USSR was writhing in the death throes of Communism and centralisation, and the Kremlin leadership had only half-a-mind on the Kuwait Crisis.

The Allied air offensive had been so successful in causing Iraqi casualties and affecting Iraqi military morale that there was hardly any need for Schwartzkopf's famous Deception Plan, as when the ground assault began there was little real opposition, with few exceptions. Allied intelligence assessments of anticipated stiff Iraqi resistance were faulty. The real impact of Allied bombing was only appreciated by the Allies as they moved into the ground attack and saw abandoned defences, thousands of enemy dead (seldom mentioned) and thousands of Iraqis waving surrender leaflets. It seems the way had been prepared by daring US Marines. Allied initial probing and feint attacks in the eastern part of the Obstacle Belt to divert attention from the westward encircling movement, became exploitive.

As Iraqi formations did not stand and fight a deadly battle it is hardly possible to detect any obtruding lessons of warfare, either new ones, or revived older ones. More to the point, it is not known whether commanding Generals on either side, many reputed to have read, and re-read, the Campaigns of the Great Captains of military history, were able to apply any of the wisdom or expertise they could have gained from them.

Later (31st March), when unsubstantiated reports began to surface that Iraqi casualties might number as many as 400,000 all told, including civilians, General Schwartzkopf was asked whether all the bombing had been necessary *(Frost Report)*, and he replied "We only had 150 people killed. And the reason why we had 150 people killed is because we so fiercely went after them, that we struck terror into their hearts". He spoke as a military commander, and not as a humanitarian.

Allied Leadership

The so-called Allied leadership was almost completely, and dominantly, American, there was no disguising the fact that it was an American show, with little more than lip-service given to the other Allies, including Britain and France, the only two European ones that produced military contingents that took part in the final ground offensive. The British changed their Prime Minister during the Kuwait Crisis, but not their policy as the new Prime Minister, John Major, continued his predecessor's loyal support for President Bush.

The prime mover and motivator in the struggle against the defiant Saddam Hussein had been President Bush, and to him must go the credit for persistence and tenacity through the lengthy period of the Kuwait Crisis, *Operation Desert Shield,* the air war and the ground assault, and he could now sit back to relax in Imperial satisfaction that a difficult and wayward problem had been solved — it just remained for Saddam Hussein to disappear into oblivion, or better still into an American prison cell to await a Show Trial, perhaps next to that occupied by General Noriega. Cheap Middle East oil had been saved for the Western world, and the might of Pax Americana had triumphed again.

During the run-up to actual combat President Bush could not believe that Saddam Hussein would not back down if the Big Stick was waved at him in a menacingly enough manner, but the Iraqi President was persistence and tenacity embodied. Bush was surprised when he realised he would have to use military force, but once he did, he could not back away, and did so with all the might at his command.

During this period it was observed that Bush at times was testy and irritable as he seemed to be waging a personal vendetta, almost a fixation, against Saddam Hussein. It was not until May 1991, when it was reported that Bush suffered a 'slight heart tremor', and had to be medicated, that it was revealed he was suffering from Grave's Disease, which when a person is under intense strain gives rise to 'atrial fibrillation'. This provoked discussion as to whether Bush's medical condition had affected his judgement at critical moments of the Gulf War. Several people questioned the extent the President's 'uncharacteristic mind-set', was affected by his hyperthyroid condition, after the Iraqi invasion of Kuwait. Previously, some tended to think of Bush, perhaps because he had been such a docile Vice-President, as being a 'concensus man', rather than a keen, decisive one.

One American commentator (*William Safire, New York Times*: 26th May) asked "Was the President 'hyped' last August 2? Did his over active gland affect his decision to launch the air war, or over the ground war, earlier this year?" and added "I believe he made his greatest historic decisions at those moments". Firm evidence is missing, but this issue may become an oft-repeated talking-point and writing-point for researchers, medical and lay, for months and years ahead.

President Bush was fully supported, and perhaps even egged on, by the ambitious James Baker, Secretary of State, a legal beaver and a fixer by some accounts, who probably had future Presidential aspirations, and who certainly shared Bush's dream of Pax Americana. Baker was responsible for cobbling together the Alliance of 30 nations against Iraq, and of keeping it together by bribes, promises and threats. A successful lawyer, Baker was adept at wheeling and dealing, and could not fully understand the Arab mind. He was unable to fathom why he could not persuade Arabs to sit down at a negotiating table to bargain with him, and then not implement an agreed deal.

Richard Cheney, Secretary of Defense, maintained a quieter profile, but was none the less dedicated to Pax Americana, wanting to effect a successful outcome to enhance the reputation of the US military establishment. Although considered by some to be a 'time-server' and a safe man, Cheney lent his weight to the build up of the Big Stick, and when that failed was wholeheartedly behind military action. These were the three key policy-making leaders, although since many others have insisted they also contributed a significant input into decision-making.

On the military side the lead actors in the Gulf War were three serving Generals. As Chairman of the Joint Chiefs of Staff, General Powell was continually in the limelight, and was conscious that he was the first Black General to hold that Office. As the senior serving officer in the US Armed Forces he was anxious to make his mark by successfully implementing badly needed major reforms.

As a veteran of Vietnam, he too was haunted by over two decades of military unpopularity, and was determined to rectify this. His main contribution to the Gulf War was to instil a note of caution and warning against premature, or unwise, action, knowing that a set-back on the battlefield would be disastrous for the reputation of American arms, especially against such a small country. He insisted that the build-up of troops in the Gulf area must be in sufficient strength to ensure victory in battle, and that an overwhelming preponderance be ready to meet any contingency, was better than not having sufficient military muscle at a critical moment. General Powell worked well with his direct boss, Cheney, but tended to be reserved when dealing with President Bush. Not being a White House 'insider', Powell knew his position, did not presume, and so survived. Had things gone badly wrong, he knew he could well be the fall guy.

As sitting Commander of the US Central Command, General Schwartzkopf was the automatic choice to become Commander of *Operation Desert Shield*. He was on the point of retirement from the Army when fame was thrust upon him. Schwartzkopf too had been anxious to improve the image of the US Armed Forces in the eyes of the American people, and was in favour of Pax Americana, although being a serving officer, he avoided political statements or comments, and strictly conformed to the Presidential line in all matters. He too had no intention of stepping out of political, or indeed military, line. The US media 'hyped' him up in the early phases of the Kuwait Crisis, ascribing to him ambitions to become a Patton, a Rommel or a Montgomery, but their sort of military opportunity never came Schwartzkopf's way.

His major contribution to American military success in liberating Kuwait was in operating the Total Force concept, being seen to have authority, and exercising it openly over all elements of the four US Services under his command. His brash, extrovert appearance pleased Americans, and won respect from the Allies. Schwartzkopf had been lauded as the 'Architect of Victory', which rather over-stated the case, as he was extremely constricted strategically by his parameters, and by both Cheney and Powell, to say nothing of President Bush's direct intervention from time to time. Whether he had a real flair for battle or not, we shall never know as the scope of his brief was so limited, his military strength so overwhelming, and the enemy so passive. Schwartzkopf became the living American symbol of victory, boosting both military morale and national pride. He was also adept at Public Relations techniques, and handling the media.

One of the most important contributors to the American success in the Liberation of Kuwait was General Charles Horner, USAF, who as CENTAF, organised, and was responsible for the operation of Allied aircraft, involving over 103,000 sorties in all. To him, almost a back-room General, and his staff, should go much of the kudos for success. Also coupled with General Horner, should be scores of other 'desk' Generals and Colonels, not known to the public, and therefore unsung outside their own Department or Branch, who so successfully organised the 'Commissariat for War'.

The Human Shield

A major factor in this saga, now deliberately played down, and sometimes even omitted when the Gulf War is discussed, especially by the USA, was the Human Shield phase, when Saddam Hussein held a number of foreign nationals hostage, many at, or near, potential Allied military targets, in Kuwait and Iraq, as a deterent against Allied attack. He was eventually persuaded to release these hostages, as being counter-productive, and a number of prominent personalities now claim some of the credit for persuading the Iraqi President to take this decision as a gesture of good faith. At that time Saddam Hussein did not think the USA had either the will or confidence to attack him and so, shrewd as he was in many ways, he fell into Bush's trap. Saddam Hussein chose to gamble, and his gamble failed.

Had Saddam Hussein retained his Human Shield it is probable that the Kuwait Crisis would have developed on the lines of the one that began in November 1979 in Iran, when American hostages were seized in the US Embassy in Tehran, and some of them held for 444 days. The President of the leading Super Power in the world was unable to do anything positive to obtain their release. If a similar situation had obtained in the Kuwait Crisis it is probable the Allied Coalition would not have held together under the strain for any length of time, and so the course of history would have changed. It is extremely unlikely that President Bush would have deliberately bombed Iraqi military targets if it would have endangered the lives of American citizens. It was Bush's lucky break, enabling him to go ahead untrammelled with the military option. The long-running 'hostage situation' in Lebanon was an indication of the value placed on the lives of their nationals by Western governments, and the kidnappers' realisation of this fact. They noted what had happened in the Kuwait Crisis and capitalised on it.

Victory

Victory can have several facets that reflect different views. The Allies claimed a glorious victory, but then later, so did Saddam Hussein. To the Allies victory meant they had driven the Iraqi invaders out from Kuwait, and complied with a UN Resolution. But it was not a complete victory to them, such as that in World War II, as the Hidden Agenda had not been accomplished. The positive side of victory for the USA was that its Armed Forces gained both self-respect and the respect of the American people. It was also a victory for American 'high-tech' weaponry, and 100,000 tons of HE munitions. The facet of victory for Saddam Hussein was that he still retained sovereign power in Iraq.

The Liberation of Kuwait will hardly qualify for a place of honour in the Roll of Great Battles, as there was little or no military opposition, and it was much too one-sided to be deemed an epic struggle. The harsh reality is that it may be remembered in future as probably the greatest 'high-tech' slaughter of the Century, exceeding that of World War II. Historians may perhaps regard it as a footnote in military history in which a 'high-tech' sledge-hammer was used to eliminate a small, inconvenient nut; or it may be seen as a heavy-handed police operation to further the cause of Pax Americana.

One American columnist (*Robert Reno, Newsday:* 8th August) wrote "I still don't get the point of what history will surely record as a wretched little high-tech police action comparable say, with Third Century struggles that accompanied the Christianisation of the Bohemian Lake tribes". Perhaps this conflict will find an historical niche somewhere in between these extremes.

Casualties

In this Liberation campaign Allied casualties were very small in number, and those of the Iraqis extremely heavy. After a series of re-assessments government figures showed that the USA had lost 266 dead, of whom 145 had been killed in action and 121 in accidents, while the British lost 24 killed in action, and the French six. At its maximum, the US military contingent numbered about 541,000, the British about 45,000 and the French about 12,000, so the ratio was extremely favourable and satisfactory. Arab States have always been reluctant to publish their own casualty lists, and this war was no exception. It is believed the Saudis lost about 38 dead, and the Egyptians about nine. It is known that other GCC States lost men in battle, but no figures are available.

The long-running mystery of the Gulf War is how many Iraqi casualties were incurred. No one seems to know, even to a few thousand, and guesstimates are all that are available. The notional figure of '100,000 dead' was the current rumour for some time. When General Schwartzkopf was asked this question (*Wall Street Journal:* 22nd March), he replied "We don't have any figure on this". That was the official line. Throughout, CENTCOM would not comment, nor would it be drawn into speculation on the Iraqi casualty issue. It seems almost as if there were a deliberate plot to keep such information from the American people, in case they learned that the war had not been as clinical as they had been led to believe.

One of the first American official statements on this issue came from the DoD, on the 22nd May, which estimated that Iraqi casualties "could number about 100,000 dead", but added this figure could be 50% out either way. By this reckoning the figure of 150,000 Iraqis could be acceptable. On the 29th, *Greenpeace* produced the first non-official comprehensive survey of the Gulf War, estimating that 100,000-120,000 Iraqi troops had been killed, and 5,000-15,000 civilians; and that 2,000-5,000 Kuwaitis had also been killed, or had died as a result of the war, or the occupation. Very much a rough rule-of-thumb calculation within very wide brackets, but all numbers quoted were very large ones nevertheless.

As late as August, the ICRC was complaining that so far it had only been able to trace a 'few hundred' Iraqi military dead, and that no details had been received of locations of mass graves. It seems that CENTCOM had forbidden such information to be passed on. Only a few lone voices continued to attempt to penetrate this wall of official silence, and it seemed as though the British, and other Westerners, were more concerned about the loss of 'wild life' and ecological damage done due to Iraqi release of oil that formed the huge oil slick in the Gulf, than to Iraqi 'collateral damage'.

The Air War

Using new concepts and weaponry, the Allied air war was undoubtedly the military technological wonder of the age, causing re-appraisals in air forces all over the world. Its main message was the dominance of high-flying Stealth aircraft with stand-off, precision laser-guided missiles and bombs, that overshadowed conventional aircraft with free-fall munitions. Despite little or no Iraqi opposition the air war did drag on for 38 days without achieving the desired result, which was to crush Iraqi national resistance completely.

Some advocated the air war should have continued longer, until it was proven that wars could be won by air power alone, and some Western commentators began to enthuse that Western air power could win a war anywhere in the world. Whether this could have been accomplished in the Gulf, and how soon, is a matter of conjecture, but certainly the Iraqis were nearing the end of their tether. In any case, President Bush's patience was running out, so this theory was not tested to its full extent.

The Pentagon made certain miscalculations, one being to anticipate a gigantic air battle, in which the Iraqi air force would be destroyed, after which attention could be given to smothering ground-based air defences, and then destroying power stations, and other sinews of war. Saddam Hussein chose not to send his air force into a suicidal battle, but it remained an Allied background worry for some time. Another miscalculation was the unexpected durability and fortitude of both the Iraqi army and people, bereft of air cover, under the continuous Allied aerial onslaught.

As the bulk of Iraqi aircraft and defence material were of Soviet manufacture, the outcome of the war affected the reputation of Soviet arms, causing anxiety within the top military leadership. Soviet strategy generally came into doubt. Later, Marshal Dimitri Yazov, then Soviet Minister of Defence, admitted that "the Soviet air defence system in Iraq had failed in most cases", adding that a "review is necessary of our attitude to our country's entire defence system" (*Krasnaya Zvezda* [Red

Star]). Soviet military planners, who had long believed their ground forces would influence any NATO-Warsaw Pact military clash, became alarmed by the new NATO Air-Land Battle strategy, designed to defeat numerically stronger forces, especially ground ones, which had been partly put into practice so successfully in the Gulf War.

Perhaps the Soviets were unduly passimistic as there had been no initial air battle, and no real test of aerial superiority between opposing aircraft, such as the US F-15 against the Soviet MiG-29, the latter being somewhat apprehensively regarded by Allied pilots. Even so the Americans claimed, seemingly without real evidence, their F-15 had exceeded their hopes and expectations.

The Tornado F-3 air defence fighter had a disappointing war, as although it flew patrols no enemy aircraft were encountered, its agility as a top superiority fighter aircraft being questioned. The Tornado GR-1 low-level bomber, performed well, but was unlucky as six were lost, but only one on a low-flying bombing mission. Later, it was stated (*Alan Clark, House of Commons*: October 1991) that three of the RAF's Tornado GR-1s were shot down by surface-to-air missiles, and one was lost due to a premature explosion of its munitions.

The causes of the other two losses were not known precisely as their crash-sites were in Iraq, and still inaccessible to inspection teams. It was said there was no common thread in the Tornado GR-1 losses, but it was confirmed the RAF was searching for a new stand-off delivery, laser-guided missile. The RAF also admitted it had been a mistake not to send Buccaneers, which had laser-guidance systems, out to the Gulf area sooner, and also that the ALARM anti-radar missiles had arrived 'only just in time'.

According to the British Defence Minister (Tom King), during the Gulf War the RAF flew over 4,000 combat sorties, dropping 3,000 tonnes of munitions, including 100 JP-233s, 6,000 conventional bombs, and 1,000 laser-guided ones; and fired over 100 anti-radar and over 700 air-to-ground missiles.

Tested or not in combat, the majority of Allied aircraft used in the Gulf War had been in service for some time, and their respective merits and demerits had been thoroughly discussed openly on many occasions. It seemed as though the USAF was determined that all types of its air-worthy aircraft, and USN aircraft as well, should 'have a piece of the action', motivated no doubt by pressure of having to jockey for a share of Defense allocations.

Even old B-52 heavy bombers probably flew their last active service sorties, despite their less than state-of-the-art navigational aids, and free-fall 'iron bombs'. B-52s flew thousands of miles just to spend a few brief minutes over target areas to 'carpet-bomb' them from great heights, often with less than pin-point accuracy. Only one B-52 was lost, when returning to its base at Diego Garcia, while another had to 'ditch' its bomb-load into the Mediterranean. The eight US B-52s positioned at RAF Fairford (UK), as from the 3rd February, flew 60 combat missions, dropping 1,150 bombs.

Despite Allied claims of munition capability, many of the Iraqi HAS and command bunkers proved stout enough to survive strikes by the GBU-27 laser-guided 2,000-lb bomb, carried by F-117A (Stealth), F-111s and F-15s. Increased penetration capability was called for, and the GBU-28 was hastily improvised, which was a 'needle' shaped bomb, claimed to be able to penetrate up to '100 feet of earth and up to 22 feet of concrete' (CENTCOM). Two only were dropped, by F-117A (Stealth) aircraft, flying at 20,000 feet, on the 27th February the penultimate day of the air war. One hit its target, a command bunker at Abu Ghaib, near Baghdad, destroying it, and 'killing many senior Iraqi officers' (CENTCOM), while the other missed its (unspecified) target.

In keeping with the NATO Air-Land Battle doctrine, General Horner, the Air Component Commander (CENTAF) blended his combat aircraft into Force Packages, that is a mixture of aircraft, each with differing specialities and capabilities, to counter as many enemy contingencies as possible. Despite a modification of this aerial strategy after the first few days of the air war the Allies let it appear that the Force Package concept continued until the end of hostilities, although this was not strictly so. For example, General Horner later stated that the only aircraft to bomb targets in Baghdad was the F-117A (Stealth), which being high-flying did not need escort planes, as it was out of reach of interdiction aircraft and ground-based missiles. This explained why Iraqi counter-measures seemed to be so random and aimless in Baghdad. A journalist re-visiting the scene after the Cease-Fire (John Simpson) said that only '30 buildings in Baghdad had been hit'.

General Horner explained the reason for his change of aerial strategy (ADJ: October 1991), and gave an example of a typical Force Package. It was probably composed of 'four A-6 bombers and four Saudi Tornados, escorted by four Wild Weasels, with five EA-6B radar-jammers, and 21 F-18 fighters carrying radar-homing missiles. Of these 38 aircraft, only eight dropped bombs, whereas 21 F-117s could drop bombs on 37 targets'. He also stated that 'Eight F-117s, with eight pilots could achieve the same results as 75 non-Stealth aircraft, with over 100 air crew'.

General Horner also stated that "Stealth aircraft enabled us to gain surprise every day of the war", and that on "Day One, F-117s flew against more than 30% of the targets. They also flew about 2% of the combat sorties of the war, blasting 30% of the strategic air campaign's target base, and only represented 2.5% of my assets".

Peace-time assessments did not always materialise as predicted, and for example, the AH-64 Apache helicopter, reputed to have a poor trials record, with its TADS capability and Hellfire laser-guided missiles, proved to be competent, and could operate adequately in both darkness and bad weather.

The circumstances of the 'flight of Iraqi aircraft', to Iran remains uncertain and controversial, and debate still falters over whether it was impromptu, a mass mutinous movement, or a shrewd plan. It was probably a forced opportunistic combination of all three, dominated by the Iraqi leader's determination to save some of his best aircraft if he could, for use after the war was over. One authority *(IISS)* stated that '115 aircraft were flown to Iran', which together with the probable 35 shot down by the Allies, only accounts for about one-third of what was thought to be Iraq's inventory. This must indicate that he still possesses about 350 combat aircraft, mostly surviving in HAS. Moreover, Iraq's fleet of some 350 military helicopters seemed to have survived virtually intact, having been widely dispersed and well camouflaged. The Iraqi problem in this respect suddenly became one of lack of spares. Common gossip has it that the Iraqi planes have all been absorbed into the Iranian air force.

Since, Iraqi pilots involved in the 'flight' (Iranian sources) have stated that as the Allies had destroyed Iraq's refining capacity, aircraft fuel was no longer available, and so offensive, or even defensive, aerial action was out of the question. Aircraft became ground targets. As it was anticipated victorious Allies would automatically seize all Iraqi aircraft, flight to Iran, fuel permitting, became a possible alternative option. Some Iraqi pilots said they sat in their cockpits for hours waiting to be given the take-off signal that the sky in the vicinity, and along the proposed flight-path, was clear of Allied combat aircraft. They insisted it was not inexperience that caused pilots to crash-land in Iran but simply shortage of fuel.

The SCUD Factor

The SCUD factor in the Gulf War was played down by the Allies, and also by Israel, to disguise the fact that the elderly, rather inaccurate, short-range Soviet ballistic missile, dismissed so curtly by General Schwartzkopf as being of no strategic and little tactical importance, caused significant apprehension as it could reach over land borders. It seemed to nullify the Israeli demand for 'secure land frontiers', and indirectly helped to force the Israelis to the Madrid Conference table. Had the Patriot, with its uncertain development record, not been available at the critical moment, or its effectiveness been less successful, the Gulf War may have taken another twist, as Israel may have forced itself into the conflict to the detriment of the Allied Coalition. The Allies dreaded SCUDs, not so much for their small conventional HE warheads, but because they could carry CW ones, a fear that did not materialise, but was later shown to be no idle threat.

The SCUD factor produced a demand by Middle East States for this weapon, and more of them if they already had a few, or better still similar missiles with ranges of up to 500 miles or more. Short-range ballistic missiles have come to be regarded as an essential mutual deterrent. Syria was quick off the mark, and it is believed that both China and North Korea began taking orders for this type of weaponry, which simply quickened the Middle East arms race.

Later, perhaps as a propaganda slight the Israelis (AFP) despite initial praise of the US Patriots, complained ungratefully, they 'were less accurate and effective than Washington had led them to believe'. The SCUD factor caused certain countries to concentrate upon developing anti-missile missile systems as a defence against such weapons. On the 15th August, the Israelis test-fired their new 'Barak-1' ship-launched anti-missile missile, having a reputed range of '11-kms carrying a 5-kg warhead'. The Israelis also continued work on the US-funded 'Arrow' project, which had reportedly been test-fired.

During the Kuwait Crisis and the Gulf War the Saudis kept a low profile regarding their own CSS-2 ballistic missiles, and did not even hint they might use them as a last resort, relying implicitly on the USA to thwart Saddam Hussein's ambitious southward glances.

The Ground War

The Allied ground offensive in the last '100 hours', gave little opportunity of assessing the merits and demerits of respective Western and Soviet weaponry, as with only few exceptions, the Iraqis did not fight back. There were, for example, no tank clashes, when it would have been seen whether the US Abrams and British Challenger tanks were superior in battle to the Soviet T-64s and T-72s, or not. Most destroyed or damaged Iraqi tanks had been hit by 'tank-killing' aircraft, such as the A-10, and Apache helicopters, armed with Hellfire missiles.

Consequently, claims by Allied advancing armoured formations have to be accepted with some reservation, and it was later admitted by the Pentagon that many more Iraqi tanks may have survived than initially estimated by CENTCOM. Allied ground forces contented themselves generally with 'speed of movement and reliability' claims. For example (ADJ) it was claimed that throughout the '100 hours, US Abrams succeeded in maintaining a 90% efficiency standard', and that on one night-move, more than 300 tanks of the US 3rd Armored Division 'covered 120 miles without a single break-down'. Praise was lavished on Bradley M-2s and M-3s, and on the effect the Hellfire anti-tank missiles had on enemy armour.

General Schwartzkopf had already stated at a CENTCOM press briefing that during the '100 hours' his armoured troops had moved 200 miles, when some of his Bradley M-2s and M-3s had recorded speeds of just under 50 mph, and that his Abrams 'went even faster'. Not to be left out the British 7th Armoured Brigade claimed it had 'fought its way 189 miles across Iraqi and Kuwaiti terrain' during which it 'knocked out 200 Iraqi tanks'. None of the disabled or captured tanks were T-72s.

Tanks in combat had technical problems to contend with which were not over-emphasised in the excitement and tension of battle, perhaps for reasons of national pride. Some of these problems were appraised by a British armoured expert (General Peter Reed, *Army Quarterly:* June 1991). He compared relative aspects of American and British tanks in view of a forthcoming competition for a major commercial contract. Reed said that the Abrams only managed 60-kms between fuel fillings, compared with 200-kms for the British Challenger, and that when stationary the Abrams had to keep the engine idling, sometimes for long periods, to provide power for the gun-turret, whereas the Challenger did not need to keep its engine running in similar circumstances as its batteries were charged by a small auxiliary engine to traverse and elevate the gun.

General Reed pointed out that US armoured forces used helicopter-carried 'fuel bladders' to top-up tanks, while the British welded extra fuel-tanks on to the sides of theirs'. Abrams had to be refilled from bowsers four or five times a day, which meant that had their been fierce enemy opposition, they would have been at a distinct disadvantage. He also pointed out that Abrams were subject to more 'sand ingestion' than Challengers, and declared that the British Warrior infantry armoured vehicle compared favourably with the US Bradley M-3. A little biased perhaps, but based on fact. The British thought so highly of their Warriors, that in subsequent defence cuts, they were not only exempted, but an additional 300 were ordered.

One weapon reported to have done very well in the Gulf War was the Multiple Rocket Launcher System (MRLS), only comparatively recently adopted by American and British armies. The MRLS had been used with devastating effect by the Soviets against German Wehrmacht gun-crews in World War II, being known as 'Stalin Organs', but for decades afterwards this weapon had largely been ignored by the West. The modern MRLS, with 12 barrels, and each rocket scattering 260 bomblets, did not cause a crater, but formed a wide 'killing area'. The British 1st Armoured Division fired 2,500 MRLS rockets.

Another innovation, also long ignored by Western armed forces was the Unmanned Aerial Vehicle (UAV), previously referred to as a reconnaissance drone, or remotely-piloted vehicle. This is a small pilotless aircraft that carried small TV and film cameras and Infra-Red sensors, and could operate up to 100 miles from base control. The Israelis had used UAVs in their 1967 and 1973 wars, and the Soviets used them at Chernobyl in April 1986, to monitor the nuclear disaster site, but in Western armies they were mostly on evaluation trials.

In 1988, the US DoD established a UAV Joint Program Office to evaluate these aerial vehicles. The most commonly used was the Pioneer, of which there were several variations. Six tactical units were deployed in the Gulf War, each of five UAVs, three with the US Marine Corps, two with the US Navy, and one with the Army *(ADJ)*. The British and French also evaluated several types of UAVs. All were used for reconnaissance purposes, and none carried munitions.

In all the Americans operated some 35 'Pioneer' UAVs, some also from the *USS Wisconsin*, which flew at heights between 3,000 and 7,000 feet, and carried out '523 missions, logging 1,559 hours flight', relaying information back to base. Only one was shot down. The Iraqis called them 'buzzards'. British UAVs, including Pioneers and the Canadian CL-89, flew over 500 missions, while the French operated the 'Mart' (a joint Anglo-French product) UAV. (Source — 9th International Conference of RPVs: Bristol [UK], in September 1991.)

Chemical Warfare

One of the main fears of Allied troops was that Saddam Hussein might unleash CW against them, but this did not happen, and some wondered why, especially as it was later revealed that he had ample CW means available, and his threat was not an empty one. The answer seems to be that Saddam Hussein was afraid of massive Allied retaliation in kind. One source, Major Johan Persson, a liaison officer with a Swedish military hospital (*Daily Telegraph*: 29th November 1991), claimed to have seen a 200-page official Allied document, outlining the Allied plan for a CW counter-offensive, which had been issued to American and certain other formations, including the British 1st Armoured Division. It was reluctantly confirmed by the Pentagon that the Allies, meaning the Americans, had both nuclear and CW weapons with them in the Gulf, ready for use if necessary, and this intention was passed on to the Iraqis.

Friendly Fire

Another unspoken fear was that of 'Friendly Fire'. In the heat and confusion of battle occasionally by mistake, miscalculation or mis-identification, troops are killed and wounded by their own side. This has been a battle hazard since firearms were invented, and before that probably mis-directed arrows hit their own soldiers sometimes. This has always been a very sensitive subject, seldom spoken about openly, or even admitted, and invariably when it happened, one suspects was usually covered up to preserve military morale and prestige.

One of the first open admissions of this subject in recent times was revealed by the Israelis (*Jerusalem Post*) that during their invasion of Southern Lebanon in 1982, 'one in five (Israeli) casualties were caused by their own fire'.

The US Freedom of Information Act forced a reluctant and belated DoD admission that 'in 28 identifiable incidents, 35 US service personnel were killed and 72 wounded by Friendly Fire', and that most of these casualties had occurred in armoured vehicles. The British admitted to losing nine soldiers from the same cause, but other national military contingents have not been so open and frank — but it can happen in any army in battle, and does: it is one of the black curses of war.

In the Gulf conflict, as was customary, different coloured cloth panels were placed on tops of vehicles and distinguishing signs painted on to prominent parts of the vehicle-body, to enable it to be easily and quickly identified from the air. Vehicle crews were responsible for ensuring their own recognition signs were in place and visible from above, but sometimes they became obscured by sand, dust or mud.

Special Forces

It is claimed that Special Forces, especially American and British, covertly played a significant role in the Gulf War, but exactly what they did, and what value it really was, we are not allowed to know, but only invited to speculate with a nod-and-a-wink as outrageously as may be wished, as whatever is written will be officially ignored. Secrecy may be justified on the score that Special Forces' techniques may be needed on some future battlefield, but it does seem as though authorities prefer them to be known for their legends, rather than their substance. A few more facts would give confidence and help appraisals.

It is said that US Special Forces used modified helicopters and land vehicles to take them into, and bring them out of, enemy terrain, as did British ones too, but General Schwartzkopf could only describe their activities as being "Like a Special Operations theme park". He confirmed "There were some direct missions. Period", an euphanism for assassinations. The Pentagon admitted that Special Forces teams had been 'inserted' into southern Iraq to 'lay laser-target markers on anti-aircraft radars, to take them out to create safe Allied flight-paths'.

The British were also reticent. At a social function the British Prime Minister, John Major, said that "SCUDs were destroyed by the SAS. They were fabulous", but gave no details. Neither did the Defence Minister (Tom King), when he claimed the SAS were in Kuwait and Iraq 'from the beginning', and that one of their tasks was to obtain evidence of atrocities. It seemed that some SAS personnel were in disguise, which one thinks would automatically render them, if captured, to be shot as spies. According to one authority *(Charles Allan)* SAS commandos captured on secret missions in search of SCUD missile sites 'had their finger-nails pulled out as part of a grim saga of torture'.

General Sir Peter de la Billiere, himself an SAS officer, confirmed (Lecture: *RUSI*, London) that their main achievement, apart from long-range information-gathering, was in destroying fixed SCUD missile-launchers, and missile command and control centres, but he avoided commenting upon successes or failures, mentioning that "There is still nothing to replace a good pair of eyes on the ground". One source *(Newsweek)* tells of a Joint SAS and Delta Force unit, supported by A-10 (Thunderbolt) tank-busting planes, that was dropped into western Iraq to hide by day and search for SCUD launchers by night, and that (27th February) it 'marked 26 SCUD missiles with laser-markers, and called in the A-10s, which destroyed them all in an air-strike'.

Allied Intelligence

Despite the plethora of Allied, mainly American, intelligence-gathering gadgets, the several Intelligence Agencies did not always get it right. After the war, General Schwartzkopf spoke of intelligence weakness, not always in a restrained manner. Later (June 1991), he told a Congressional Hearing that the "Intelligence provided to me was so seriously flawed, as to be almost useless", and that it was "caveated, disagreed with by footnotes, and watered down to the point of confusion". Short comings were usually put down to lack of corroborating human intelligence, in other words, lack of spies on the ground. Some intelligence assessments were unsatisfactory, and sometimes there was hesitation in sharing intelligence with Allies.

American General Leonard Perroots, a Specialist Consultant to the US Defense Intelligence Agency (DIA), later alleged (on a *BBC TV Panorama* programme: 25th March), that the Soviets had supplied the British with information about SCUDs, including the fact that they could remain 'fully-fuelled' for much longer periods than US Intelligence Agencies thought, but remarked that this did not seem to have been passed on. He spoke of lack of intelligence co-operation, and confirmed that the 'six helicopters in Iraqi colours' had been carrying American Special Forces personnel, and that 'uniformed' Saudi authorities on the ground 'jumped the gun'. The Saudi claim that they were Iraqi defectors had to be retracted publicly.

Perroots also spoke of the danger of unchecked, and out-of-date intelligence, which could affect selection of Allied targets. He said that

125

the precision-bombing of the 'Baby Milk factory' (23rd January) was a mistake, and that the attack mounted against the Almiriya air-raid shelter (13th February) 'had not been based on the most current information'.

The Allied Naval War

The main task of Allied naval forces was to enforce the economic blockade at sea against Iraq, and this was done effectively. Most of the alleged embargo-busting occurred on Iraq's northern and eastern borders. As Iraqi naval opposition was negligible, and was soon 'blown out of the water', this meant long days of dull routine, of searching ships for contraband, and watching out for mines, which consequently attracted less media attention. Allied naval units took part in bombarding land targets, using both carrier-based aircraft and launching '285' Tomahawk cruise missiles. Allied naval forces claimed to have brought down a few Iraqi planes.

One British naval authority, Captain Sharpe (Editor of *Jane's Fighting Ships*) wrote that not enough credit had been given to the British Navy, which patrolled and controlled the sea-lanes leading to Iraq and Kuwait, commenting that "European naval collaboration was pathetic . . . and only the British, Dutch and possibly the Australians, were able to work within the US Tactical Naval Command'. He deduced that "There's a long way to go in terms of multi-national co-operation". The naval scene in the Gulf was obviously very much an American dominated one.

However, British naval helicopters claim to have sunk, or disabled, 15 Iraqi patrol boats, and detected 228 mines, of which it destroyed 113, while opening the sea-lanes into Kuwait (*Preliminary lessons of Operation Granby*). Towards the end of the war, the British Navy claimed its radar capability had improved so rapidly that its Marconi Type-1022 radar was able to detect F-117A (Stealth) aircraft up to a distance of 40 miles.

On one occasion, just after the Battle for Kafji, Allied intelligence detected several small Iraqi craft hugging the coastline in inshore waters, when an Exocet MM-40 missile, fired from one of the missile boats that escaped from Kuwait ahead of the Iraqi invasion, scored a direct hit on one of them. This success surprised Allied ships in the vicinity as the 'homing heads' of the Exocet missile were particularly affected by 'ground clutter' (*ADJ*). An *Aerospatiale* spokesman claimed it was the only Exocet missile fired during the Gulf War.

Allied Morale

It was generally agreed that Allied morale during the Gulf War was consistently high throughout, which is what could be expected as a majority of the service personnel were volunteers, and enemy opposition was negligible. It was feared however, that as the Phoney War dragged on, owing to harsh living conditions and boredom, morale might deteriorate, and indeed a relief rotation scheme had been planned by the Pentagon.

Western Allied troops found themselves in a strange Muslim land, with unfamiliar customs they had to respect. There were bans on alcohol, Christian worship, Western-style entertainment and contact with Saudi women. The ban on alcohol was welcomed by Western Allied commanders as it obviated many disciplinary problems commonly associated with troops on active service; church services were carried out covertly (shades of early Christian exigencies), and although Western entertainers visited the troops to give concerts, they had to be circumspect. Friction with the Saudi people was largely avoided as Western military contingents were in remote desert areas well away from them.

One of the best kept secrets of the Gulf War was the *Princess* Cunard cruise liner (with 900 cabins), moored just off Bahrain, which was used as a facility for three-day 'Rest-and-Recreation' leave for US personnel, on board which alcohol and female company were available, and a host of American Show Bizz Stars visited to entertain the troops. Undoubtedly this was good for the morale of the fortunate few American service personnel lucky enough to be selected for R-&-R, but had this become generally known, it might have had an adverse effect on wives and folks back home. The *Princess* remained at its moorings off Bahrain until September.

The British were keen to accredit their good morale and performance to their Regimental *esprit de corps*, most being professional soldiers who served together in the same regiment or unit for years. The 'regiment' was their rallying symbol and family. This was a professional assertion, weakened somewhat by a certain amount of cross-posting of personnel to make units up to strength for active service, which seemed to make little difference to the state of morale, and simply reinforced the old military maxim that there are no bad soldiers, only bad officers.

The Media

Most people admit that a degree of media censorship is essential in a war situation no matter how much a democratic country may value its cherished free speech and free Press, but there are always arguments about how much latitude should be allowed. Afterwards there are inevitable media complaints over how censorship restrictions were implemented, particularly if the media feels it had been blatantly used by the government, or that information not strictly of sensitive military value had been kept from it. So it was after the Gulf War.

Western media was persuaded by their governments to accept Press Guidelines, which was censorship in another guise. TV teams and journalists accredited to CENTCOM had 'minders', who over-saw them, and their copy before it was dispatched, and were restricted in movement 'due to combat conditions'. Later, General Schwartzkopf openly boasted he had used the media to aid his famous Deception Plan.

Both CENTCOM and Western military establishments remained 'economical with the truth', and lent themselves to deception, the excuse being that Saddam Hussein relied upon Allied media for information about Allied intentions and activities, as his own external intelligence service hardly existed, and he had neither satellite observation nor aerial surveillance. Non-Western members of the Allied Coalition all had their own national built-in censorship as a permanent feature, and so were no problem to CENTCOM in this respect. A four-man CBS TV team that avoided its 'minder', strayed into 'No Man's Land' to be picked up by an Iraqi patrol, but were released unharmed on the 2nd March.

Strict censorship was operated inside totalitarian Iraq, where Saddam Hussein skilfully manipulated international TV teams and journalists in Baghdad throughout the Phoney War, especially during the Human Shield phase. Media personnel were controlled by 'minders', their copy was censored, and their movements severely restricted.

The major media feature of the Gulf War on the news scene was the appearance of CNN, an international news-gathering and reporting organisation. CNN was largely unknown to the British public as its news programmes were not beamed to the UK, although they were to over 70 other nations across the world. CNN did a deal with Saddam Hussein enabling its TV team to remain in Baghdad, and to use government communications, including a 'four-wire' arrangement, through Jordan, for its transmissions to be relayed direct to its HQ in Atlanta City (USA). This caused some inter-media friction, bringing accusations of collaboration with the enemy.

Allegations against CNN were answered by Ted Turner, founder of CNN (*Frost on Sunday: TV AM: 27th October*), who admitted that CNN had been used by Saddam Hussein, saying that it was an international news organisation, not interested in deep analysis and propaganda, and was above narrow nationalism, even though the USA was involved in a war. He insisted that although his TV team had been restricted in scope, it was better to have some news from a beleaguered capital, than no news at all. Turner countered allegations, pointing out that the whole of the Western media had been used by CENTCOM during the Gulf War, adding that "The USAF 'footage' taken on fighter and bomber aircraft on their bombing missions, has still to be released". He was correct: some of it probably never will.

Women at War

Some 33,000 American Servicewomen saw active service in the Gulf War, of whom eleven died, five in action, and two were taken POW. Three were killed in the SCUD strike on US barracks near Dhahran; one, a medical staffer, was killed in a minefield giving medical attention to an injured helicopter pilot; and the other died when the helicopter she was in came under enemy fire. One woman, a Doctor, attending an injured person in a helicopter crash, was captured, and the other woman POW was in a vehicle that ran into an Iraqi patrol.

A number of women served on a few USN warships in the Gulf, and adjacent waters, which seems to have been a fairly successful experiment, women having separate quarters off-duty. The main opposition came from naval wives back at base. One report, on the USS Acadia, a repair ship, which had Servicewomen aboard, stated that '36 were pregnant, 14 before they sailed and 22 when on shore leave'.

The ban on women serving on British naval craft was only lifted in February, and the only British warship with women aboard in the Gulf was HMS Brilliant, but no special problems were reported.

International Terrorism

It was anticipated by the Allies that Saddam Hussein might instigate a wave of international terrorist attacks against Western targets to undermine national resolve. A scare occurred on the 5th February, when mysterious code signals, similar to those relayed by the BBC to the French Resistance during World War II, emanated from Radio Baghdad. Western Allies waited, but international terrorism hesitated. Up to that moment some 80 acts of terrorism had occurred relating to the Gulf War situation in countries as far apart as Britain, Greece and Thailand, but all were small explosions, with no loss of life, and were regarded as impromptu opportunity exploits by local groups. On the 19th February, Saddam Hussein called upon "All free peoples to strike at the centre of American, and other Coalition interests", but this exhortation was disregarded.

The main reason why international terrorism failed to come to the aid of the Iraqi President, was lack of opportunity and support facilities. The international terrorist underground in Western Europe was more or less shattered, as was that in Eastern Europe, while there never had been one in the USA. Syria, formerly a terrorist-supporting State, since it had been 'bought' by the USA, had rounded up its terrorists suspects and dissidents and packed them into detention camps; while Gaddafi of Libya, tightened his firm grip on terrorists hiding in his country as he feared a repeat of the American attack on Tripoli in April 1986, if he stepped out of line. Generally, Western and other, vulnerable countries, aware of the potential danger from international terrorism, put out their drag-nets, deporting or detaining suspects, and taking extra precautions at airports and ports. One source (John Simpson) accredited Yasir Arafat, of the PLO, with persuading international terrorist leaders to abstain from terrorist activity, but one feels this may be too farcical to be taken seriously.

9

The On-Going Sequel

The Allied Liberation of Kuwait did not solve any problems, but was instrumental in generating more. Its sequel can be summed up briefly as an on-going one in which problems created more problems, and gave a boost to the robust arms race that was still in progress in the Middle East Region. Events in the region were overshadowed by the falling apart of central authority in the USSR, which left the USA as the dominant Super Power in the world, which made its Pax Americana complex increasingly hard to hide and deny.

When the slaughter at Mutla Ridge ceased, and comparative silence fell on that bloody battlefield, embarrassing questions began to be asked. Was it so essential to mount such a vicious air and ground assault on demoralised Iraqi units that were scurrying to quit Kuwait as quickly as they could, when General Schwartzkopf had given hedged promises not to attack them if they withdrew, provided they left their guns and tanks behind? Detractors also asked whether it had been necessary to instigate such devastating air missions, over Iraq, which was beyond the scope of UN authority, and why estimates should not be released of Iraqi civilian casualties they had caused?

Saddam Hussein still remained in power with a small core of his army, although badly battered and disorganised, remaining intact on Iraqi soil. It became increasingly apparent that the Iraqi arsenal and armament industries had not been as badly crippled as CENTCOM had so enthusiastically and confidently claimed. This prompted another question — 'What had been achieved?' A question that was hard to answer.

In view of his obvious personality clash fixation with Saddam Hussein, many were surprised by President Bush's seeming moderation in ordering a cessation of hostilities on the 28th February. In hindsight it is known that had the fighting continued for a day or so longer Allied ground forces would have soundly defeated the remnants of the Iraqi army in southern Iraq, and could easily have entered Basra, perhaps even pressing on to Baghdad itself, to demonstrate to the world who the winner really was. Allied token forces could have sheltered under the UN flag.

Instead, the Allied pause gave Saddam Hussein time to recover, to re-organise his army, and strengthen his grip on power. Bush's official explanation was that to advance into Iraq in military force would have been to exceed UN authority — but there was more to it than that. Bush would have had to carry his Allies with him, and especially would he have had to convince the whole Allied Coalition that this was the correct course to take. Also, Allied troops would have been entering a potentially very hostile country as aggressors, when lines of communications would have been vulnerable to sabotage and partisan action.

One feels that Bush must have been sorely tempted, but his military advisors, whatever they said afterwards, were at that critical moment in favour of caution. Perhaps the most significant factor, one that had been censored, was the uncertain morale of certain USAF pilots, who reputedly had expressed reluctance to continue to bomb a defeated army and a civilian population.

The Cease-Fire

From the 28th February to the 3rd March, a sort of hazy limbo hovered over the Kuwait battle areas, while Allied troops buried Iraqi dead, usually in mass graves, sometimes it seems without properly recording names of individuals, and herded Iraqi POWs and refugees. Such Iraqi military personnel as could, scrambled back to their own country. On the 3rd, General Schwartzkopf led a team of senior Allied officers to meet a team of Iraqi ones, led by General Hussein Rashid, to discuss a cease-fire. As the victorious General, Schwartzkopf emphasised that all UN conditions must be rigidly observed, especially those pertaining to the destruction of all Iraqi weapons of mass destruction. These discussions did not produce any positive result, so it was merely agreed that for the moment the *de facto* cease-fire should continue.

At this stage it should be emphasised that the US Administration thought it would be only days, or even hours, before Saddam Hussein would be deposed by a military junta, so there was little point in prolonging discussion with the Iraqi team, that soon, it was hoped, would have a new master, when serious business could commence. By the 3rd March, anti-Saddam Hussein disturbances were developing in Basra.

In fact, cease-fire details took some time to hammer out, during which period Saddam Hussein not only survived in power, but successfully crushed both a Shia and a Kurdish insurrection. On the 15th March, President Bush and the British Prime Minister, John Major, met at the

Bermuda Summit. Both were disturbed about the way things were progressing in Iraq, and wondered whether or not to step in and give military aid to the southern Shias. This did not happen as it was thought that a threatening military demonstration might be sufficient to bring Saddam Hussein to heel, and two US divisions (the 3rd Cavalry and the 101st Mechanised) were ordered to advance some 30 miles or so into Iraqi territory, and re-occupy positions they had previously briefly held along the line of the southern watershed of the River Euphrates, near the towns of Samawa, Nasiriya and Suk ask-Shuykh.

On the 1st April, there were still 277,000 US troops (CENTCOM) deployed on Iraqi territory, covering a 250-mile 'front'. Iraqi troops were supposed to remain north of this 'front', and on the 2nd, CENTCOM complained they had approached within 1,000 yards of it in the Umm Qasr area. It was not until the 3rd April, after a week of intensive American lobbying at the UN, that the Security Council approved Resolution 687, based on an American draft, which covered a formal cease-fire. This was accepted on the 6th, by the Iraqi representative at the UN (Abdul al-Anbari).

UNIKOM

UN Security Council Resolution 689, of the 9th April (approved on the 11th) created a De-Militarised Zone (DMZ) between Kuwait and Iraq, extending '10-kms into Iraq and 5-kms into Kuwait'. It authorised the deployment of the 1,140-member (later increased to 1,500) UN Iraqi-Kuwait Observation Mission (UNIKOM), for which all five Permanent Members of the Security Council were to provide military personnel. UNIKOM, which was to have 300 unarmed military Observers, as well as engineers and infantry, with fixed wing aircraft and helicopters, was to patrol the 120-mile length of the DMZ, and also to monitor the Khor Abdullah channel. Commanded by an Austrian General (Gunther Greindl), UNIKOM was in position by the end of April. UNIKOM evolved to have about 400 personnel, including 300 Observers from 33 countries (IISS).

US troops established two camps for refugees (run by the US 404th Civil Affairs Company), one near the border town of Safwan, and the other at Abdali, to which flocked hordes of refugees, including Iraqi Shias and other anti-Saddam Hussein individuals, hoping for American protection. By the end of March it was claimed these two camps had already fed over 40,000 refugees which included Iraqi POWs who did not wish to return home again.

As US troops thinned out from the DMZ prior to evacuation from Kuwait, many refugees were transferred to a Saudi camp at Rafha. The Safwan refugee camp was closed on the 6th May, after an airlift of '8,371' refugees had been transferred to Rafha. About 6,000 refugees, being some 2,000 Iraqis and 4,000 Bidoun, remained in the Abdali camp. The last British troops pulled out from Kuwait in July, and American ones in September.

POWs

Unfortunately as seems inevitable in Middle East conflicts, POWs fared badly, and exchanges dragged haltingly and painfully on. In early March, the ICRC stated the Allies held at least 63,000 POWs, of whom it had already registered over 50,000; but numbers were uncertain. The Allies estimated that Iraq continued to hold over 8,000 Kuwait POWs, including some senior officers, but the Kuwaiti representative at the UN (Mohammed Abdul Hassan), insisted the number was '8,600 Kuwaiti POWs, and 22,000 civilians'. General Schwartzkopf put the number of Kuwaitis in Iraqi hands as being 'about 40,000'. Arguments continued over numbers of POWs and civilians held by respective sides. The British had taken about 8,000 POWs, and the French about 3,000.

During the first week in March, 44 Allied POWs, mainly Westerners, were handed over by Iraq, and later (in August) the Allies released news that Allied POWs had been ill-treated in captivity, and some tortured (*Charles Allen*). On the 11th March, Iraqis refused to accept a batch of 500 Iraqi POWs, owing to lack of transport to collect them, asking for assistance with vehicle fuel for this purpose. Later, on the 26th July, when taxed with delays in POW exchanges, Iraq stated it was prepared to hand over all its Kuwaiti POWs to the ICRC, but was still waiting for positive responses. It came to be accepted the Iraqis were still holding back about 2,000 Kuwaiti civilians.

Kuwait

Back in Kuwait City, when Allied guns fell silent, a short period of anarchy ensued as Kuwaiti vigilantes appeared and roamed the streets unhindered by Allied armed forces which were reluctant to interfere with Kuwaiti 'internal politics', searching, arresting and generally wreaking vengeance on suspected collaborators, and occasionally killing their victims. Kuwaiti vigilante wrath fell on Palestinians and the unfortunate Bidoun. It is suspected that many old scores were paid off in this brief rampage.

Suddenly, the Palestinians were the 'baddies', it being alleged their community (still thought to be some 250,000 strong) had been infiltrated by members of the Arab Liberation Front (ALF) and the Palestinian

Liberation Front (PLF), both supported by the Baghdad government, to implant pro-Iraqi sympathies. In any case Arafat had openly sided with Saddam Hussein, and was accordingly seen as a major Kuwaiti enemy. A Kuwaiti brigade had been allowed to enter Kuwait City with Allied troops and was at large, but its activities were uncertain, except that it is known it detained many suspected collaborators.

Those who had dismally forecast that if it came to the military option there would be little left of Kuwait City standing to liberate, had not been entirely accurate. It had been deliberately spared from Allied bombing, and most of the damage had been done by departing Iraqis. It is true that Kuwait City presented a picture of a devastated, looted and sacked city, but structural damage to major buildings, many of concrete construction, was less than anticipated. Sewerage and desalination works had been deliberately wrecked, as had generating capacity, but inhabitants had been able to exist at a primitive level, some faring better than others, allegedly due to collaboration with Iraqi occupiers. Allied troops made a start at clearing roads and demarcating minefields, searching buildings for booby-traps, and restoring water, electricity and sewerage services.

A heavy pall of toxic smog and smoke hung over Kuwait City, and the Allies made preliminary attempts to assess the number of oil-wells that were ablaze, or pouring out volumes of thick black smoke, and to figure out how this gigantic problem should be tackled.

Stunned and sunk into inertia the Kuwaiti government-in-exile seemed at a loss as to what to do, and its hesitation to quickly re-enter Kuwait City, led to allegations that it was waiting for the Allies to restore order, and for all the anti-Sabah family undesirables to be detained, before it was considered to be safe for the Emir, his government and his entourage to return to his domain. Eventually, on the 4th March, Crown Prince Sheikh Saad al-Sabah, in a long motorcade of black bullet-proof limousines, with outriders and a strong military escort, arrived in Kuwait City.

The Crown Prince, appointed Military Governor by the absent Emir, imposed a night curfew on the 5th, and decreed Martial Law. His actions brought some amelioration of the anarchy, and a degree of stability began to return to the city, although it is believed that 'Death Squads' continued to operate at night, some allegedly with the cognisance of the al-Sabah regime. It was not until the 18th May, that all Kuwaiti citizens were ordered to hand in all unauthorised weapons in their possession. The USA was later criticised for turning a blind eye to the activities of the Death Squads, especially when mass graves of many killed after the Liberation were discovered.

The absence of the Emir and his seeming reluctance to hurry back to Kuwait was commented upon unfavourably. His spokesman explained the delay was due to the fact that the Royal Palace in Kuwait City was not yet ready for occupation and that it would be unfitting to his style and dignity to return until it was made habitable. Hostile critics commented that he seemed to be waiting for 'gold taps to be fitted in his bathroom'. The thought of returning immediately to share the discomfort of his subjects did not seem to occur to him.

Belatedly, due to pressure from barely concealed Western media hostility, on the 14th March, the Emir, and his retinue, also in a long motorcade of black bullet-proof limousines, with outriders and military escort, returned to Kuwait City. The Emir disappeared behind the doors of his Royal Palace, where he remained for quite a while.

Other Kuwaiti exiles were also slow to return, although many were officially discouraged from doing so until adequate supplies of water and electricity were available, and it was not until May, they began to return in number. By this time there was a small outflow from Kuwait City, ostensibly for health reasons, due to the heavy pall of toxic smoke that hovered over the country from burning oil wells.

Rumours of continued mass arrests and ill-treatment of prisoners in Kuwait attracted the attention of *Amnesty International*, which sent a fact-finding mission. It reported that over 2,000 alleged collaborators, largely Palestinian, and some Iraqis, were detained, and that some 700 of them were to be arraigned for trial before Special Courts. *Amnesty International* confirmed ill-treatment of prisoners, and some instances of torture. These Special Courts awarded arbitrary sentences, including the death penalty. Later, due to American pressure, death sentences on 20 accused, including three women, were commuted.

Mass deportations were made of Palestinians, supplemented by many leaving voluntarily due either to being unable to obtain employment or being alienated by the general attitude of reprobation against them. The Palestinian community in Kuwait soon sank to the 150,000 mark, and in the following months dropped still further to about 75,000. Asian workers were brought in to fill jobs vacated by Palestinians.

It was not long before discontented muttering was heard in the Diwaniyas, and more generally too. The first surprise act of dissidence (to the Emir) came from a group of senior military officers, who presented a petition requesting the removal of both Sheikh Nawaf al-Sabah, the Defence Minister, and Sheikh Salim al-Sabah, the Interior Minister, for failing to remain at their posts when the Iraqis had invaded Kuwait.

Discontent materialised on the 1st April, in an 'opposition' rally in Kuwait City, demanding the restoration of the National Assembly. The Emir replied on the 7th, making his first public speech since his return, announcing that there would be elections for the General Assembly — but not until October 1992. The Emir was clearly playing for time, but as an interim measure he said he would permit elections for 50 seats open to citizens on the suspended Kuwaiti Advisory National Council, formed at the eleventh hour before the Iraqi invasion; the other 25 members were nominated by the Emir. Elections were held, but were boycotted by what had come to be called the 'Pro-Democracy Movement'.

By this time the attitude of the Emir, and his delay in instituting democratic reforms, was causing some concern in the USA. On the 14th June, in answer to a Senatorial question of "What did we win in Kuwait?", Secretary James Baker admitted that "Kuwait does not have the optimum type of regime". This was the first overt American criticism of the Emir of Kuwait.

Meanwhile, international oil fire-fighting teams had been brought in to Kuwait to douse fires and cap oil wells. Despite initial Kuwaiti lethargy, tactfully referred to by Americans as 'bureaucracy', progress was made. American fire-fighters included the famous Texan, Red Adair, who also came up against Kuwait lethargy, and at a US Congressional Hearing (in June) he criticised Kuwait's handling of its oil disaster, and its government's "Mickey Mouse" approach to the problem.

At first it had been thought the whole task might take up to three years, but as work progressed, and more international oil fire-fighting teams were brought in, and as experience was gained, the speed of progress increased, and all '640 burning oil wells' were doused by early November (*Daily Telegraph*, 1st October 1991). On the 6th of that month, the Emir solemnly 'threw a switch' to ceremoniously quench the 'last blazing oil well' in Kuwait (which had to be specially re-kindled for the purpose). The Kuwaiti government estimated the total war damage to its oil industry to be over $75-billion.

By this time the Kuwait oil industry was picking up again, and producing some 13,000 bpd (excluding the 165,000 bpd, being its share from the Neutral Zone). It was however, admitted that 'over 240 oil-lakes, holding more than 25-million barrels', had still to be cleared, and that most of the oil wells themselves had still to be restored into working order. It was forecast that full oil productivity, of up to 1.5-million bpd, would be reached by the end of 1992.

In the meantime, despite its vast invested wealth, Kuwait experienced a cash-flow and an oil-income flow problems, and had to resort to large scale borrowing. On the 3rd June, Kuwait asked GCC States for a 'loan of some oil', but this request was rejected on the ground they did not 'have any to spare'. Arab fraternal feelings seemed to be weak. On the 9th, King Fahd, of Saudi Arabia, visited Kuwait, and congratulated the Emir on his "wise policy of reconstruction" — but still did not lend him any oil.

Kuwait exported, on the 25th July, its first consignment of crude oil since the Iraqi invasion, by which time it was already pumping some 115,000 bpd, which again excluded its share from the Neutral Zone. Refining at one of Kuwait's three oil refineries, began on the 27th August, which removed the need to import vehicle fuel and other refined products.

The Damascus Declaration

Foreign Ministers of Egypt, Syria and the six GCC States, met in Damascus on the 5th-6th March, and made what became known as the 'Damascus Declaration'. This called for a Joint Arab Defence Force to maintain security in the Gulf, to consist mainly of Egyptian and Syrian troops, that would 'guarantee the security and peace of Arab countries in the Gulf Region', in return for which GCC States would pay Egypt and Syria a reputed $15-billion. The envisaged strength of the Joint Arab Defence Force was to be about 150,000 troops, of which Egypt would provide about 100,000. Its purpose was to be a buffer between Kuwait and Iraq.

Iran, a major, non-Arab Gulf State, objected to this, not welcoming the intrusion of 'outsiders' (meaning Egypt and Syria) in Gulf affairs. Israel was not in favour either, but said it would not oppose if it were part of wider negotiations. The cautious Israeli attitude was summed up by an Israeli comment that an "eight-plus-one" (meaning the eight Arab States and Israel) could suddenly become "eight-against-one".

As it mistrusted the leaders of both Egypt and Syria, Kuwait was not happy with the Damascus Declaration, and was reluctant to entrust its national security into their hands, but did not directly oppose it, as the Americans thought it was a good idea. The Emir really wanted the USA to be his guarantor, but the US Administration was coy and reluctant to position armed forces in the Middle East on a permanent basis, as Western troops on Arab soil would be seen as aggressors, would also be a catalyst for destabilisation, and would provide fuel for anti-Western propaganda. The Emir had already invited Western Allies to provide a defensive force for Kuwait, but the British had refused point-blank, the French were non-committal, and the Americans said they were unwilling.

President Bush thought it was sufficient that CENTCOM, in any emergency, could quickly project military force into the Gulf area from adjacent bases, such as Incirlik, in Turkey. General Schwartzkopf stated (on the 24th) that there was no intention to retain a permanent American military base in the Gulf, but did favour a 'staff facility' in Bahrain, for a 'few hundred staff officers'. The Saudis supported this, which would mean that Western 'infidel' troops would not be on sacred Saudi soil. This suggestion stalled, as did suggestions for such a facility to be positioned on Bubiyan Island, or in Oman or Qatar.

Discussions on the Joint Arab Defence Force tailed off, and on the 8th May, President Mubarak of Egypt, stated he would withdraw his remaining troops from Kuwait and Saudi Arabia, already down to some 38,000. The Syrians had already withdrawn their contingent. Optimism was giving way to scepticism, tribal isolation and inertia, as Arab Gulf Rulers seemed to be content to remain under the assumed, but undefined, protection of the American *Desert Shield* attitude.

Following the somewhat contrary Kuwaiti statement that the USA would not be granted permission to have a permanent military base in Kuwait, the government formally invited Egypt to station troops in the Emirate. This re-aroused Mubarak's interest and he agreed (on the 2nd July) in principle, but negotiations dragged on, there being arguments over the size of the proposed military contingent, and its cost.

A feeling the Allies were tending to lose interest in the defence of Kuwait, probably caused the Kuwaiti government to over-emphasise an incident that occurred on the 28th August, when it was claimed that an Iraqi invasion force had landed on Bubiyan Island, and was confronted by Kuwaiti Coastguards, when '46 Iraqi soldiers in disguise were detained, and more than 30 others escaped'. A protest was made to the UN, and a UN team was sent to investigate, which questioned the individuals captured, but could find no evidence of an Iraqi military landing, and formed the opinion that they were a group of civilians intent on salvaging abandoned Iraqi equipment and blankets for commercial reasons. The Kuwaiti motive for exaggeration was made to try to prove that Iraq was still dangerous, and that Kuwaiti defence should be given a higher American priority.

Secretary James Baker persisted, and eventually a Ten-Year USA-Kuwait Defence Agreement, was signed on the 19th September, which provided for the Americans to stock-pile weapons and munitions in Kuwait, the use by US armed forces of Kuwaiti ports and other facilities, and for Joint US-Kuwaiti defence exercises. Baker had wanted more than this, hoping to tie the other GCC States into the agreement, which of course implanted a firm American military footprint on Kuwait, and torpedoed the Damascus Declaration. The first Joint US-Kuwait military exercise was held in November. Somewhat predictably Baker had stated "In no way does this open the door for permanent military bases in Kuwait" (Washington Post).

Egypt

Having been snubbed by the Kuwaitis, and indirectly by the Americans, President Mubarak was not in a happy frame of mind. He was also concerned about the appearance of non-Arab involvement in Arab Gulf affairs, by an excess of American pandering to Turkey, and by French overtures to Iran. Unswerving in his support for the USA in the Kuwait Crisis and Gulf War, Mubarak was disappointed by the size of his reward. His aim was to make Egypt the dominant country in the Middle East, and he had already made a prestige gain by persuading the Arab League to return to its old HQ in Cairo.

Mubarak complained that wayward Syria, back in the Arab fold again, had been given financial aid by the Allies, while Egypt had merely had a few international debts written off. This was partly true as the 'Paris Club' (of 17 industrial nations) agreed to cancel more Egyptian debts, but this belated act only reduced the total amount owing (some $50-billion) by about half. However, the USA had promised Egypt a $1.6-billion arms package, which included another 46 F-16 combat aircraft (to add to the 100 previously delivered), 80 Maverick missiles, and 1,500 bombs, that included 48 'smart' and 240 cluster ones. President Bush prodded a reluctant IMF into lending Egypt $372-million to enable it to carry out an 18-month economic reform plan.

Syria

Western Allies were reluctant to fully accept Syria as a 'reformed' Ally, in view of its former record as a Soviet satellite state, and its reputation for supporting international terrorism, but had gone cautiously along with James Baker, who had tempted Syria into the Allied Coalition by financial offers. Syria was a confrontation state, and was regarded with extreme hostility by Israel. On the 11th March, Syria was openly praised for its support by Secretary James Baker, and some Western nations that had broken off diplomatic relations with that country, slowly resumed them again. The Western attitude towards Syria remained suspicious and cautious. It was not until the 11th July, that Britain was persuaded to drop its opposition to EC arms sales to that country.

Syria had been at loggerheads with most Arab League States, especially Egypt, for some years. It had been the only Arab country to support Iran in the Iran-Iraq War, and had differences with Turkey over the distribution of water resources. Turkey suspected that Syria was supporting and training Turkish Kurdish 'rebels', some of whom were reported to be in camps in the Bekaa Valley, in Lebanon. Syria was in military occupation of some two-thirds of Lebanon, the Bekaa Valley being a sort of No Man's Land, which had become a sanctuary for dissident and terrorist groups of various affiliations. The Syrian fear was that Turkey might be provoked into sending a military force into Lebanon, to eliminate the Turkish Kurdish dissident camps, and perhaps remain in occupation.

The Allies were startled to learn that during the second week in March, the one in which Baker had praised Syria, it had reportedly received 24 SCUD-Bs, with 20 mobile launchers, from North Korea, paid for reputedly with Saudi cash. This also caused Americans to look sideways at the Saudis, but nothing was said. A little later it was thought that Syria ordered more SCUD-Bs and some SCUD-Cs from both China and North Korea, and was also negotiating with China for a number of M-9s (reputed range of 600-kms). This alarmed both the USA and Israel, but little could be done about it. To censure Syria might mean alienating that country, and Baker reasoned it was better to have Syria within the Allied Coalition than outside it; while to censure Saudi Arabia was out of the question.

US Arms Policy Review

Startled by the volume of arms flowing into the Middle East region, especially from free-trading China and North Korea, President Bush ordered an 'Arms Policy Review' by which he hoped to gather Western arms-producing countries into a US-dominated regulating body. There was no disguising the fact that a robust arms race was in progress in the Middle East, fuelled by both China and North Korea, over which the USA had neither control nor influence. These two maverick countries were already providing an estimated 15% of arms flowing into the Middle East, and were gearing themselves up for increased production.

The US Arms Policy Review was selective and excepted arms destined for Israel, and the $1.6-billion arms package for Egypt, while Turkey was considered to be outside the Middle East region for this purpose. The Israelis had been promised another 50 F-15 combat aircraft, 600 kits to up-date their US 175mm self-propelled guns, and more Patriots. Representatives of the Five Permanent Members of the UN Security Council, meeting in London in October 1991, agreed, unconvincingly, to declare the Middle East to be a 'Weapon Free Zone'. Unfortunately, there seems to be no real substance behind the facade of the talks, but that each participant merely hopes to persuade the others to cease trading in arms, thus leaving this commercial field open only to himself.

The Middle East Peace Conference

In his speech to the US Congress (6th March) President Bush had triumphantly outlined his view of the 'New Order' in which he envisaged a re-alignment in the Middle East with Israel and the Arabs ranged against Iraq. He indicated that Israelis should trade 'land for peace' with the Arabs, and in particular return the Israeli-occupied Golan area to Syria, now an American Ally. The Israeli Prime Minister, Yitzak Shamir, flatly stated that the Golan area was not negotiable.

Greatly encouraged by his success in persuading certain Arab States to join the Allied Coalition, and to remain in it for the duration of the war, Secretary Baker embarked upon a far more ambitious project — to solve the so-far intractable Palestinian Problem. He decided to convene a Middle East Peace Conference, when Israelis and Arabs would sit down together to work out a peace formula under his guidance. Baker shuttled endlessly between Capitals, using all his wheeling and dealing skills to bring this about.

Israelis had never been keen on such a conference, feeling that the Soviet Union and Arab States would gang up against them, wanting instead to negotiate with each Arab confrontation state individually for peace, when the question of the Palestinian Problem could be regarded as a peripheral issue that could be side-tracked until in the fullness of time it would go away. The Israelis had in mind the Egyptian-Israeli peace accords. Israel was soon putting forward conference conditions that Palestinians would find unacceptable, hoping to shift blame for any failure to attend on to the Arabs.

Disregarding completely Bush's 'land for peace' suggestion, Israelis embarked upon a major scheme to bring hundreds of thousands of Soviet Jews to Israel, and continued also to found new Israeli settlements along the 'Green Line' (the border between Israel proper and the Israeli-Occupied Territories), and also in the Occupied Territories. For example, the Israeli Housing Minister (Arik Sharon) openly stated he was planning to increase the Jewish population in the Golan area from '11,000 to 22,000' (*Jerusalem Post*).

Additionally, Israel applied to the USA for 'guarantees' to the tune of $18-billion, to pay for re-settling the Soviet Jewish immigrants. Bush asked the Israelis to pend this application for four months, which meant until after the proposed conference, as a means of ensuring Israeli attendance. This roused opposition from the American Jewish lobby, and a head-on collision with the White House was narrowly averted when it backed away in the face of Bush's determination.

The Middle East Peace Conference was eventually convened in Madrid, on the 30th November, where Arabs and Israelis sat down at the same table facing each other — a miracle in itself. After delegates slanged each other in opening addresses, the Conference was adjourned. Further meetings took place, in a negative atmosphere of Israeli non-co-operation and stone-walling.

Saudi Arabia

After the Liberation of Kuwait, Saudi Arabia sat tight. King Fahd and his government realised what a narrow escape it had been, but were loath to admit their vulnerability. The impact of over half-a-million 'infidels', who included Jews, on its sacred soil, with female American soldiers carrying guns, driving vehicles, and sometimes being in command of men, caused Islamic shudders. Abrasive and pushy American suggestions that reforms should be instituted to incorporate Democracy and Human

Rights, was a Saudi in-house worry, which it was hoped would disappear with the exodus of Western soldiers, and as their withdrawal was even more rapid than their build-up, the Saudi government did not fret overmuch. As a concession to the Americans on the 15th April, King Fahd announced that a Commission would be appointed to study the introduction of a Consultative Council — but that was all, and no further progress along this avenue can be detected.

Saudis demanded from their Western Allies huge quantities of modern 'combat-proven' arms. Promises were made that did not seem to be in accordance with the spirit of the US Arms Policy Review. Saudi Arabia was to have an additional 24 F-15s, 4 AWACS, 5 aerial tankers, 36 Apache helicopters, 2,400 Maverick missiles and 250 Bradley armoured infantry vehicles. It was planned to double the strength of the Saudi army, re-organise it on divisional lines, and to equip it with US M-60A3 tanks and Bradleys.

The Saudis comforted themselves they still had over 30 Chinese CSS-2 medium range ballistic missiles, which they had no cause to use during the Gulf War, but were there to fall back on in case of dire emergency, and of which the Western media had been thoughtful enough to omit all mention during hostilities.

The main overt external threat to Saudi Arabia was still Iraq, as long as Saddam Hussein remained in power, but Saudis were quietly confident that the American *Operation Desert Shield* concept lingered on for their protection, thus obliterating worry in that respect. The Saudis 'bought' the friendship of the Soviet Union, long a hostile power, by extending a loan of $1.5-billion in August, and also improved contacts with China.

However, the Saudis knew their real covert enemy was Iran, which had inherited the ambitions of the late Ayatollah Khomeini. A resurgent Iran posed a distinct danger, and Saudi fear was that the Tehran government might, if opportunity offered, instigate insurrection amongst the eastern Shias, and from that base, hop westward to seize the 'Custodianship of the Two Holy Mosques'. Severed owing to Iranian political activity during the Haj, full diplomatic relations with Iran were resumed, and the Saudi government turned an overtly friendly face towards Tehran.

Jordan

Jordan came out of the Liberation of Kuwait period badly as it was seen by the Allies, and the USA in particular, to be openly siding with, and supporting, Saddam Hussein. At the best Jordan was regarded as an 'unreliable neutral'. As over half the population of the country were Palestinians who were continually mounting rowdy pro-Saddam Hussein demonstrations in Amman, had King Hussein not associated with their sentiments he would have been toppled from power, when his Kingdom would have degenerated into chaos. Throughout this period supplies continued to arrive at the Jordanian port of Akaba, to be transported by road into Iraq. Israel, regarded by the USA as a 'reliable neutral', did little to obstruct this traffic through the narrow Strait of Akaba, although, in theory at least, a UN economic embargo was in force against Iraq.

King Hussein made a speech on the 6th February, in which he alleged the real American purpose was the destruction of Iraq, and the 're-arrangement' of the Middle East, with the ultimate aim of bringing it "under direct foreign hegemony", which placed him in American eyes, firmly in the Iraqi camp. This half-truth hurt very much. The Saudis had already turned against Jordan, terminating their interim oil supplies, ceased trading with it, and expelled Jordanian diplomats. It was estimated the Gulf War cost Jordan about $8-billion in lost production, trade and overseas remittances.

After the *de facto* cease-fire, US Congress (on the 22nd March) formally terminated all military and economic aid to Jordan, but allowed humanitarian aid to continue. However, when James Baker began to lobby for support for his Middle East Peace Conference project, he turned and smiled at Jordan. By the end of April, King Hussein had abandoned the cause of Islam and Arab nationalism, as expounded by Iraq, and resumed his former pro-Western stance. By mid-May, King Hussein had agreed to send a Joint Jordanian-Palestinian delegation to the proposed conference. The resumption of US military aid, to the tune of $29-million, was promised.

Turkey

During the Liberation of Kuwait campaign Turkey had been loyal and helpful to the Allied cause, and was waiting anxiously for its reward. President Ozal had hoped for the disintegration of Iraq, and anticipated that his claim for oil-rich adjacent territory would be sympathetically considered by the victors. When, on the 8th March, Defense Secretary Cheney stated that "A divided Iraq would not be a good thing", Ozal realised this was not going to happen, and so he lowered his sights. Ozal knew only too well that the ending of the Cold War, and the possible disintegration of the USSR, meant that the strategic value of Turkey to the USA had decreased considerably.

Ozal began to turn his attention towards developing good regional relations with Iran. He was also waiting for UN embargoes against Iraq to be lifted so that he could once again establish good trading links with that country. Preparations were made to re-open the twin oil-pipelines from the Iraqi border to the Yumurtalik berths. Turkey also showed an interest in a possible Afghanistan-Iran-Turkey strategic *bloc*. Ever-willing to trade with the USSR, and to barter food and consumer goods for Soviet oil and natural gas, Ozal proposed a 'Black Sea Economic Co-operative Zone', of the Soviet Republics of Azerbaijan, Georgia and Ukraine, which was also to include Bulgaria and Rumania, designed to isolate Greece. Turkey offered to help the SSR of Azerbaijan develop its oil and petrochemical industries.

Somewhat concerned that Turkey appeared to be looking regionally for trade and security, instead of towards NATO territory, President Bush, when he visited President Ozal in Istanbul (21st May), proclaimed that the USA wanted a "Strategic relationship with Turkey", emphasising again that it was the corner-stone of American foreign policy in the region. Ozal pressed for what he thought he could get, specifying more modern arms, asking for another 80 US F-16 combat aircraft, and more assistance in developing his military assembly plants. Turkey was already assembling F-16s, but only contributed some 5% local material to the product. Ozal wanted an agreement that would cater for some 95% Turkish-manufactured parts.

President Bush was cautious of over-commitment towards Turkey as he was unsure of its continued pro-Western stance. Although President Ozal could remain in Office until 1997, his ruling Motherland Party (he was the founder-member), now led by Prime Minister Mesut Yilmaz, could not be certain of retaining power at the soon-to-be-held General Election. Bush had been wise. The Turkish General Election (20th October) returned an uneasy coalition government, which was faced with the major problem of whether it should develop a European, or an Asian outlook.

Allied Victory Parades

By the beginning of May, Allied military contingents were fast winding down in the Gulf area; the last USAF air patrol was carried out on the 6th of that month, and the US 3rd Armored Division was in the process of pulling out, leaving just one brigade behind for a short while longer. By the 8th, all US armed forces had withdrawn from southern Iraq and responsibility for the security of the people in the DMZ was given over to UNIKOM. The British had only about 2,500 troops remaining in the area, most being at Jabayl (Saudi Arabian port) busily shipping home their equipment, with only a 1,000-man battle group remaining in Kuwait. The French had already departed.

Previously, on the 20th April, General Schwartzkopf, and his '400 staff officers', departed from Riyadh to their home base at Tampa (USA). On arrival they found that the initial flush of wild, popular victorious enthusiasm, was beginning to wane, and efforts had to be made to keep it at a high pitch until the Victory Parades were over. Schwartzkopf, regally welcomed as the 'Hero and Architect of Victory', was feted and showered with honours, American and foreign. He was a ready-made, perfect example of a victorious American military leader, returning in true Roman-style from the wars.

A Grand Victory Parade, an almost all-American show, was held in Washington on the 8th June, in which some 8,600 Gulf War veterans took part, while over 80 aircraft flew overhead. This was followed by a picnic and a spectacular firework display in the evening. It had been anticipated that over one million spectators would turn out to witness the Parade, but (estimates vary widely) probably only about 200,000 did so. Whatever the correct figure was, it was a somewhat disappointing response.

New York City Fathers were determined to up-stage Washington, and held their own Victory Parade on the 10th, the estimated cost of $3-million being found by the City, supplemented by contributions from commerce and the public. The main body of the Parade consisted of some 25,000 service personnel, American and Allied, but also included Veterans of Foreign Wars. Controversy surrounded the Parade, as diverse groups, such as homosexuals and other fringe factions, edged in, and a few anti-war demonstrations occurred. A protest against the presence of the Syrian flag was made by relatives of victims of the Lockerbie Air Disaster, on the grounds that Syria supported international terrorism, and was in some degree responsible, which caused the Syrian military contingent to withdraw.

General Schwartzkopf himself led the New York Victory Parade on foot (for a short distance), along Wall Street, the famed 'Valley of Heroes', when specially shredded paper was produced to provide an old time traditional 'ticker-tape' welcome. Again spectator support was less than hoped for, most estimates putting it at the one-million mark. On the 9th August, General Schwartzkopf retired from the Army, handing over CENTCOM to General Joseph Hoar, a Marine officer.

The US DoD was not keen on prolonging the euphoria of victory any longer than essential, as it was in the process of implementing a massive military re-organisation, that meant severe cuts, which were to include the elimination of six army divisions, two aircraft carriers, and the run down of the overall strength of the Armed Forces to 1.65-million.

The British government was less than enthusiastic about a Grand Victory Parade, and had to be prodded by public opinion into authorising a low-profile 'Welcome Home Parade' through the City of London, on the 21st June. It consisted of about 1,000 Gulf War veterans, while overhead flew 21 helicopters and nine other aircraft. Similar 'qualified rejoicing' Parades were also held in certain provincial cities.

British Defence Minister (Tom King) was anxious to get these formalities, described indiscreetly by one of his officials as "a tiresome necessity", over as soon as possible, in case they roused latent British jingoist emotions, such as had surfaced so inconveniently during, and after, the Falklands Campaign (1982), as he was about to announce some swingeing Defence cuts, when names of some famous British regiments, each with scores of Battle Honours gained over three centuries, were to disappear from the Army List.

The French held their usual colonial-victory-type Parade in Paris down the Champs-Élysées, led with panache by the Band and Pioneers of the Foreign Legion, followed by veterans of the Daguet Division, with representative aircraft flying overhead. A reasonably rousing reception was given to this Victory March, and medals were distributed.

Then the matter seemed to be forgotten by the French Government, anxious to renew favourable trading contacts with Middle East states, both victors and vanquished. The French Defence Ministry was also about to make severe Defence reductions, and did not want to arouse hostile popular protest. The French 'Armée 2000' plan for 'rationalisation' meant the disbandment of certain formations, and a reduction in overall strength. The French Government was in the process of re-orientating from a passive NATO membership to a more active role in the WEU.

On return home, Arab Allied military contingents involved in the Gulf War, held their own Victory Parades in their respective Capitals, and then the matter was pushed aside, as their government reverted to involvement in post-Gulf War, inter-Arab, and anti-Israeli politics.

Payment for the Gulf War

Victory Parades over, the US Administration could revert to a matter that was causing some concern, that of the slow Allied response in paying their promised contributions to the Gulf War chest. Already (22nd March) certain defaulters had been named publicly, which included Germany, Japan and Saudi Arabia. The USA had hoped the whole cost of the Gulf War would be covered by Allied promises, but it had to produce an interim $15-billion to meet immediate costs, and provide a 'cushion' in case Allied pledges did not cover all costs.

Contributions continued to be slow to arrive. The US Budget Director (Richard Darman) told the House of Representatives (31st July) that additional costs incurred by the military operation were expected to total $61-billion, that foreign contributions received amounted to $46-billion: but that Saudi Arabia and Kuwait each still owed $12.5-billion, and that other back-sliders included Germany, Japan and the UAE. In November, it was stated (Reuter) that Kuwait had paid almost all the '$22-billion owed' to the USA for the Liberation campaign, and that the remaining $1-billion owing would be paid in before the end of the year. Saudi Arabia had been forced to raise a loan of $4.5-billion, the first foreign one it had made for two decades.

Post-War Iraq

In late March 1991, a UN Relief team visiting Iraq on a fact-finding mission, reported that Allied bombing of the country had caused 'near apocalyptic results' and had reduced it to the 'pre-industrial age'. The UN team expressed concern over lack of medicines, food, fuel and transport, while shattered sewerage systems indicated the need for a crash programme of innoculations to ward off epidemics.

Against this background, Saddam Hussein had appeared on television on the 2nd March, for the first time since the early part of the Gulf War, calm and urbane, to rally his armed forces and his people, against an anticipated Allied incursion. To the surprise of many, Iraqis tackled their monumental reconstruction tasks in an almost phoenix-like manner, and for example, by the end of the month electricity had been restored to Baghdad. Certain major international television and news networks had been allowed to send teams to Baghdad, which reported both devastation and reconstruction.

President Bush's speech (6th March), indicating that Allied troops would not be marching against him, enabled Saddam Hussein to get on with the task of quickly re-organising his army to tackle the Shia opposition which had flared up in southern Iraq. Two Republican Guard mechanised brigades from the Turkish frontier area were moving southwards, while new army formations were being assembled with men and material from broken units.

On second looks, it was estimated (IISS) that Saddam Hussein still had 380,000 mobilised troops (with some 650,000 reserves), about 2,300 tanks and up to 4,500 other armoured vehicles, which made the Iraqi army the largest in the Middle East, with the sole exception of that of Egypt. He also had at least 250 combat aircraft, and practically all his 350 helicopters. His restricting problems were lack of spares and shortage of fuel.

Also on the 6th, Saddam Hussein appointed General Hussein Kamil, his cousin, to be Defence Minister, to mastermind the military shake-up, in which 'heads rolled'. All dissidence, reluctance and lack of full commitment in the armed forces was crushed ruthlessly. On the 16th March, Saddam Hussein promised he would implement major democratic reforms; and on the 22nd, re-shuffled his Cabinet. Taha Ramadan became a Vice-President, to join the only Vice-President, Taha Moheiddin Maarouf, the only Kurd in the Iraqi top leadership strata. Saadoun Hammadi became Prime Minister (vice-Saddam Hussein who had also held that appointment), and Ahmad Hussein became Foreign Minister.

Taking this as a sign of weakness, President Bush called (on the 24th) for a 'Man of Peace' to lead the Iraqis, insisting that he did not want Iraq to be 'Lebanonised'. Bush qualified his comments by adding that he did not expect Saddam Hussein to fall from power until the end of the year. This was a considerable lowering of sights. The Iraqi President meantime maintained his attitude of Strategic Defiance.

The Shia Uprising

The first sign of a 'popular revolt' against Saddam Hussein surfaced in Basra as early as the 1st March, as demoralised Iraqi troops, shouldering their way northwards, attempted to cross the almost bridgeless Shatt al-Arab waterway in whatever craft or makeshift rafts they could lay their hands upon. In Basra, local Baath Party leaders, and even senior military officers, became targets, and then victims, of angry, disillusioned Shia mobs. In addition, military discipline had broken down in some formations, there were arguments, and even in-fighting between commanders, soldiers, units and factions, some wanting to stand and fight, and others who did not.

Anti-Saddam Hussein demonstrations in Basra developed ferociously and speedily, although the 3rd March has become the usually accepted date of the commencement of the southern Shia Uprising. Originally a civilian opportunist outburst, as it gathered momentum, parts of the city were taken over by the 'rebels'. This was regarded by the Allied media as the expected inevitable reaction to the Iraqi defeat. It gave the US Administration smug satisfaction, and enhanced its belief that the Iraqi leader would not last very long. Later, Shia opposition sources alleged that on the 3rd March, Bush had authorised a dialogue to be opened with the Shia 'rebels', and even approved secret CIA aid for them, but the Americans were faced with the problem of which Shia opposition movement to support.

There were at least three main, separate externally-backed Shia opposition groups — IING, SCIRI and JACIO (Joint Action Committee of Iraqi Opposition). IING (Iraqi Independent National Group), led by Hassan al-Naqib, was Saudi-backed; the Saudis favouring an Iraqi government being formed under Ibrahim al-Daoud, a former Iraqi Defence Minister, then in exile in Saudi Arabia.

President Bush's speech to Congress (6th) was also a green light for Saddam Hussein to turn his full attention to crushing the Shia Uprising. Dispatching his hard-line General, Ali Hassan al-Majid, who had conducted the 1988 campaign against northern Kurds, and used Chemical Warfare means against them at Halabja, now Interior Minister, with orders to crush the rebellion at all costs, and with no holds barred. The Iraqi President ordered pay increases and bonuses for army personnel, and announced amnesties for draft dodgers and deserters. He also sent Baath Party leaders south to re-assert Party discipline on the population.

In short, Iraqi armed forces crushed the Shia Uprising with fire-power and brutality, but it took a few days, owing to insufficient troops immediately available to dampen down the whole region quickly. In the cities, as military units gained a hold on one sector, the 'rebels' switched to another, and as troops turned to move against them again, the 'rebels' tended to back-infiltrate; a process that was repeated several times.

On the 9th, a SCIRI statement, issued from Beirut, claimed that already 30,000 people had died during the Shia Uprising, and that fighting was still in progress. On the 12th, it was reported that Karbala and Nejaf had been 'recaptured' by government troops, where considerable damage had been done to buildings by artillery fire, and many people had been killed. Additional reports indicated that violent unrest had broken out in Saddam City and Shula (Shia districts of Baghdad), but these disturbances were quickly crushed. By the 15th, Shia refugees flooding southwards from Basra into the DMZ, confirmed that Iraqi troops had regained their grip on the city.

In the last week of March, foreign journalists, who were taken on a tour of southern Iraqi cities, reported scenes of devastation, with 'rotting corpses on the streets' (Reuters). It is generally accepted that by mid-March, Saddam Hussein had effectively subdued his southern Shia region. The famous Golden Dome of the Karbala Mosque had been badly damaged by gun-fire and it was not re-opened for worship until the 2nd September.

According to a later US Senate Foreign Relations Committee Report (of the 2nd May), at the height of the Shia Uprising a group of Iraqi senior army officers had approached the JACIO, then in Beirut, and offered to support it, if all factional differences were set aside. However, one stumbling-block condition was that the USA must give support to JACIO, which had not been forthcoming.

Iran

Relations between Iraq and Iran remained very stiff and formal, with the 'flight of Iraqi aircraft' still unexplained, but the Iranian government did show a deep concern and interest in its Shia co-religionists in Iraq, and their struggle against Saddam Hussein. As early as the 4th March, the *Tehran Times* in an effort to internationalise the situation, gave editorial support for the Shia Uprising, when it was knife-edged and tense. So tense in fact, that Saddam Hussein sent Saadoun Hammadi to Tehran, reputedly in an attempt to persuade the Iranian government to allow some form of power-sharing over the Iraqi Shia south, between the Baghdad government and the Iranian-backed SCIRI. But within days, the tide had turned, and the situation in southern Iraq changed, with Saddam Hussein battering his 'rebels' into submission, when the Hammadi ploy was no longer necessary.

During the course of the Shia Uprising the Tehran government maintained a disapproving attitude towards Iraq, and decreed that the 18th March was to be observed as a Day of National Mourning for the 'Massacre of the Iraqi People', and for the 'desecration of the Holy Shrines of Karbala and Nejaf'. The Speaker of the Iraqi National Assembly accused the Iranian government of sending armed forces into Iraq to assist the 'rebels'. This was denied by Tehran. The Iranian Majlis held a special session (24th March), to discuss the situation in Iraq, which condemned Saddam Hussein's treatment of Iraqi Shia leaders, especially Grand Ayatollah Abu Qassim al-Khoei, of Nejaf (who had been detained), and pledged support for the 'Uprising of the Iraqi Muslim Nation'.

Iraqi Shias who sought refuge in Iran were housed in camps adjacent to the border. Later, after the collapse of the Shia Uprising, when Allied troops were rapidly withdrawing from Iraq and Kuwait, Prince Sadruddin Aga Khan, Head of the UN Inter-Agency Humanitarian Programme for Kuwait and Iraq, claimed (10th May) that "the West has ceased to pay attention to the continued plight of Shia refugees in Iran". Later still, on the 11th June, the Tehran government called upon the UN 'to protect 500,000-900,000 Shias, reported trapped in the southern Iraqi marshes . . . surrounded by 100,000 Iraqi troops and airborne units'.

Iran had made a start at clearing and rebuilding its Shatt al-Arab port of Khorramshahr, but progress was very slow, Western countries hesitating to provide financial support as they were suspicious that the Tehran government was still involved in Lebanese Hostage incidents. However, France made a special effort to improve its relations with Iran, and that country was visited by the French Foreign Minister (Roland Dumas) who was anxious to obtain a 'large piece' of the Iranian $130-billion reconstruction programme.

Iran was also engaged with the Chinese in a $200-million nuclear research programme, and was almost openly working to obtain a nuclear weapon. The main Iranian nuclear centre was at Moellewm Kalayeh, in the Qazin mountains, some 70 miles north of Tehran, where Chinese nuclear scientists were working. This site was open to normal IAEA inspections, but it was suspected that vital parts of this nuclear project were being carried out at a number of other secret sites. It should be noted that China had not signed the 1968 Nuclear Non-Proliferation Treaty, but that Iran had.

Exiled Shia Opposition

Despite the failure of the Shia Uprising, illicit Shia radio stations in Iran, Syria and Lebanon, continued to falsely claim that a number of Iraqi cities and towns were held by Shias opposed to Saddam Hussein. A Joint Conference had been held in Beirut (11th-13th March), attended by about 400 Iraqi opposition representatives, of some 20 groups. The main front was JACIO, composed of 17 groups, to which were added two London-based ones: the Nationalist Iraqi Constitution, led by Salah Omar Ali, and the Free Iraqi Congress, led by Saad Saleh Jaber. The single Sunni representative was Kayreddin Hasib. Neither IING nor SCIRI attended this Conference.

At this Conference a Four Point Manifesto was issued, which in brief called for support for the Uprising, unification of Iraqi opposition parties, the formation of a provisional government, and 'free and direct' elections — when Saddam Hussein was overthrown. Later (6th May), JACIO called, this time from Damascus, for the removal of Saddam Hussein, and the establishment, of a 'democratic government'. But the moment of opportunity had passed, and it was now only a voice crying in a wilderness created by Saddam Hussein.

The Kurdish Insurrection

Hot on the heels of the Shia Uprising came a Kurdish Insurrection in the northern Iraqi mountains, instigated by the two main Iraqi Kurdish opposition groups, the Patriotic Union of Kurdistan (PUK), led by Jalal Talabani, and the Democratic Party of Kurdistan (DPK), led by Masoud Barzani, which in mid-March occupied a number of cities and towns in Kurdish territory, including Kirkuk, Arbil, Dohuk and Zhako.

Having dealt with the Shia Uprising, Saddam Hussein turned and marched his troops against the dissident Kurds, and it is reputed that in the punitive campaign that ensued they killed over 50,000 Kurds, drove Kurds from their villages in terror, and caused a mass exodus of Kurdish refugees into adjacent regions of Turkey and Iran. Winter conditions still obtained in the northern mountains, and Kurdish families left in the open were perishing.

Forbidden the use of fixed-wing aircraft by the UN, Iraqi troops used helicopters, of which they had ample, with drastic effects. Two Iraqi combat aircraft were shot down by the Americans, one on the 20th, near Takrit, and the other on the 22nd, near Kirkuk. Saddam Hussein had trailed his coat to his cost. The Americans meant business.

UN Security Council Resolution 688 was rushed through (on the 5th April) to try to protect the Kurds from Saddam Hussein's wrath. The

Resolution condemned the repression of the Iraqi civilian population, demanded access into Iraq for humanitarian organisations, and that Saddam Hussein co-operate with the UN Secretary-General. The Allies considered this UN Resolution to be the authority for intervention, and during April, detachments of American, British and French troops entered northern Iraq to establish 'Safe Havens' for Kurdish refugees of whom it was reported that over 13,000 had already perished on the mountain slopes, both to care for them, and to protect them from Iraqi government vengeance.

The Allies pressed Saddam Hussein into having talks with the Kurds about autonomy, which began in Baghdad. Leashing back his troops, he stood off, while protesting against Allied infringement of Iraq's sovereignty. The Safe Havens were able to give limited help to Kurdish refugees and temporary security. A tiny UN Observer Mission (of ten men) was set up to deter confrontation between Kurds and government troops, but it was too minute to be effective, and was soon withdrawn.

There was some talk amongst the Allies of forming a Rapid Reaction Force, to operate from the Incirlik NATO base, in Turkey, but little positive came of this before Allied detachments were withdrawn from Iraq, leaving the Kurds to seek their own salvation. Saddam Hussein immediately suspended the autonomy talks in Baghdad: they had only been a ploy to keep the Allies quiet until their armed forces had quit northern Iraq.

It should be noted that Turkey, like Iraq, had a long-running Kurdish insurgency problem, and both countries had previously co-operated with each other in measures against their 'rebels' in border areas. The Turkish government did not share the Allies' concern for the well-being of Iraqi Kurds, and Turkish armed forces gave only a minimum of assistance.

Iraqi Internal Affairs

In a speech to the Iraqi people on the occasion of the anniversary of the founding of the Baath Party (8th April), Saddam Hussein claimed a victory in the 'Thirty-fold Aggression', a term that had come to be used for the Liberation of Kuwait campaign, also claiming that the Iraqi armed forces had smashed opposition in all cities in the country. He said this had been an external plot to tear Iraq apart. Iraqi media began referring to Bush as 'President Halagu', after Genghis Khan's infamous grandson, who had razed Baghdad to the ground. Saddam Hussein then embarked upon regularising his armed forces, with emphasis on the Republican Guard, disbanding the notionally one-million strong Popular Army militia. Later, he appointed General Iyad Fathi al-Rawai, Commander of the Republican Guard, to be Chief of Staff.

On the political side, the ban on Iraqis travelling abroad was lifted (11th May), although exit visas were required (and were hard to get), and money could not be taken out of the country. Next, on the 23rd May, the dreaded Revolutionary Court, which had such a black record in dealing with political offenders, was abolished. Further, on the 4th July, the Iraqi National Assembly approved plural representation, while reserving the right of the Baath Party to be politically active within the armed forces, a move that had to be ratified by the Revolutionary Command Council, where it stalled. On Iraq's National Day (17th July), Saddam Hussein, back in his old confident form again, gave a rousing speech, urging everyone "to unite to re-build our nation".

On the economic side, UN sanctions were pinching hard, but the population seemed to be able to get by just above primitive existence level, it is thought helped somewhat by sanction-busting through both Turkey and Iran. Iraq re-opened its first oil refinery, claiming that it would soon be producing two-million gallons of petrol and other refined products.

On the 3rd May, the UN Security Council stated that it was up to individual countries whether to unfreeze any Iraqi assets held by them, but the response was poor. In September, the UN Security Council agreed to allow Iraq to export oil, through the Turkish twin pipelines, to the value of $1.6-billion for a period of six months. The money was to be used only for humanitarian purposes, the UN Fund for War Victims and UN costs of destroying Iraq's weapons of mass destruction. But Saddam Hussein would not agree to the UN conditions.

Non-Conventional Revelations

Once the Cease-Fire conditions had been accepted by Saddam Hussein the Allies, especially the USA, were anxious to step inside Iraq proper, to assess and oversee the destruction of that country's 'non-conventional' weaponry, which was done under the guise and authority of the UN. The Pentagon wanted to find out just how advanced the Iraqis were in the military nuclear, chemical and biological fields, and in ballistic missile development — or indeed, if they had any of this weaponry at all.

The UN ran into stubborn opposition as once again Saddam Hussein fell back on his Strategic Defiance policy. A saga of Iraqi deceit and delaying tactics ensued, which was countered step by step by American persistence, as more authority was sought, and obtained, under successive UN Security Council Resolutions, which compelled the Iraqi leader to give way an inch at a time, to reveal more vital information, or to allow UN monitoring teams more latitude.

As this tussle draggingly unfolded, the enormity and advanced state, of the Iraqi arsenal of non-conventional weapons, was gradually exposed in its terrifying starkness to astound and shock Western Allies, and the world at large. It was soon accepted from evidence unearthed by UN and IAEA monitoring teams that not only would Saddam Hussein have probably been able to produce a nuclear warhead 'within months, rather than years', but that he had already obtained ingredients that put him on the path towards developing a hydrogen bomb.

What was almost as shattering, and embarrassing, to certain Western governments, was the disclosure that a multiplicity of Western firms had long been supplying Iraq with essential ingredients and components for mass destruction weapon projects. Loop-holes in both national and international regulations against such exports gaped wide open for all to see, while the list of Western suppliers, together with items supplied, grew longer as UN monitoring teams unearthed more evidence. This fascinating saga of detection is still on-going and Western governments are on edge as to what may be revealed next. Here it is only necessary to mention a few significant steps in this hunt.

It was not until April, that Saddam Hussein was persuaded to provide the required lists of non-conventional weapons in his armoury, when it was declared that Iraq possessed, amongst many other items, '50 SCUD missiles, including 30 with chemical warheads . . . and 10,000 chemical bombs'. It was denied that Iraq had any biological weapons at all. Dissatisfied, the UN and IAEA pressed for further details, especially regarding the amount of weapon-grade uranium at the two Iraqi nuclear reactor sites just south of Baghdad, which had been hit by Allied bombs during the Gulf War. After an interval, they were informed that all 'weapon-grade uranium' there had been buried beneath bomb-damage rubble.

UN and IAEA monitoring teams, whose task was to check, and over-see the destruction of all Iraq's non-conventional weapons did not gain entry into that country until the third week in May, and then their freedom of movement was restricted. Not until well into June, after the monitoring teams had been refused access to certain nuclear sites, due to American pressure, did Saddam Hussein give the required permission.

On the 15th August, UN Security Council Resolution 707 was approved, requiring Iraq to allow the monitoring teams to use both aircraft and helicopters to over-fly Iraqi territory to search for suspected locations, but these flights were restricted by Saddam Hussein. That month the Iraqi President agreed to destroy his stocks of CW material on condition the process was supervised by Iraqi officials only, but this was not acceptable by the UN, meaning of course, the USA.

A high-level Iraqi scientist had defected to the USA, and was providing information that had to be checked out, but Saddam Hussein's delaying tactics were so obstructive and blatant, that the frustrated President Bush threatened to resume aerial attacks against Iraq unless UN conditions were complied with. Under US *Operation Determined Resolve*, American combat aircraft were placed on an alert, a threat that successfully extracted further details. In July, Iraq admitted (*Times*: 9th July 1991) possession 'of 48-lbs of enriched uranium, which had been regularly inspected by the Vienna-based IAEA', and also that it had '24 nuclear facilities'.

In August, the location of the long-denied 'Super Gun' was discovered, where already the 'Baby Babylon' gun project, a smaller prototype, with a 14-inch calibre and a 172-feet long barrel, was assembled ready for firing. Barrel sections and other parts of the so-called 'Doomsday Gun', which had a 39-inch calibre, and if it had been proved viable, would have been able to project a shell a claimed 600 miles, were discovered. Also, in August, a major Iraqi CW arsenal was detected, and Saddam Hussein admitted to experimenting in germ warfare.

In September, a UN monitoring team unearthed a wealth of incriminating material at the Record Building of the Iraqi Atomic Energy Commission, in Baghdad, and was taking documentation away, when it was held for four days in the car park, Iraqis demanding the documents be left behind. Eventually, the UN team, with its welter of documentary evidence, which included personal files on all involved in nuclear projects, was allowed to take it away for examination. This evidence showed the immensity of the Iraqi non-conventional programmes, the amount of sensitive materials Iraq had accumulated, and revealed how embargoes had been avoided, or ignored, and which Western Governments had been conveniently commercially-blind to such transactions.

The sad epilogue is that if Iraq has been able to progress so far along the military nuclear path, how far along this route has its neighbour and enemy, Iran, which has made little secret that it is striving towards military nuclear status, progressed? Or how far along the military nuclear path are Egypt, Pakistan, or a score or so other nations suspected of working to achieve this military goal. Or, indeed how many 'nuclear bombs in the basement' does Israel have?

President Bush was wise to have provided extra funding for his predecessors' GPALS (Global Protection Against Limited Strikes), a project designed to provide some protection against 'rogue nuclear missiles', or even ones launched by accident, or mechanical fault, which was becoming elbowed out by other US vested Defense interests. GPALS will include ERINT (Extended Range Interceptors); the US-funded and Israeli-developed Arrow, with a range of some 50 miles; and the THAAD (Tactical High Altitude Air Defence), with a range of about 100 miles: both being anti-missile missiles.

About the Liberation of Kuwait

(August 1990 – March 1991)

APPENDICES

"A"   The Arab League

"B"   The Gulf Co-operation Council

"C"   United Nations Security Council Resolutions

"D"   Nations contributing to the Allied Coalition

"E"   Naval Contributions and Deployment

"F"   Allied Ground Forces

"G"   Operation Desert Storm Command Structure

"H"   Allied Combat Aircraft Operating in the Gulf

"I"   Order of Battle: Ground Forces

"J"   Further UN Security Council Resolutions

The Arab League

The Arab League was founded in March 1945, and consists of 21 Arab countries (including 'Palestine') which are:–

Algeria – Bahrain – Djibouti – Egypt – Iraq – Jordan – Kuwait – Lebanon – Libya – Mauritania – Morocco – Oman – Palestine – Qatar – Saudi Arabia – Somalia – Sudan – Syria – Tunisia – the United Arab Emirates – and Yemen.

The aim of the Arab League is to strengthen the close ties between Arab sovereign states in order to co-ordinate their policies and activities for the common good of the Arab World.

Representatives from each member-country form the Council, the supreme body, while the General Secretariat carries out decisions of the Council.

Egypt was suspended in March 1979, for making a Peace Accord with Israel, and the Arab League HQ moved from Cairo to Tunis. Egypt was reinstated in May 1989, and the HQ moved back from Tunis to Cairo.

The Secretary General, Chedli Klibi (a Tunisian) resigned in September 1990, after Saudi criticism, and in May 1991, Ahmad Abdul Meguid (an Egyptian) was appointed to that post.

Gulf Co-operation Council

The Gulf Co-operation Council (GCC) was formed in May 1981, and consists of six sovereign "Traditional" Arab Gulf States, being:–

Bahrain – Kuwait – Oman – Qatar – Saudi Arabia – and the United Arab Emirates.

The aim of the GCC is to establish co-ordination, integration and co-operation in economic, social and cultural affairs between member countries.

The Supreme Council consists of Heads of member countries, which meet in alternating countries. The Secretariat is based in Saudi Arabia. The Secretary General is Abdullah Yacov Bishara (a Kuwaiti).

In August 1990, the GCC condemned Iraq's invasion of Kuwait, and agreed to reinforce its Rapid Deployment Force, so that GCC troops could join the US-led multi-national force in northern Saudi Arabia.

The United Arab Emirates comprise the Emirates of Abu Dhabi – Adjman – Dubai – Fujairah – Ras al-Khaimah – Sharjah – Umm al-Qaiwain. (All formerly British Trucial States.)

UN Security Council Resolutions

No. 660 (2nd August 1990): Condemned Iraqi invasion of Kuwait — demanded Iraqi withdrawal — and called for a negotiated settlement.

No. 661 (6th August): Imposed mandatory sanctions on Iraq and Kuwait.

No. 662 (9th August): Declared Iraqi annexation of Kuwait null and void.

No. 664 (18th August): Demanded the release of 'foreign hostages'.

No. 665 (25th August): Gave authority to deploy maritime force against sanction-breaking — to use such measures commensurate to the specific circumstances as may be necessary to inspect and verify cargoes.

No. 666 (13th September): Humanitarian aid to civilian population of Iraq.

No. 667 (16th September): Condemned Iraqi violation of diplomatic premises in Kuwait.

No. 670 (25th September): Placed an Air Transport embargo on Iraq.

No. 674 (29th October): Condemned hostage-taking.

No. 677 (29th November): Condemns Iraqi attempts to modify the demography of Kuwait.

No. 678 (29th November): Authorised the use of force to evict Iraq from Kuwait — unless Iraqis quit Kuwait by the 15th January 1991.

Nations Contributing to the Allied Military Coalition

Argentina	Germany	Pakistan
Australia	Greece	Poland
Bahrain	Italy	Qatar
Bangladesh	Kuwait	Saudi Arabia
Belgium	Morocco	Senegal
Canada	Netherlands	Spain
Czechoslovakia	New Zealand	Syria
Denmark	Niger	UAE
Egypt	Norway	United Kingdom
France	Oman	United States

= 30 countries

Plus — an Afghan Islamic Resistance Detachment (500)

National Naval Contributions & Deployment

(mid-January 1991)

IN THE GULF:

United States

Midway carrier: with eight warships and two supply ships;
Missouri battleship: with one warship and one supply ship;
Eight warships, four mine-hunters and two supply ships.

Britain

Four warships, three mine-hunters, six supply ships and two landing craft.

Canada

Two warships and one supply ship.

Denmark

One warship.

France

One warship and one supply ship.

Norway

One supply ship.

(NB: The Soviet Union had two warships and two supply ships in the Gulf, which were not part of the Allied Command.)

IN THE ARABIAN SEA:

United States

Wisconsin: battleship with five warships and one supply ship;
Ranger: carrier with five warships and two supply ships;
30 amphibious craft.

Argentina

Two warships.

Australia

Two warships and one supply ship.

Belgium

One supply ship and two mine-hunters.

France

Four warships and two supply ships.

Italy

Three warships and one supply ship.

Spain

Three warships and one supply ship.

IN THE RED SEA:

United States

Saratoga: carrier with seven warships, and three supply ships;
Kennedy: carrier with six warships and two supply ships;
Theodore Roosevelt: carrier with five warships and two supply ships.

France

One warship.

Greece

One warship.

IN THE EAST MEDITERRANEAN

United States

Five amphibious ships.

Italy

Two warships.

Germany

Five mine-hunters.

Sources: Pentagon, Armed Forces Journal, Sunday Times.

Allied Ground Forces

(mid-January 1991)

United States	Armoured and Airborne — 225,000 (1,900 tanks) Marines — 90,000 troops (500 tanks).
Saudi Arabia	40,000 troops (200 tanks).
Egypt	35,000 troops (200 tanks).
Britain	25,000 troops (170 tanks).
Syria	12,000 troops (200 tanks).
France	10,000 troops (72 tanks).
Pakistan	8,000 troops.
Bangladesh	6,000 troops.
Morocco	1,200 troops.
Senegal	500 troops.
Niger	500 troops.
Czechoslovakia	300 troops.

The **GCC** States of **Bahrain, Kuwait, Oman** and **UAE** contributed a combined force totalling 10,000 troops (50 tanks).

Sources: USCENTCOM, Sunday Times.

Appendix "G"

Operation Desert Storm – Command Structure

USA:

George Bush — President of the USA.

Richard Cheney — Defense Secretary.

General Colin Powell — Chairman of the US Joint Chiefs of Staff.

General Norman Schwartzkopf — Commander, US Central Command (CENTCOM). His HQ in Saudi Arabia was known as CENTCOM-FORWARD.

Lt-General Calvin Waller — Deputy CENTCOM.

Component Commanders were:

Lt-General Charles Horner (Air Force) — CENTAF.

Lt-General John Yeosock (Army) — ARCENT.

Vice-Admiral Stanley Arthur (Navy) — NAVCENT.

Lt-General Walter Boomer (US Marines) — MARCENT.

Colonel Jesse Johnson (Special Operations Command) — SOCOM.

Saudi Arabia:

Prince Sultan Ibn Abdul Aziz — Defence Minister.

General Prince Khaled bin Sultan — Commander of the Saudi Air Force — and nominally C-in-C of all Allied and Saudi Forces on Saudi territory.

166

Allied Combat Aircraft Operating in the Gulf

(mid-January 1991)

USA:

Incirlik (Turkey)	— 72 F-111s; 20 F-117A (Stealth); 3 AWACS.
Diego Garcia	— 28 B-52s.
Cairo (Egypt)	— 25 B-52s.
Abu Dhabi	— 44 F-16s.
Bahrain	— 48 F/A-18s; 20 A-6s.
Doha	— 72 F-16s.
Jabayl	— 72 A-10s.
Tabuk	— 38 F-111s; 6 TR-1s; 12 EF-111s.
Thumrait	— 15 F-15s.

Britain:

Bahrain	— 12 Jaguars.
Dhahran	— 32 Tornados.
Seeb	— 3 Nimrods.
Tabuk	— 18 Tornados.

France:

Hufuf	— 16 Mirages; 14 Jaguars.

Italy:

Abu Dhabi	— 7 Tornados.

Kuwait:

Tabuk   — 15 Mirages.

Saudi Arabia:

Dhahran   — 53 Tornados; 20 F-15s; 30 Hawks; 5 AWACS.

Khamis Mushayt   — 15 F-5s; 20 F-15s.

Tabuk   — 15 F-5s.

Taif   — 15 F-5s; 20 F-15s.

US Carrierborne Aircraft

East Mediterranean   — 20 F/A-18s; 20 A-6s.

Gulf and Gulf of Oman   — 80 F/A-18s; 80 A-6s.

Sources: USCENTCOM, Sunday Times, AFJI, Jane's Defence Weekly.

Order of Battle: Ground Forces

US CENTCOM (Forward):

US 18th (XVIII) Airborne Corps (General G. Luck):

— 1st Cavalry Division
— 101st Airborne Division
— 82nd Airborne Division
— 24th Mechanised Division
— *French:* 6th (Daguet) Light Armoured Division.

US 7th (VII) Army Corps (General F. Franks):

— 1st Armored Division
— 3rd Armored Division
— 1st Infantry Division
— *British:* 1st Armoured Division.

US Marine Corps (General W. Boomer):

— 1st Marine Division
— 2nd Marine Division.

Saudi Task Forces (included Kuwaiti and other GCC National contingents).

Pan-Arab Contingent (included Egyptian Divisions and other Arab contingents).

Sources: CENTCOM, Pentagon and AFJI.

Further UN Security Council Resolutions

After hostilities ceased several UN Security Council Resolutions were approved relating to the Gulf War, which included:–

No. 686 (2nd March 1991): Demanded Iraq's acceptance of all previous relevant Resolutions — called on Iraq to cease hostilities — to release all POWs — and give assistance to identify and locate mines and other explosives.

No. 687 (3rd April): Required Iraq to submit information on all chemical and biological weapon stocks held.

No. 689 (9th April): Authorised the establishment of UNIKOM and the DMZ.

No. 692 (20th May): Established a Compensation Fund to be formed from Iraq's oil exports to pay for damage incurred by foreign governments and nationals in the Gulf War.

No. 699 (17th June): Ordered Iraq to bear the full cost of destruction of proscribed weapons and ammunition.

No. 707 (July): Demanded that Iraq allow UN monitoring teams to overfly its territory, to search for suspected weapon sites.

The Second Gulf War

The Liberation of Kuwait

INDEX

The following will NOT appear in the index as they appear on most pages:

America (n) (s)
Arab(s)
Gulf
Iraq (i) (s)
Kuwait (i) (s)
Saddam Hussein
USA (US)

Abbas, Gen Saad – 62
Abdali – 133-4
Abu Abbas – 55
Abu Dhabi – 30; 42
Abu Ghaib – 119
Abu Musa – 26; 54
Abu Nidal – 55
Abu Zimbal – 23
Achille Lauro – 55
Adair, Red – 137
Adami, al- – 7
Adana – 65; 77
Adjman – 30
Advisory National Council (Kuwait)
  – 136
Afghan – 29
Aga Khan, Prince – 151
'Air-Land Battle' concept – 69; 118-9
Akaba – 144
Algeria – 19; 24
Algiers – 2
Algiers Treaty – 14
Ali Baba – 2
Allied Air Plan – 68-69
Allied Coalition (Alliance) – 41; 43;
  52; 54-5; 78; 110; 112; 120; 128;
  132; 140-1
Almiriya – 126
Amman – 43; 55; 82
Amnesty International –13; 22; 24;
  31; 136
Anbari, Abdul al- – 133

Ankara – 46
Arab Co-operation Council (ACC) –
  15; 23; 27; 41
Arabian Peninsula – 10-11; 15; 19
Arabian Sea – 97
Arab Gulf States – 8; 16; 20; 28; 32;
  138
Arab League – 10-1; 17th; 19th;
  23-4; 139-40
Arab Liberation Front – 134
Arab Magreb Union (AMU) – 24
Arab Nation – 8; 22
Arab States – 9; 14; 26; 40; 54; 81;
  116; 142
Arbil – 152
Arafat, Yasir – 5; 26; 32; 54; 57;
  130; 135
Argentinia (n) – 23; 45
Armed Services Committee (US
  Senate) – 60; 85
Armilla Patrol – 43
Arms Policy Review – 141; 143
Ash Shubah – 101
Asia (n) (s) – 2; 136
Assad Dam – 26
Assad, President – 25-6; 41; 54
Ataturk Dam – 26; 31
Australia – 45; 126
Austria – 56
Azerbaijan – 145
Aziz, Tariq – 161, 101

Baath (Regional) Party – 13-14; 25-6; 153-4
Babran, Mudar – 27
Babylon – 32
'Baby Milk Factory' – 96; 126
Baghdad – 2; 4; 6-7; 9; 13; 33-4; 50-3; 55-6; 61-2; 65; 70-1; 74; 87; 96-7; 119; 128; 132; 135; 148; 150; 153; 156
Bahrain – 27-8; 42-3; 88; 127; 138
Baker, James – 10; 16-7; 19-20; 35, 40, 42; 44-7; 60; 113; 137; 139-42, 144
Bakh, President – 14
Bangkok – 2
Bangladesh – 42; 88
Basra – 1; 10-11; 57-8; 62; 89; 104; 108; 132; 149-50
Barzani, Masoud – 152
BBC – 89
Beiruit – 3; 150; 152
Bekaa Valley – 140
Belgium – 44-45
Bendjedid, President – 24
Berlin Airlift – 85
Berlin Wall – 38
Bermuda Summit – 133
'Bidoun' – 134
Billiere, General – 86; 125
Bishara, Abdullah – 28
Bnaid al-Gar – 3
Bombing Encyclopaedia – 67; 69
Border Guards (Kuwait) – 1
Britain (ish) – 6; 11-12; 14; 25; 27; 29; 37; 41; 43-4; 46; 52; 56; 71; 86; 92; 96; 110-12; 117; 123-4; 126; 129; 134; 140; 145-7; 153
Bristol – 123
Brooke Amendment – 41
Brussels – 44
Bubyan – 11-12; 58; 138-9
Bulgaria – 145
Bull, Gerald – 33
Bush, President – 10; 14; 16; 18-9; 35; 37-41; 43-5; 47; 49; 51-3; 55; 57 63; 66; 69; 83; 85; 93; 95; 97; 99; 105; 107-8; 112; 115-7; 131-2; 138; 141; 145; 148-9; 155

Cairo – 13; 17; 19; 23; 26; 139
Canada – 33; 45
Caractus – 39
Caribbean Basin – 36-7
Carter, President – 35; 39
Casablanca Summit – 23
CENTCOM – 36; 38-9; 48; 53; 67; 71-4; 79; 86-9; 94-6; 100; 102; 104-6; 109; 116-7; 119; 121; 128; 131; 133; 138; 146
CENTCOM-FORWARD – 66
Chemical Defence Unit – 62-3
Chemical Warfare – 15; 23; 25; 33-4; 100-1; 120; 123; 150; 155-6
Cheney, Richard – 10; 18; 35; 57; 85; 95; 100; 113-4; 144
Chernobyl – 122
Chevenement, Jean-Pierre – 44; 87
China (ese) – 14; 17; 21; 26; 29-30; 32; 38; 47; 53; 61; 70; 121; 140-3; 151
CIA – 9; 25; 88-9; 149
Civil Defence (Iraq) – 62-3
CNN – 81-2; 128
Cold War – 17; 40; 69; 144
Communist(s) – 34
Conferences of Arab Popular Forces – 55
Convention of Uqair – 11
Croaskery, Donald – 6
Cuba – 18; 37; 47; 61
Cuellar, Perez de – 52
Cyprus – 31

Daily Task Plan – 66
Damascus – 152
Damascus Declaration – 138-9
Daoud, Ibrahim – 149
Darman, Richard – 147
Dasman Palace – 2
Dawa – 2; 34
'Death Squads' – 135
Democratic Party (USA) – 57
Democratic Party of Kurdistan – 152
Denmark – 44
Department of Defense – 36; 53; 80; 93; 116; 123-4; 146
'Desert Rats' – 86

DFLP – 55
Dhahran – 18; 20; 42; 75-6; 99; 129
Dhofar – 29
DIA – 88; 125
Diego Garcia – 66; 85; 119
'Diwabiya' – 12
DMZ – 133; 145; 150
Doha – 42
Dohuk – 152
'Doomsday Gun' – 156
Dortyol – 18
Dubai – 30; 42
Dugan, General – 50
Dumas, Roland – 151
Dutch – 126

Eagleberger, Lawrence – 78
Egypt(ian) – 9; 15; 9; 22-4; 26; 34;
   41; 59; 101; 111; 138-42; 156
Eight-Point Peace Plan – 97; 101
Emir (of Kuwait) (see Sabah) 1
Euphrates (river) (Valley) – 26; 31;
   96; 104; 106; 133
European Community (EC) – 17; 31;
   40; 44-7; 69; 72; 112
Exercise 'Imminent Thunder' – 91
Exercise 'Internal Look; 90' – 48
Exercise 'Peninsular Shield' – 28
Exxon Valdez – 93

Fahd, King – 9; 18; 20; 137; 142
Falklands Campaign – 80; 147
Fao – 32
Farnborough Air Show – 70
Fasht al-Dibal island – 28
Fatah – 54
Fatah-RC – 55
'Force Packages' – 73; 119
France (ench) – 14; 17; 20-1; 24; 27;
   32-3; 43-4; 46; 56; 70; 83; 86-7; 92;
   101; 103; 112; 116; 123; 129; 134;
   138-9; 145; 147; 151-2
Franco-Iraqi Friendship Society – 44
Free Iraqi Congress – 152
'Friendly Fire' – 123
Fujairah – 30

Gaddafi, Colonel – 24; 129

Gates Commission – 35
GCC – 7; 10; 19; 27-8; 42; 87-8; 111;
   116; 137
Geneva – 61
Genghis Khan – 153
Georgia – 145
German (y) – 41; 44; 84; 86; 111; 147
Gigli – 46
Glaspie, April – 10
Glosson, General – 67-8
Gorbachev, President – 25; 46-7; 49;
   97; 101
Greece (Greek) – 44-5; 129
'Green Line' – 142
Greenpeace – 116
Greindl, Gunther – 133
Grenada – 36-7
Gulf Finance Co-operation Group –
   46
Gulf of Oman – 52

Habash, George – 55
Habib, General – 87
Hafar al-Batin – 7; 28; 42; 75; 86;
   98-9
Haifa – 75
Hail – 20
Haj – 21-2; 143
Halabja – 34; 150
Halaby, General – 87
Halago – 153
Hammadi (Hamadi), Saadoum – 95
   6; 149; 151
HAS – 70-1; 79-80; 92; 119-20
Hasib, Keyreddin – 152
Hassan, King – 24; 41
Hassan, Mohammed – 4; 134
Hawatmeh, Nayef – 55
Heath, Edward – 56
Helsinki Summit – 43; 47; 49
Hillah, al- – 33
Hoar, General – 144
Hormuz (Strait) – 29
Horner, General – 66; 68; 73-4; 78;
   114; 119
Hufuf – 42
Human Rights – 5; 22
'Human Shield' – 51; 57; 83; 89;

114-5; 128
'Humint' – 67-9
Hussein, Ahmad, – 149
Hussein, Ali, Colonel – 6
Hussein, King – 9; 27; 43; 54; 57;
143-4
Hussein, Naquib al – 149

IAEA – 151; 155-6
ICO – 17; 42
ICRC (Red Cross) – 54; 117; 134
IDF (Israeli Defence Force) – 78
IFF (Identification) – 78
IING – 149; 152
IMF – 22; 27; 46; 140
Incirlik – 46; 65; 77; 138; 153
India – 21
Individual Ready Reserve (US) – 36
'Intifada' – 54
Iran(ian) (s) – 2; 8; 14; 21; 23; 27-8;
31-2; 34; 53-4; 115; 120; 143; 150-
2; 154; 156
Iran-Iraq War – 2; 14; 21-2; 27-8; 30;
32-3; 43-4; 62; 69; 76; 79-80; 92;
140
Iraq-Soviet Friendship Treaty – 32
Islamic Fundamental(ist)(s) (ism)
– 8; 14; 23; 27; 31-2; 35; 51
Islamic Revolutionary Guards Corps
– 32
Israel(i)(s) 14-5; 23-4; 26; 33; 36; 42;
54; 57; 75-6; 78; 121-2; 124; 138;
141-2; 147
Italy – 44-5; 57; 71

Jabayl – 21; 42; 145
Jabril, Ahmad – 55
JACIO – 149-50; 152
Jahra – 2; 52; 108
Japan – 41; 45; 57; 147
JCS (US) –37-8; 48-50; 110; 113
Jedda – 31
Jerusalem – 21
Jihad – 19; 41
Joint Arab Defence Force – 138
Joint Information Bureau – 80
Jordan(ian)(s) – 15; 19; 26-7; 41; 43;
54; 78; 81; 143-4

Joze, Pierre – 103

Kadhima – 52
Kamil, General – 148
Karates – 46
Karbala – 21; 150-1
Kassem, President – 11; 13
Khairallah, General – 62
Khafji – 93-4; 126
Khalid, Prince – 60
Khamis Mushayt – 20; 42
Khazraji, General
Khobar al – 76
Khoei, Ayatollah – 151
Khomeini, Ayatollah – 14; 21; 27-8;
31; 143
Khor Abdullah – 11; 34
Khorramshahr – 151
King Abdul Aziz Air Base – 20
King Fahd Air Base – 20
King, Tom – 72; 118; 124; 147
KIO – 13
Kirkuk – 152
KTO – 88-92; 94; 98; 100; 104; 107-8
Kurds – 26; 29; 31; 34; 62; 140; 150;
152-3
Kuwait Air Force – 7
Kuwait armed forces – 6-7
Kuwait City – 1; 4-5; 51; 57; 101;
104; 106; 134-6
Kuwait Governate – 6
'Kuwaiti-17' – 2
Kuwait navy – 7
Kuwait Protectorate – 11

Latvia – 47
Lebanon(ese) – 10; 25-6; 36-7; 115;
124; 140; 151-2
Libya(n)(s) – 19; 24; 55; 129
LIVs – 38
'Lockerbie disaster' – 55; 146
London – 146; 152
London Declaration – 17; 40
Luttwak, Edward – 50
Luxembourg – 44

Madrid – 120; 142
Majid, General – 6; 62; 149

Major, John – 112; 124; 132
Martial law – 135
Mashad – 2
Marine Corps (US) – 36; 38; 60; 83; 85; 91; 94; 101-2; 111; 123
Mauritania – 19; 24
Mecca – 20-2
Media – 127-8
Media Response Teams – 80
Medina – 20-1
Mediterranean – 10; 22; 25; 30; 119
Mesopotamia(n) 10-1; 32
Middle East Peace Conference – 141-2; 144
Military Airlift (US) – 84
Military Sealift (US) – 84
Mina al-Ahmadi – 93
Mishab – 93
Mitterrand, President – 86
Moellenm Kalayeh – 151
Morocco(n) (s) – 19; 24; 41; 57; 88
Moscow – 17; 25; 101
Mossad (Israeli) – 33
Motherland Party – 145
'Mother of all Battles' – 98
Mubarak, President – 9; 23; 41; 58; 138-40
Muharraq   12
Mujahideen – 29
Mukhabarat – 2; 5
Mutla Pass (Ridge) – 108; 131

Nasiriya – 104-5; 133
National Assembly (Kuwait) – 12; 58; 136
National Assembly (Turkish) – 46
National Democratic Alliance (Jordan) – 55
National Democratic Party (Egypt) – 23
National Guard (Kuwait) – 7
National Guard (Saudi) – 21
National Guard (USA) – 36
National Iraqi Constitution – 152
National Military College (Iraq) – 13-4
National Progressive Front (Syria) – 25

NATO – 30-1; 36; 44; 46; 65; 69; 72; 84; 110; 118-9; 145; 147; 153
Nejaf – 21; 1501
Nejd – 11
Netherlands – 44
Neutral Zones – 9; 11; 137
'News Pool ' – 80
New York – 146
'New World Order ' – 49
Nida, al- – 52
Niger – 42
Noreiga, General – 39; 112
North Korea – 76; 121; 140-1
Nouman, Aziz – 62
Nuclear – 74
Nuclear Non-Proliferation Treaty – 151
Nuclear Research Centre – 33
'Nuclear Winter ' – 40

'Obstacle Belt' – 87; 89-92; 94-5; 98-9; 101-2; 107; 111
Oil Slick – 93
Oman – 27; 29; 40; 42; 88; 135
OPEC – 8-10; 12; 19; 29-32
Operation Daguet – 80
Operation Dessert Sabre – 98
Operation Desert Shield – 19; 40-2; 44-6; 48; 50; 55; 60; 64; 66-7; 71; 85; 87; 112; 114; 138; 143
Operation Desert Storm – 64; 69; 72
Operation Determined Resolve – 155
Operation Eagle Claw – 35
Operation Granby – 72-3; 86; 111; 126
Operation Just Cause – 30; 39
Operation Spinx – 33
Operation Urgent Fury – 36
Ottoman (Empire) – 11; 19; 31; 46
Ozal, President – 45-6; 144-5

Packard Commission – 37-8
Pakistan – 32; 42; 156
Palestinians – 2; 5; 27; 55; 78; 134; 136; 143
Palestine Problem – 19; 141-2
Panama (Canal) – 39

Paris – 147
Paris Air Show – 70
'Paris Club' – 140
Patriotic Union of Kurdistan – 152
Pax Americana – 18; 39-40; 49;
    112-4; 116; 131
Peace Accord – 57
Pell, Claiborne – 60
Peninsular Shield Force – 28
Pentagon (US) – 35-7; 49; 57-9; 63-4;
    69; 74; 84; 88; 90; 97; 102; 108-9;
    117; 121; 123-4; 127
People's (Popular) Army (Iraq) – 4-5;
    33; 154
Perroots, General – 125
Persson, Johan – 123
PFKG – 5-6
PLF – 54-5; 135
PFLP – 55
PLO – 5; 19; 26; 43; 54; 57
PNSF – 26
POLISARIO – 24
Popular Congress (Jedda) – 58
Portugal – 44
POW(s) – 53-4; 71-2; 103-6; 129;
    132; 134
Powell, General – 1; 59; 74; 85; 88;
    95; 100; 107; 113-4
Primakov, Yevgeny – 97
Princess – 127
Pro-Democracy Movement (Kuwait)
    – 137
'Psy-Ops' – 105

Qaboos, Sultan – 29
Qarah Island – 92
Qatar(i)(s) – 27-9; 42; 88; 94; 138
Qazin mountains – 151

RAF (British) – 72-3; 96; 118-9
Rafha – 87; 98-101; 133-4
Rafsanjani, President – 97
Ramadan, Taha – 148
Ras al-Khaimah – 30
Rashid, General – 62; 132
Rawai, General – 153
Reagan, President – 17; 35-8
Red Sea – 22; 40; 97

RCC (Iraq) – 9; 54; 56; 154
RDF (US) – 7; 28; 42
RDJTF (US) – 36
Riga – 57
Riyadh – 18; 21; 66; 75-6; 145
Roquejoeffre, General – 86
'R&R' – 59; 127
Rumaila (oil-field) – 8
Rumania – 32; 145

Saadi, Saleh – 152
Sabah, al-, Crown Prince – 2; 135
Sabah, al-, Emir – 1; 10-11; 136-8
Sabah, al-, family – 2; 5; 11-2; 58;
    135
Sabah, al-, Nawaf – 3; 136
Sabah, al-, Salim – 136
Saddam City – 150
Saddamiya al- Mitla – 52
SADR – 24
'Safe Havens' – 153
Safwan – 108; 133
Saladin – 13
Saleh, Ali – 152
Salman – 103
Samawa – 133
Sarkhou, Doctor – 4
Saud, King – 19
Saudi Arabia(ian) (s) – 2; 7; 12; 14;
    16; 18-22; 26-8; 41; 43-4; 46-8; 52;
    54; 58-60; 65-6; 71; 74-6; 80-1;
    83-4; 87-8; 91; 98-9; 101; 103; 106;
    111; 125; 127; 138; 141-4; 147-8
SBS – 92
Schwartzkopf, General – 37; 48; 50;
    59-60; 66; 74; 76; 79; 84; 86; 90;
    92-5; 98-9; 104-7; 111; 114; 116;
    120-1; 124-5; 127; 131-2; 134; 138;
    145-6
SCIRI – 34; 149-52
Scowcroft, Brent – 40
Sea Island – 93
SEAL teams – 92
Seeb – 42
Selective Reserve (US) – 36
Senegal – 42
Shamir, Yitzak – 141
Shamshal, General – 62

Shamrani, Captain – 74
Sharjah – 30
Sharon, Arik – 142
Sharpe, Captain – 126
Shatt al-Arab – 11; 34; 53; 109; 149; 151
Shevardnadze, Edvard – 17; 47
Shia(s) – 2; 21; 29; 34; 133; 143; 149-52
Shula – 150
Shuwaikh barracks – 2; 7
SOCOM – 91-2
South Africa – 24
Soviet Union (Soviets) (See USSR) – 14; 17; 20; 34; 56; 74; 7-8; 121-2; 140; 142-3
Spain(ish) – 24; 44
Special Courts – 136
Special Forces – 33; 37-8; 87-8; 91-2; 94; 100; 124-5
'Strategic Defiance' – 51; 56; 59; 149; 154
Strategic Defense Initiative – 36
Suk ask-Shuykh – 133
'Stalin organs' – 122
Sulayil oasis – 21
Sultan, General – 62
Sultan, Prince – 56
Sunni(s) – 21; 29; 34; 152
'Super gun' – 33; 156
Syria(n) (s) – 10; 12; 19; 24-6; 31; 55; 57; 59; 87; 121; 129; 138; 140-1; 146; 152

Tabuk – 20
Tactical Naval Command (US) – 126
Taft, William – 84
Taif – 2; 7; 9; 12; 20
Taha, Moheiddin – 148
Takrit – 13; 151
Talabani, Jalal – 152
Tallil – 105
Tampa (Florida) – 53; 59; 145
Tehran – 22; 34; 95; 115; 143; 151
Tel Aviv – 74; 76
Terrorism – 129
Thailand – 129
Thatcher, Prime Minister – 17; 37;

43; 52
'Thieves Market', Baghdad – 2
'Thirty-fold Aggression' – 153
Thrumrayt – 42
Thuwait – 33; 74
Tibet – 21
'Tienanmen Square ' – 61
Tigris (River) (Valley) – 13; 31; 106
Total Force concept – 36; 110; 114
Trucial Treaty (States) – 11; 29
Tripoli (Libya) – 130
Tunisia – 19; 24
Turkey(ish) – 17-8; 26; 30-1; 41; 44-6; 57; 111; 138-41; 144-5; 148; 152; 154
Turner, Ted – 128

UAE – 9; 27; 29; 42; 44; 88; 147
UK (See Britain) – 37
Ukraine – 145
Umm al-Maradim – 93
Umm al-Qaiwain – 30
Umm Qasr – 11; 34
UN – 10; 17-19; 43; 47; 52-3; 56; 60-1; 97; 107; 110; 115; 131-3; 139; 144; 152-6
UNIIMOG – 30
UNIKOM – 133; 145
US Air Force – 71-2; 83; 111; 118; 131; 145
USA-Kuwait Defence Agreement – 139
US Navy – 7
USSR (See Soviet Union) – 17; 25; 27; 32; 36; 47; 56; 76; 111; 131; 144-5

Velayati, Ali – 54
Victory Parades – 145-6
Vietnam – 35-6; 38; 48; 50; 59; 66; 80; 84; 80; 110; 113

Wadi al-Batin – 89; 99; 104
Wahabi(i)(s) – 21; 58
Waldheim, Chancellor – 56
Warba – 11-2
Warsaw Pack – 118
Washington – 21; 40; 100; 146

Webster , William – 60
Wehrmacht – 122
'West Bank' – 27
WEU – 44
Woerner, General – 39
'Women at War ' – 129
World War I – 11; 14; 19
World War II – 12; 35; 45; 86; 102;
  115; 122

Yanbu – 18; 45
Yazov, Marshal – 117
Yemen – 15; 17-9; 42; 47; 55; 61
Yilmaz, Mesut – 145
Yugoslavia – 32
Yumurtalik – 18; 30; 145

Zhako – 152

FORMATIONS

US

7th Army Corps – 85; 98-9; 101;
  104-6
18th Army Corps – 85; 98-101;
  104-6
1st Cavalry Division – 84
2nd Armored Division – 84
3rd Cavalry Division – 133
3rd Armored Division – 121; 145
24th Mechanised Division – 84
82nd Airborne Division – 18; 38; 84
101st Air Assault Division – 38; 103;
  105
101st Aviation Brigade – 64
11th Air Defense Artillery Brigade
  – 84
1st Marine ExpeditionaryForce – 84
404th Civil Affairs Company – 133

British

1st Armoured Division – 86; 104;
  122-3
4th Armoured Brigade – 86
7th Armoured Brigade – 86; 104;
  122

French

6th (Daguet) Light Armoured
  Division – 86; 100; 103; 147

Egyptian

3rd Mechanised Division – 87
4th Armoured Division – 87

Syrian

9th Armoured Division – 87

Kuwait

6th Brigade – 106
35th Armoured Brigade – 87

Iraq

2nd Army Corps – 62
3rd Army Corps – 62; 88
4th Army Corps – 88
Republican Guard – 1; 4; 33-4; 57;
  62; 79; 88; 90; 104-6; 108; 148; 153

ARMOUR

Abrams (M1A1) – 23; 84; 121-2
Bradley M-2 – 121; 143
Bradley M-3 – 121-2
Centurion – 7
Challenger – 86; 121-2
Chieftain – 7; 27; 88
ERC-90 – 86
GIAT-10 – 86
M-60 – 87; 143
M-84 – 88
T-55 – 90; 108
T-64 – 108; 121
T-72 – 87-8; 90; 108; 121-2
VAB – 86
Vickers (Mk-1) – 7
Warrior – 122

AIRCRAFT

A-4 – 71
A-6 – 65; 71; 119
A-10 – 121; 125
'Adnan' – 68; 79
Alpha Jets – 30
AWACS – 20; 68; 75; 143
B-52 – 66; 74; 100; 118-9
Boeing 707 – 67
Buccaneer – 73
C-5 – 84
C-130 – 84; 86
C-141 – 84
EA-6B – 65; 119
EC-130H – 65; 73
EF-111A – 65
F-4G – 65
F-5 – 20; 27
F-15 – 18; 65; 70-1; 73-4; 118-9; 141; 143
F-16 – 45-6; 70; 73; 96; 140; 145
F-18 – 7; 67; 71; 119
F-111 – 46; 65; 73; 93; 119
F-117A (Stealth) – 39; 45; 64-5; 73-4; 119; 126
Hawk (Trainer) – 7; 29
Ilyushin-76 – 68
J-6 – 33; 70
J-7 – 33
Jaguar – 72
MiG-29 – 70; 79; 118
MiG-25 – 70
MiG-23 – 70; 79
MiG-21 – 33; 70
MiG-19 – 30
Mirage F-1 – 7; 27; 33; 70; 75; 79
Mirage 2000 – 27
RC-4C – 67
RC-135 – 67
SU-25 – 70; 79
SU-24 – 70; 79
SU-22 – 79
SU20 – 79
Tornados – 20; 29; 43; 65; 67; 71-3; 118-9
TR-1 – 67
U-2 – 67

HELICOPTERS

Apache (AH-64) – 64; 95; 119; 121; 143
Blackhawk – 105
CH-58 – 95
Chinook – 91
Gazelle – 23
'Huey' – 105
Lynx – 23

BOMBS

BL-755 – 72-3
Durandel – 72
GBU-27 – 64; 119
GBU-27/109 – 64
GBU-28 – 119
JP-233 – 118; 72
Rockeye – 73

MISSILES, ETC

AA-6 – 70
AA-7 – 70
Abbas, al- – 76
Arrow – 78; 131; 156
AS-10 – 70
AS-14 – 70
Barak-1 – 121
Condor-2 – 23; 33
Dong Feng-3 (CSS-2) – 21; 121; 143
Exocet – 7; 33; 70; 126
FROG-7 – 7-8
HAWKs – 7-8; 78
Hellfire – 64; 119; 121
HOT – 7
Hussein,al- – 76
M-9 – 26; 140
Maverick – 23; 140; 143
Patriot – 76-7; 79; 120-1; 141
Roland – 70
R-550 Magic – 23; 70
SAM-2 – 70
SAM-3 – 70
SAM-6 – 70
SAM-9 – 70

SCUD – 25; 75-9; 100; 120-1; 124-5;
   129; 140; 155
Shahine – 20
SS-21 – 25
SS-23 – 26; 76
Stinger – 29
Super R-530 – 7
Swingfire – 23
Tomahawks – 65; 97; 126
TOW – 7; 23

UNMANNED AERIAL VEHICLES

CL-89 – 123
Mart – 123
Pioneer – 123
UAVs – 122-3

EQUIPMENT, ETC

ALARM – 118
ASARS – 67
ERINT – 156
FLIR – 66
GCI – 68; 70
GPALS – 156
GPS – 66; 68
J-STARS – 67; 76
LANTIRN – 75
Marconi-1022 – 126
MPS – 68
TADS – 119
THAAD – 156

MAJOR NAVAL CRAFT

HMS Brilliant – 129
Clemenceau (French) – 44-5
USS Eisenhower – 40
USS Kennedy – 40
USS Missouri – 60; 97
USS Saratoga – 40
USS Wisconsin – 123